DATE DUE

The Touch of the Past

The Touch of the Past: Remembrance, Learning, and Ethics

Roger I. Simon

THE TOUCH OF THE PAST
© Roger I. Simon, 2005.

First published in 2005 by
PALGRAVE MACMILLAN™
175 Fifth Avenue, New York, N.Y. 10010 and
Houndmills, Basingstoke, Hampshire, England RG21 6XS
Companies and representatives throughout the world.

PALGRAVE MACMILLAN is the global academic imprint of the Palgrave Macmillan division of St. Martin's Press, LLC and of Palgrave Macmillan Ltd. Macmillan® is a registered trademark in the United States, United Kingdom and other countries. Palgrave is a registered trademark in the European Union and other countries.

ISBN 1–4039–6746–6
ISBN 1–4039–6747–4

Library of Congress Cataloging-in-Publication Data

Simon, Roger I.
    The touch of the past : remembrance, learning, and ethics / Roger I. Simon
        p. cm.
    Includes bibliographical references and index.
    ISBN 1–4039–6746–6—ISBN 1–4039–6747–4 (pbk.)
        1. Public history. 2. Memory—Social aspects. 3. History—Philosophy.
    4. History—Psychological aspects. 5. History—Study and teaching. I. Title.

D16.163.S56 2005
907'.2—dc22   2004057310

A catalogue record for this book is available from the British Library.

Design by Newgen Imaging Systems (P) Ltd., Chennai, India.

First edition: April 2005

10 9 8 7 6 5 4 3 2 1

Printed in the United States of America.

For Kim and Sharon

CONTENTS

Contents

ILLUSTRATIONS

CREDITS

The book cover painting *Sounds of Silence* by Samuel Bak is reproduced courtesy of Pucker Gallery, Boston, MA.

The counter-Columbus Quincentenary poster "Autodescubrimiento" by Rodrigo Bentancur and Elizabeth Dante is reproduced with the permission of Joanne Kowalski (for the Estate of Rodrigo Bentancur) and Elizabeth Dante.

The engraving of Spanish atrocities in the context of New World colonization by Theodore de Bry is reproduced courtesy of the James Ford Bell Library, University of Minnesota, Minneapolis, Minnesota.

The painting *Columbus Landfall* by William Snyder is reproduced courtesy of the family of William Snyder.

The painting *The Landing of Columbus in San Salvador, October 12, 1942* by John Vanderlyn is reproduced with the permission of the United States Capitol Historical Society.

Images from Karen Atkinson's art installation *Remapping Tales of Desire*, 1991 are reproduced with the permission of the artist.

The painting *White Crucifixion* by Marc Chagall is reproduced with the permission of the Estate of Marc Chagall/SODRAC (Montreal) and the Art Institute of Chicago.

The photograph of children selling sweets in the Lodz Ghetto is reproduced with the permission of the Ghetto Fighters' House Museum, Israel.

The poem "Wagon of Shoes" by Abraham Sutzkever is cited with the permission of the University of California Press.

The poem "Flower" by Abraham Sutzkever is cited with the permission of Mosaic Press (Oakville, Ontario).

Excerpt from the poem "Lithuania" by Myra Sklarew is cited with the permission of Azul Editions, 7804 Sycamore Drive, Falls Church, Virginia.

Excerpts and video sampling of the testimony of Rita Hilton are cited and reproduced with the permission of the United States Holocaust Memorial Museum.

Excerpts from the video testimony of Paul Kagan are cited with the permission of the Canadian Jewish Congress Archives (Montréal).

Excerpts from the video testimony of Zena G (T-1399), Beba L. (T-426), Samuel B. (T-618), and Mira B. (T-257) are cited with the permission of the Fortunoff Video Archive for Holocaust Testimonies, Yale University Library.

Excerpts from interviews appearing in the film "The Partisan's of Vilna" are cited with the permission of Aviva Kempner, Ciesla Foundation.

INTRODUCTION

Remembering Otherwise: Civic Life and the Pedagogical Promise of Historical Memory

The only philosophy which can be responsibly practiced in the face of despair is the attempt to contemplate all things as they would present themselves from the standpoint of redemption . . . Perspectives must be fashioned that displace and estrange the world, reveal it to be, with its rifts and crevices, as indigent and distorted as it will appear one day in the messianic light. To gain such perspectives without velleity or violence, entirely from felt contact with its objects—this alone is the task of thought . . . [But this is] utterly impossible because it presupposes a standpoint removed . . . from the scope of existence, whereas we well know that any possible knowledge must not only be first wrested from what is . . . but is also marked, for this very reason, by the same distortion and indigence which it seeks to escape . . . Even its own impossibility [thought] must at last comprehend for the sake of the possible. Beside the demand thus placed on thought, the question of the reality or unreality of redemption itself hardly matters.

Theodor Adorno, 1974, 247

There is a saying attributed to the Rabbi Israel Baal Shem Tov, the eighteenth-century founder of the Hasidic movement, that "forgetting leads to exile; remembering leads to redemption." Today, few can utter this proverb without equivocation. Elie Weisel has recognized as much, stating that, until he visited Bosnia, he always believed remembrance would lead to redemption, now he was not so sure.[1] In Bosnia in the mid-1990s, Weisel witnessed the lethal consequences of practices of remembrance that reproduced forms of enmity in which one's identity is enhanced by the removal and annihilation of another. Within this prospect of remembrance, hate is engendered by memory and returns recursively to simplify memory. Clearly, redemption will not be realized amid such dynamics of remembrance; this underscores Adorno's insistence that for the sake of the possible, one must comprehend the impossibility of redemptive thought from the standpoint of an unredeemed world. Yet, given the light shed by the proposition that the antonym of "forgetting" is not "remembering" but the prospect of justice (Yerushalmi, 1989, 117), the irresolvable difficulties of redemptive thought do not release one from the obligations of remembrance. Indeed, these obligations require a reappraisal of the links between civic life, historical memory, and the educative force of various practices of remembrance. At stake in such a reappraisal is a response to the question of the political character of remembrance; more specifically, how and why a social, and often conflictual, practice of remembrance might be central to establishing the conditions necessary for democratic life. While, clearly, the substance of what constitutes democratic life is by no means settled, at minimum, I assume, it includes a framework of sociality that recognizes the fact of human plurality and hence the realities of lived specificity, difference, and disagreement. Furthermore, I am assuming that such a framework must make possible a sense of agency and futurity through forms of communication that enable learning about and from the lives of others and the consideration of the transformative actions necessary for living in a changing, increasingly interdependent society.

The social practice of remembrance is inherently implicated in enduring questions regarding the viable substance of human sociality, questions that include the problem of human connectedness across historically structured differences of time and place. Jules Michelet, one of the great social historians of nineteenth-century France, wrote of his labors in archives: "I have given to many of the disregarded dead the assistance that I shall myself need. I have exhumed them for a second life . . . They live now among we who feel ourselves to be their parents, their friends. Thus is made a family, a city community of the living and the dead" (cited in Steedman, 2002, 71). Michelet was here commenting on the historian's implication in the ongoing formation of a culture in which the past matters to the present. He understood well the promise of remembrance, that it is always about the future. Hannah Arendt made a similar point when she wrote: "In the last analysis our decision about right and wrong will depend upon our choice of company, with whom we wish to spend our lives. And this company is chosen through thinking in examples, examples of persons dead or alive, and in examples of incidences, past or present" (cited in Beiner, 1992, 113). Thinking Michelet through Arendt, a community of the living and the dead is not only the reference point for our judgments, it also starts to lay out the terms for the relationship between history and public life from which we can truly learn something that might broaden our perspectives, rethink our assumptions and organizing frameworks, subject our institutions to critique, and found the bases for new thoughts and actions.

A number of years ago, I was asked to provide a conference presentation on the topic of "global memory." Knowing full well the imbrication of the Kantian vision of a universal history with the record of European imperialism and colonialism, the very notion of a "global memory" seemed problematic, to say the least. Yet, the ethical impossibility of such an idea made it all the more interesting to consider. Could there be a non-Eurocentric model of cosmopolitical sociality that might take one beyond those practices of history that delimit a scene of recognition of self and other within either the reductive humanism of progressive enlightenment or an authenticating ethnos with its own counter-memories and rigid identity positions? It is through the consideration of this question that I have become concerned with the conditions and practices within which one might encounter the testamentary traces of the lived experience of specific historical events in ways that open human sociality to the possibilities of democratic transformation. To me, this practice of social memoration, of remembrance, must be considered a form of indeterminate critical pedagogy, a practice of inquiry and learning in which the logos interrelating one's past, present, and future social relations are subject to critique and re-formation.

Thus, while the mediation of memories within practices of remembrance constitutes one of the founding signs of civic life, the motivated, authorized character of that *civitas* is very much an issue of pedagogy, of how such mediations construct the substance and terms of one's connection to those who have gone before us. Whatever symbolic duration the past may attain it owes to a trans-generational covenant with the present—a covenant enacted through the modes and institutions of representation, distribution, and reception. Much, then, depends upon the substance of our practices of remembrance, practices that constitute which traces of the past are possible for us to encounter, how these traces are inscribed and reproduced for presentation, and with what interest, epistemological frame, and structure of reflexivity we might engage these inscriptions—remnants in the guise of stories, songs, images, and objects. On such terms, practices of remembrance are not just a problem of representation. More importantly, practices of remembrance are questions of and for history as a force of inhabitation, as the way we live with images and stories that intertwine with our sense of limits and possibilities, hopes and fears, identities and distinctions.

The historical memories enacted in a society are commonly constituted within two basic forms of remembrance. Both of these forms, in quite different ways, attempt to address the problem of social adhesion. In the first form, remembrance practices link meaning and identity within collective rituals that attempt to build a social consensus by invoking iconic memories that mobilize affective structures of identification. On such terms, remembrance attempts to mobilize corporate commitment based on the psychic dynamics of recognition and identification. In the second form, remembrance practices are more overtly hermeneutic. They organize and legitimate discursive structures—the "lessons of history"—within which basic corporate commitments might be rationally articulated. Here, remembrance attempts to constitute mutual understanding and social coherence through an assent to a communal life grounded in norms embraced as indexical to civility and justice. Both of these practices attempt to secure representations of the past that might be integrated into the social practices of everyday life by underwriting the enduring values and social forms that organize and regulate these practices. In this respect, each of these memorial functions contains a specific pedagogical force intended to articulate a communal definition of the future. In these practices of remembrance, there is a prospective orientation that seeks to legitimate and secure particular social relations, making normative claims on the conduct of human behavior.

Neither of these options for remembrance, however, is able to embrace the breaks that the memory of social disaster introduces into national and local communal aspirations that view history as being not only in a state of partial disclosure with a yet unrealized potential to be made whole, but as text inscribing a series of narrative instances whose specificity is sacrificed in the mobilization of significations capable of instantiating and sustaining unifying ideologies. Furthermore, neither option is helpful in relation to the question of how we might reformulate a public historical consciousness in such a way that the study of the past might become central to new democratic forms of community, founded not on the terms of autochthony and/or relations of production and exchange, but formed in relation to an incommensurable outside—what Edith Wyschogrod calls "a community of hospitality" (1998, 241). If we are to explore such a possibility, we will have to consider a form of public history that opens one to both the demand of, and responsibility to, the alterity of the historical experience of others—an alterity that disrupts the presumptions of the "self-same." Furthermore, to begin to think through practices of remembrance differently, clarifying their ethical, pedagogical, and political implications, we need another understanding of the futurity inherent in remembrance. This means becoming less concerned with the consolidating identificatory effects of practices of historical memory and attending more to the eruptive force of remembering otherwise.

Hence, for over a decade, I have been concerned with the remembrance of events informed by systemic mass violence, and, specifically in this context, practices of remembrance within which an assembled testament of words and images not only bear witness to specific histories of violence and violation, but are given over as a difficult inheritance to those called to receive it. In this sense, my focus has been on practices of remembrance that have a transitive function; that is, they may be conceived as putting forward expressive actions that "pass over" and take effect on another person or persons. This notion of transitivity is central to my purpose here. Understanding documentary words and images as transitive acts means that while they provide partial accounts of past experience that are subject to norms of historiographic judgment, they also openly arrive in the public realm making an unanticipated claim that may wound or better, instantiate a loss that haunts those to whom these claims are addressed. This claim carries the possibility of an interruption of one's self-sufficiency, demanding an attentiveness to an otherness that resists being reduced to a version of one's own stories. This promise of "the touch of the past" opens up the possibility of learning anew how to live in the present with each other, not only by raising the question of to what and to whom I must be accountable, but also by considering what attention, learning, and actions such accountability requires.

As the enactment of historical memory, the movement of testament is always caught up in the obligations expected by the transitive testamentary act—the act of writing, speaking, imaging—so as to bear an educative inheritance to those who "come after." It is how one conceives of this inheritance and on what terms one is prepared to engage it that is the critical determinate of the substance of the links between historical memory and civic life. At stake is whether one is able to realize the responsibilities of an ethical relation to past lives, traced through a testament of disaster that does not efface its own historical disfiguration. At issue in such responsibilities is an anticipation of a future that might become conceivable and concrete yet remains indeterminate, dependent on the substance of time through which testament may be transformed into inheritance. This time of coming-to-inheritance has important implications for the future of sociality. It holds the possibility of a transformative learning that is quite different from the dominant social functions of historical memory, anticipating practices necessary for sustaining democratic communities. Thus, my concern here is not with memory as a component of the founding ethos of national or communal identity, but rather as a condition for the learning necessary to sustain the prospect of democracy.

Public Life, Publicity, and Public Time

Zygmunt Bauman (1999) suggests that social solidarity has served in all societies as a shelter and guarantee of certainty and thus has enabled the trust, self-confidence, and courage without which the exercise of freedom and willingness to experiment are unthinkable (30). Over the last several decades, such a solidarity has been eroded by neoliberal theory and practice. Despite a greater awareness of the inequities among various societies that make up the "global community" and the important work in social justice of transnational nongovernment organizations, there is a current retrenchment of interhuman commitments to either family ties or national, regional, and/or ethnocultural assertions of unity. As democratic dissent and questions of global justice are stifled in its name, this reemerging return to traditional forms of communality is nothing to celebrate. Such a reduction is now reestablishing the "natural force" of a sovereign ego seeking its "place in the sun," eviscerating civic life in the name of patriotism. If there is to be an alternative to this stagnant horizon of community defined through usurpation and violence, what is needed is the reformulation of the prospect of a human solidarity that might reinvigorate new forms of relation within which one might conceive of a "public life." Given that public life is not exclusively related to institutions of the state but includes fundamental questions regarding the organization of everyday life as well, we need to consider the possible forms of sociality integral to rebuilding public life on terms that keep open the critique and redefinition of communality. What forms of sociality are integral to rebuilding solidarity beyond those based in proclamations in the name of familial, ethnocultural, kerygmatic, and/or national identities with their condensation of common understandings and commitments on figures of esteem, grief, or anger? What are the requisite practices integral to the reconstruction of forms of sociality that might secure the possibility, in Derrida's words, of a "democracy to come" (1997, 2000)?

What Derrida anticipates is a public life given substance by its own indeterminacy—what Claude LeFort terms an "indeterminacy as to the basis of power, law and knowledge, as to the basis of relations between self and other" (1988, 19). As Derrida (2000) suggests, there is an irrecusable insufficiency "between the 'idea of democracy' and that which presents itself in its name." In this sense, "democracy" is the name for a political regime that "declares its historicity and its perfectibility, [carrying] in its concept the dimension of inadequation and that which is to come." Thus, a democratic public life requires explicit activity that subjects existing practices to continual critique and the conflictual work of repair, renewal, and invention of desirable social institutions.

But what might be the grounds on which to establish a process of amelioration and perfectability that might realize a "public life" adequate to the idea of a "democracy still to come?" Although differing as to the substance of how public deliberation regarding social institutions can and should be articulated, most social theorists concerned with prospects for democracy have argued for some version of a public sphere within which the substance of the social is debated and negotiated. At stake here is the question of publicity, the particular ways of being-in-relation that come to bear on the conditions for the formation and sustainability of democratic life. While this brief introduction is not the place for a reconsideration of the voluminous literature on the substance of publicity, I do want to, at least, signal a vastly under-discussed dimension of this concern: the integral role of learning in any adequate notion of public life.

Rather than securing the character of public life through proscriptions that define its conditions of membership and participation, we might begin by asking what it means to enact "publicity," turning public life into a question of how the substantive quality of sociality is performed. For sure, to enact public life means to have opinions and offer them for debate and decision regarding aspects of one's life with others. But, in addition, if a democratic public life requires the ongoing deconstruction of the institutions of sociality, then it seems to me that enactment of publicity also requires being open to the realities of the incommensurable character of the experiences of others. "Publicity," then, emerges as a quality of human expressive activity that constitutes, inhabits, and also breaches the interior of social subjects. On these terms, a public sphere becomes not only that ensemble of practices that increase the possibility for a public articulation of experience, but also a condition of exposure to an outside that is also an instability within—a condition, as Tom Keenan (1998) says, "of vulnerability." This condition is not one of the emergence of homogeneity, unanimity, and confirmation. It becomes the activity within which the meaning and unity of the relation between the self and social is at once constituted *and* put at risk. It implies a praxiological commitment within which one is challenged to accept the loss of what is familiar and recognizably reassuring, a principled action through which public quality of social life is brought into being by what is outside of it—precisely through an otherness that interrupts the self-complacency of common grounds and exposes the responsibility of proceeding without any epistemological or ontological certainty. On such terms, the substance of "the public sphere" is not to be limited to a discussion of institutions, sites, and spaces, but must include an inquiry into what situated practices will support listening, learning, conversation, and debate capable of reassessing the political, cultural, and moral dimensions of the organization of social life.

Hence, within a publicity requisite for a "democracy still to come," the social is not only a space for the articulation and negotiation of visions through which to mobilize action, but also that movement in which the promise of democracy becomes the frame within which a radical form of learning is enabled. On these terms, the telos of the activity of being-in-common is a displacement of the secure subject within an encounter, which Derrida 2002 has termed the "*arrivant*" (the event-arrival). Within this moment, what arrives or who arrives and arrives to me supposes an irruption that punctures the horizon, interrupting any performative organization, any convention, or any context that can be or could be dominated by the conventionality of others. At this moment, publicity becomes thinkable as the necessary condition for the learning, possible when presented with a testament attempting to convey something of an existence outside ourselves. It is the very possibility of such learning that opens up the work of inheritance required by a democratic social. Following Cornelius Castoriadis (1997) and Henry A. Giroux (2003), it is a moment I have designated as "public time."

As Castoriadis has emphasized, references to public time should not be reduced to a system of sociotemporal benchmarks for ordering collective action (calender-time, clock-time)—a time independent of our participation in it. Quite differently, public time may signify a "dimension where the collectivity can inspect its own past as a result of its own actions, and where an indeterminate future opens up as a domain for its activities" (281). Not homogeneous and empty, public time is the instantiation of a particular relation among the fragmented moments of the present, past, and future. It is a moment in which learning is not simply the acquisition of new information, but an acceptance of another's testamentary address as a possible inheritance, a difficult "gift" that in its demand for a non-indifference, may open questions, interrupt conventions, and set thought to work through the inadequate character of the terms on which I grasp myself and my world. This is thought that needs the other, thought that lives through the life of another with the implication that we are dependent on an other for what is ours. On these terms, knowing is not a timeless attunement to timeless truths, but a temporal process within which one experiences the actualities of the public realm. Thus, public time presents the question of the social— not as a space for the articulation of preformed visions through which to mobilize action, but as the social relations in which the very question of the possibility of democracy becomes the frame within which a necessary radical questioning and learning is enabled. Such questioning and learning underwrites Giroux's understanding of public time (2003, 9) as that realm within which a collectivity can consider and critique its own past as the result of its own actions, and, through this activity, open an indeterminate future for civic life. On these terms, existing institutions and forms of authority are put into question through critical judgment and a commitment to linking social responsibility and social transformation.

As conceived above, public time opens new considerations regarding the possibility of public history. For those of us interested in the educative potential of documentary words and images, the question is not only how such material may serve an evidentiary function, but also how an enacted provision of testament might initiate a reconsideration of the force of history in social life. Rather than assuming that the public realm is constituted through a time contingent space of appearance or a shared will inspiring all to collective deliberation, we might rethink the force of history from within Benjamin's notion of a secret agreement between past generations and the present that will not be settled cheaply (Benjamin, 1968). From the perspective of public time, this agreement may be understood as the acceptance of the past's claim on the interminable redemptive struggle toward a "democracy still to come." To fulfil this agreement requires not just grasping such words and images as documents that put forth claims regarding a particular historical truth, which may be then subjected to verification, explanation, and judgment, but it also means apprehending these words and images as a transitive bearing of witness, the constitution of testament as gift, a provision of the possibility of inheritance with all its disruptive risks and possibilities.

Animated within specific forms of social organization of the relation of the living and the dead, the testament offered through practices of remembrance anticipates a conceivable, yet indeterminate, future, dependent on the substance of the public time through which documents of witness not only take their place in an evidentiary record, but may be transformed into a historical inheritance. Neither flow, container, nor scarce resource, such a de-formalized public time is conceivable as an event, a time caught up with that which happens. This time of testament and the coming-to-inheritance has important implications for the future of sociality and directly binds the future of civic life with considerations of remembrance. Remembrance, enacted as a moment of public time, holds the possibility of a transformative learning quite different from the dominant social functions of historical memory, anticipating the learning necessary for sustaining democratic communities.

The Touch of the Past

The question remains, however, how might the presentation and engagement with documents of historical witness initiate the work of inheritance through which one can experience a questioning of and transformation in one's own unfolding stories and the frames on which one might argue for a possible future. Clearly, the presentation of documents from a testamentary archive is no assurance of the pedagogical possibilities inherent in public time. While the event of public time cannot be prescribed, *one can pose questions* as to the conditions within which the gift of testament might initiate learning, not only about another's experience, but from the performative claim that the transitive aspect of that testament makes on one's attention and concern. Such questions take on a perhaps more insistent yet problematic quality when faced with testamentary documentation of those whose lives have been subject to systemic mass violence. When subject to a testament attempting to bestow such memories, I find myself commanded by the traces of those past to see, hear, and remember in ways that take such testament into account. But then, how should I do so? What forms of remembrance can both give and do justice to this violence and its pervasive lethal consequences? The question is not optional. While some may naively think that others should put their past differences behind them in the search for a workable peace, others are wise enough to recognize that the task of working for social transformation is not to forget the past, but to remember it otherwise. Foundational to the notion of remembering otherwise is not only the adjudication of responsibility and the provision of just reparation; it also includes the production of a historical imaginary within which it is possible to rethink as sensible and justifiable those practices that establish one people's exploitation, dominion, or indifference with regard to others. Such a historical imaginary will require forms of remembrance within which it is possible to trace the social grammars that structure confrontations with difference, confrontations in which ontological rather than ethical questions seemed to have taken precedence in the determination of how we should act toward those who are not immediately recognized as approximate versions of ourselves. To realize such a conception of remembrance, one will need practices of memory that are not tied to the consolidation of the corporate entities whether in the guise of state nationalism, ethnocultural hubris, or religious triumphalism. Rather, remembering otherwise will proceed from those practices of remembrance whose overriding consideration is the question of what it might mean to take the memories of others (memories formed in other times and spaces) into our lives and so live as though the lives of others mattered. This suggests a new cosmo-political form in which one is open to "translating" cultures and histories in ways that make it possible to reassess and revise the stories that are most familiar to us (Simon, 2000).

As such concerns are not only political and personal but fundamentally pedagogical, much of my work in education has included an attempt to explore how cultural workers can evoke "the touch of the past," constructing practices of remembrance that might alter the way the past is made present in desires, plans, and actions. To be touched by the past is neither a metaphor for simply being emotionally moved by another's story nor a traumatic repetition of the past reproduced and re-experienced as present. Quite differently, the touch of the past signals a recognition of an encounter with difficult knowledge (Britzman, 1998) that may initiate a de-phasing of the terms on which the stories of others settle into one's experience. This experience is quite outside of the binary between that of a presumed resurrection of the past so that it lives on as if a contemporary event in the present, and that of a historiographic rendering of the past as irrevocably past, with no immediacy except through acts of document interpretation evident within historical accounts. Rather, at stake in the touch of the past is the welcome given to the memories of others as a teaching—not simply in the didactic sense of an imparting of new information—but more fundamentally as that which brings me more than I can contain. To be brought more than one can contain is not a condition in which one becomes a symptom of a history one cannot possess, but rather a condition of possibility for true learning—one which bears the risk of being dispossessed of one's certainties.

This book presents a series of essays that in various ways have attempted to address the problem of welcoming and hence learning about *and* from the testament of others. All the essays explore issues in the context of the problems of remembering aspects of historical events which incorporate, as one aspect of their specificity, violence perpetrated on persons because of their membership in a larger group conceived of in terms of particular common characteristics. Written over a period of fifteen years, they represent an extended work-in-progress set in the context of the study of remembrance as integral to the possibilities of social transformation.

Most often, my approach to writing is to set such activity as an occasion for thought, for thinking through a perspective on specific events, texts, images, or objects that have drawn my interest and concern. The texts in this volume are no exception. In the early 1990s, when I first turned to a sustained study of questions of historical memory and its relation to civic life, I became interested in and engaged with what became known as the "counter Columbus Quincentenary movement." As the five hundredth anniversary of Columbus's landfall in North America was approaching, a widespread significant social movement was formed in an attempt to force a reappraisal of Columbian cultural memory. It seem to me that a consideration of the pedagogical strategies and tactics of this movement might be a good place to begin my studies of practices of remembrance and their relation to historical memory. Chapter one is a synthesis of two previously published papers in this regard and opens the question of what might be understood as insurgent forms of remembrance.

Chapter two continues on with this question of insurgency, but this time focuses on Marc Chagall's remarkable *White Crucifixion*, a painting at the

Art Institute of Chicago, which literally stopped me in my tracks when I first encountered it. What is considered here are the discursive frames through which Chagall's image might open up a transformative reconsideration of the relationship among Jews, Judaism, and Christian theological concepts in the face of the memory of the Holocaust. I had first become interested in questions of Holocaust memory in the late 1970s during my participation in a national project for videotaping Holocaust-related testimony of survivors living in Canada. At the time, given that my primary research and writing had been focused on other concerns and that I had begun to grasp the substantial difficulties of confronting the problems of remembrance regarding this particular history, I concluded that a serious consideration of such concerns would have to wait. Ten years later, as I turned to a study of remembrance and civic life, I returned to these issues. Chapter three (written with Claudia Eppert) was my first attempt to think through the knotty ethical and pedagogical problems of the relationship between testimony and witnessing. Not unsurprisingly, then, this text focuses on a specific contentious moment in a particular video testimony attempting to articulate a framework from within which one might approach the place of such documentation in practices of remembrance.

Those of us living in Canada in the early 90s were confronted with two events that bear heavily on social questions of memory in this country. On December 6, 1989, fourteen women at a polytechnic university in Montréal were systematically selected and murdered by a man who entered the university with an automatic rifle (letting the men in the classroom go free). Since that time, the question of whether and how this date should be remembered has been an ongoing concern, especially for those of us concerned with systemic prevalence of male violence against women. Chapter four presents the work of Sharon Rosenberg and myself reporting on our attempt to raise such questions with a group of university students in a teacher education program. Unavoidable as well, for those of us in Canada, were the events of the 1990 Kahnasatke Mohawk armed resistance to the appropriation of their burial grounds near Oka, Quebec, and hearings and reports of the 1991–1996 federally appointed Royal Commission on Aboriginal Peoples. Along with my work on the counter-Quincentenary movement, these events initiated a study of the problems of responding to the testamentary records gathered by the Royal Commission. Set within a growing interest in questions of testimony, Chapter five considers the problems that might be associated with a non-Aboriginal's listening to and learning from the accounts of the 1956 forced removal of the Sayisi Dene from their homelands in northwestern Manitoba.

More recently, my work on remembrance practices has returned to questions of Holocaust memory, and, in particular, practices that instantiate a remembrance of the events of the Vilna and Lodz ghettos established by the Nazis during World War II. In this context, together with graduate students working under a funded research project, I have been pursuing the development of a methodological framework within which one might engage and consider a multi-modal archive of testamentary material consisting of diaries, memoirs, photographs, state documents, material artifacts, poetry, and songs, all referencing various aspects of ghetto life. Our intent here has been to explore the conditions under which the assembly and bestowal of this testament may initiate the promise of public time. Chapters six to eight report on various aspects of this work. Through a series of examples, Chapter six (written with Claudia Eppert, Mark Clamen, and Laura Beres) introduces a set of readings given to the archival materials at hand that attempt to grapple with the dynamics of the taking in of these traces as a part of the work of inheritance. Chapter seven (written with Mario Di Paolantonio and Mark Clamen) presents an extensive theoretical consideration of the ideas developed in relation to our practical pedagogical work. Chapter eight returns specifically to questions of viewing video testimony (again, with regard to particular testamentary fragment), but, in doing so, attempts to clarify what might be at stake in the "event-arrival" of such testament—a moment within which one might begin a reappraisal of the conventional frames of the public representation of Holocaust history established over the last twenty five years.

Together, these essays are representative of an enduring commitment to clarifying the conditions within which one might productively encounter that moment when practices of remembrance begin to enact a historical consciousness with radical possibilities. This would be a consciousness that enacts, in the words of Levinas, "the urgency of a destination leading to the other and not an eternal return to self. . . . [It is] an innocence without naivete, an uprightness without stupidity, an absolute uprightness which is also an absolute self-criticism, read in the eyes of the one who is the goal of my uprightness and whose look calls me into question" (Levinas, 1990b, 48). My hope is that others might find these words useful in thinking through possible practices of remembrance that unsettle enough to enable a reworking of one's relationship to the world and others, seeing the openings inherent in an incomplete present, and deepening one's commitments to justice now and in the world to come.

As these essays have been written over a substantial period of time, the chapters in this book have been edited for consistency in terminology and the elimination of redundancies. Taken as a whole, they provide an emergent perspective on the critical investigation of the relation of remembrance and learning that continues to inform much of the substance of my ongoing work. Much of the material in this book has appeared in print in a somewhat different form. Chapter One draws from material published in *Cultural Studies,* Vol. 7, No. 1 (January 1993), pp. 73–88 and *Educational Foundations,* Vol. 8, No. 1 (Winter 1994), pp. 5–24. A version of chapter two was published in *Review of Education/Pedagogy/Cultural Studies,* Vol. 19, Nos 2–3, 1997, pp. 129–192. Chapter Three is a substantially reedited version of a paper that appeared in the *Canadian Journal of Education,* Vol. 22, No. 2 (Spring 1997), pp. 175–191. Chapter Four appeared in *Educational Theory* Vol. 50, No. 2 (Spring 2000), pp. 133–155. A previous version of chapter five will appear in Peter Sexias (Editor), *Theorizing Historical Consciousness*. Toronto: University of Toronto Press, 2004. Versions of chapters six and seven have appeared in *Review of Education/Pedagogy/Cultural Studies*, Vol. 22, No. 4, 2000, pp. 285–322, and the internet journal *Culture Machine*, No. 4 (February 2002). http://culturemachine.tees.ac.uk/

Much of the writing in this volume was developed in the context of the work of the Testimony and Historical Memory Project at the Ontario Institute for the Studies in Education at the University of Toronto. This project has been generously supported by two successive three-year grants from the Social Sciences and Humanities Council of Canada: Project Grant No. 410–96–1461, *When History "Comes Alive": Interrogating the Use of Testimonial Practices in the Formation of Social Memory* and Project Grant No. 410–990–321, *Witness-as-Study: Remembrance as a Practice of Learning*. I have been fortunate to be able to work with a group of remarkable scholars who, at different times, have been associated with the Testimony and Historical Memory Project, either in the context of its research efforts or its open seminar. These scholars include Mark Clamen, Lynne Davis, Susan Dion, Mario Di Paolantonio, Claudia Eppert, Lisa Farley, Blake Fitzpatrick, Chris Hiller, Irene Kohn, Kyo Maclear, Margaret Manson, Amish Morrell, Joseph Rosen, Sharon Rosenberg, Julie Salverson, Lara Sauer, Florence Sicoli, and Jessica Ticktin. Our conversations have been the foundations of many of the ideas to be found throughout the chapters. Additionally, the work presented here has been invaluably informed by the draft text comments and associated conversations with the following friends, family, and colleagues: Michael Bodemann, Deborah Britzman, Michael Chervin, Philip Corrigan, Joanne Dillabough, Stephen Feinstein, Richard Fung, Bob Gibbs, Henry Giroux, Michael Levine, Laura Levitt, Bart Simon, Kim Simon, and David Slocum. Special thanks go to Sharon Rosenberg whose persistent supportive nudging convinced me of the value of compiling this volume. As well, this book is invaluably indebted to Kim Simon and Lynne Caldwell's remarkably patient and insightful editing. Kim's persistence and dedicated work was crucial to the revisions made to previously published work. Finally, without Wendy Simon's enduring love, support, and companionship, none of this would have been possible.

Rosseau, Ontario
June 2004

CHAPTER ONE

The Pedagogy of Remembrance and the Counter-Commemoration of the Columbus Quincentenary

> The aim of judgment in historical or literary-critical discourse . . . is not that of determining guilt or innocence. It is to change history to memory: to make a case for what should be remembered, and how it should be remembered. This responsibility converts every judgment into a judgment on the person who makes it.
>
> Hartman, 1989, 80

During a sabbatical leave in the spring of 1992, I began to take a serious interest in the cultural pedagogy being practiced within the continental social movement organized to contest the celebration of the five hundredth anniversary of the arrival of Christopher Columbus on the coast of the landmass now known as North America. This counter-commemorative pedagogy took many different forms, at times surfacing within the commercial minutia of everyday life. While renting an apartment in Berkeley for a few months, I received a mail-order catalog (addressed to "current resident") inviting me to acquire an assorted set of contemporary American middle-class kitsch. Amid the plethora of procurable objects, which included audio cassettes of *Classic Bob and Ray*, Sterling Silver Teddy Bear earrings with matching necklace, a book entitled *The Best of the Old Farmer's Almanac*, and my choice of three different M.C. Escher silk neckties, was a T-shirt on which was printed a picture of a fifteenth-century sailing ship and the inscription "How could Columbus have discovered America when Native Americans were already here?" Accompanying the image of this item of apparel was the text: "This shirt poses an intriguing question and reminds us all that our continent's heritage goes back a lot further than 1492." The counter-commemoration clearly had not eluded commodification.

Yet, commodification does not necessarily imply trivialization. Indeed, in my view, consideration of this simple T-shirt can serve as a productive entry into the study of a problem of crucial, contemporary concern: the construction of a pedagogy that may help elicit the re-formation of historical memory, consciousness, and imagination. To begin, it is instructive to trace the production and marketing of the counter-commemorative shirt in its cultural context. In the months leading up to the occurrence of the Quincentenary, there was an extensive production and distribution of materials based on various aspects and assessments of Columbus's life and achievements. These included books, films, TV and radio programs, theater performances, and rap songs as well as buttons, decorative and declarative fabrics, calendars, puzzles, and games. While most of these commodities were intended to financially exploit a commemorative interest (in either its celebratory or contentious form), it would be a mistake to dismiss their cultural significance. No doubt, it is important to reserve a degree of cynicism for the interest in history promoted by educators and entrepreneurs on the major anniversaries of past events.[1] However, such reservations do not negate what should be grasped about the counter-Columbian commodity forms mentioned above. As forms of historical representation, they stand as claims on our understanding of the past seeking to either maintain or reinterpret dominant narratives, revive marginal ones, or bring to light those formerly suppressed, unheard, or unarticulated. In other words, they represent a portion of the complex cultural processes of the production, organization, legitimation, and contestation of historical memory; processes whose form and substance are simultaneously pedagogical and political. Neither a faculty of a single mind nor the discursive organization of what an individual has seen, done, felt, and thought, historical memory is constituted through social practices of remembrance wherein specific images and narratives are put forward as the terms on which to articulate a collective historical imaginary. Cultivated through the materially and socially organized activities of listening to and conversing with others, reading text, and engaging various forms of media and art, this historical imaginary is a relational concept that gives sense to one's temporal existence, thus, making it possible for events not personally experienced to become an active force in one's thinking, emotional attachments, and ethical commitments. It is in this respect that a historical imaginary can become a significant factor in constituting the possible interpretations held and actions undertaken within a community.

It is essential for anyone interested in questions regarding the significance of the past in the present to consider the functional relationship between historiographic inquiry and any given set of practices of historical memory and the imaginary that they support. While insurgent practices of historical memory can, at times, contest the silences and legitimations structured into officially sanctioned history, it is important to acknowledge that remembrance is a selective cultural practice that can also be a prop of power and authority, as well as an impetus to the reproduction of hatred and violence. In this light, historical discourse is needed to challenge historical memory and re-pose the essential questions about the relation of history to the social institution of memory. At least in democratic societies, it remains vital that the formation of historical memories be enriched in a shared dialog with historians. This is not to cede sole authority to historians to define the substance and significance of the historical memory. Rather, as Michael Frisch (1990) suggests:

> Historians must not treat historical intelligence as a commodity whose supply they seek to replenish . . . Whether one is talking about the history of a war or the memories of old residents in a crumbling ethnic neighborhood, what we need are works that will search out the sources and consequences of our active ignore-ance. We need projects that will involve people in exploring what it means to remember, and what to do with memories to make them active and alive, as opposed to mere objects of collection. (26–27)

It is just such projects that define the point of entry for educational thought regarding the formation of historical imaginaries. When, as educators, we intentionally try to affirm or transform established practices of historical memory through person-to-person encounters or the staging of engagements with text or image, we deploy what I will call pedagogies of remembrance. As a pedagogical form, remembrance incorporates a set of evaluations that structure what memories should inform our social imagination as well as a detailed, structured set of operations for presenting and engaging historical representations intended to provoke and solidify particular affect and meaning (Giroux, 1992; Trend, 1992).

In enacting such pedagogies, one must be sensitive to the range of modalities through which remembrance stages the possibility of the past, making an educational claim on the present. Acknowledging and grappling with the complexity of this assumed educative relationship between the present and the past is important to those of us who—as cultural workers and teachers—create, organize, distribute, and structure engagements with the traces and representations of the past. While social and material investments in historical memory proceed from the very human hope that the past has something to teach us, remembrance as a practice of pedagogy requires the recognition that there are alternative and conflicting ways of constituting its lessons, each with a distinct pedagogical and political character. Here, I am not concerned with the myriad of reasons that justify the full exercise of a historical imagination. I am also bypassing the educational argument that the teaching of history as a method of inquiry is of importance in formulating critical thinking skills. My focus is the claim that knowledge of the past is important because it can make a difference in the present.

It is in this context that I now want to return to the counter-commemorative pedagogies initiated in regard to the Columbus Quincentenary. Clearly, these pedagogies were intended to be insurgent and transformative forms of remembrance that would contribute to the redefinition of the historical imaginary operative for most North Americans. The importance of this agenda needs to be understood in light of the fact that societies have differed in the degree to which their citizens have been able to contest the hegemonic practices of remembrance. In democratic communities, we at least acknowledge *in principle* that previously established historical memories, informed and sustained by established practices of remembrance, should be open to critique and contestation. Thus, democracy entails an ongoing tension between a retention of affirmed shared memories and the preservation of the possibility that such memories can be challenged and altered. In other words, democrats cherish, rather than dismiss, practices of counter-memory, which can call into question both the social imagination previously secured by particular remembrances and the social interests and ethical vision supported by such an imagination. Such a process does not mean mindlessly accepting all contesting counter-memories, but means learning how to hear what is being asserted within them and seriously considering the claim they make on our understanding of the present. In North America, such a practice might valuably take the form of what Guillermo Gomez-Pena (with a little help from Mikhail Gorbachev) has astutely called "gringostroika"(Martinez, 1991); a process of self-criticism and renewal that opens possibilities for change in the basic terms of reference of the relation among citizens, their environment, and their state.

Considering remembrance as a contested activity, it is virtually self-evident why the controversy over how to commemorate Columbus's landfall remains so important. At minimum, the struggle is over how the event is to be defined, what and whose stories and images are worth remembering, as well as what it might mean to learn from different representations of the past. While there are a range of issues that could be addressed regarding how one could and should remember events initiated by the European arrival in the Americas, my own interest is in how non-natives living in Canada and the United States might embody within "living memory" the invasion, appropriation, exploitation, attempted genocide, and colonialization of indigenous peoples.

Stating my agenda in these terms in no way displaces what I see as an interrelated project defined by indigenous communities in response to the Columbus Quincentenary; that of commemorating 500 years of native resistance to invasion and its aftermath. Indeed, the essential first step for the non-native in confronting the issue of colonialization of indigenous peoples is to attend to indigenous efforts to reclaim, name, and tell their own histories—histories that are informing the struggles for Aboriginal self-determination taking place throughout the Americas. In fact, with justification, one can conclude that for non-natives like myself, now should be a time, not for speaking and writing, but for listening.

The importance of such listening cannot be overstated. Yet, in my view as an educator, such a self-limitation would be a mistake; a mistake because it suppresses the corollary educational questions: who is listening, what is heard, and what is learned? Non-native educators have the responsibility of recognizing that they have a role to play in influencing what is heard in their communities when listening to indigenous accounts of the history of the continent. Indeed, the question of how to initiate "gringostroika" is *our* question. Recovered histories and the availability of stories previously suppressed do not ensure that they will be intertwined within historical imaginaries and communal identities. Clearly, such voices have the potential to challenge dominant memories and the social order they underwrite. However, if remembrance practices are only concerned with "correcting memory" and do not explicitly function to renew a reconstructed living memory for a community, the potential insurgency in such practice will be greatly diminished.

To get a better sense of what is at stake here, consider a few of the possible positions that non-natives frequently adopt when they encounter the indigenous narration of colonialization and resistance:

(1) *Relative indifference.* In this position, one listens openly but simultaneously distances oneself from a story through an insistent wondering "what does this have to do with me?"

(2) *Defensive skepticism.* In this position, one listens for historical inaccuracies that might justify a narrative's dismissal.

(3) *Ethnographic curiosity.* In this position, one confers on the story and the storyteller the status of "objects" whose meaning must be rendered familiar to the listener *on the listener's own terms*; this position breeds a delusional empathy often expressed as "how terrible, I understand how you must feel."

(4) *Self-identification.* In this position, there occurs an intense identification with the persona of the story, which in the case of nonindigenous North Americans, at times, results in prideful arrogance, self-suffering guilt, or the displacement of one's own historically and materially rooted identifications by the incorporation of a sense of the indigenous Other defined within a specific, limited comprehension of difference.

In my view, none of these positions are adequate ways of "listening" to indigenous accounts of colonialism and resistance—narratives that are fundamentally constructed within and across very disparate and unequal terms for relating with and experiencing difference. What it is that can be heard from these positions presents little basis for the transformation of a historical imaginary in ways that might impact on one's actions and the ethical character of nonindigenous identities and commitments. As a way of exploring alternative possibilities, it is my working premise that to listen differently—to hear in a way that what is heard becomes a part of one's living memory—is a task that parallels attending to First Nations' histories.

One way to come at this problem is to consider the implications of the supposition that what is heard and remembered as non-natives listen to indigenous narrations is very much linked to how non-natives remember and make intelligible the practices of colonialization initiated and sustained by Europeans and European-derived communities. Within this premise, to alter what is heard in First Nation accounts, not only must one engage in an active re/membering of the actualities of the violence of past injustices, but one must also initiate remembrance of the emergence, circulation, and maintenance of the discursive practices that underwrote the European domination, subjection, and exploitation of indigenous peoples.

To elaborate on this pedagogical claim and develop its implications, I return to the counter-commemorative T-shirt mentioned at the beginning of this chapter. Compared to books, films, and more complex art forms, the printed T-shirt might seem trivial—a rather bare iconographic statement with a minimum of narrative and always in danger of reduction to a commodity cliche. Yet, such forms of apparel have become pervasive in North America and shirts with images and text designed to instigate forms of remembrance are now a cultural commonplace. Indeed, the form contains its own unique set of pedagogical dynamics. A sign carried by bodies, the inscribed T-shirt brings its referent close to us; it declares the entry of history into our lives and confronts others we meet with our declared relationship to the past. Intersecting with other circulating discourses, it makes history topical within the everyday and attempts to define an image-text that has the potential for mediating relationships between people. As a public act of remembrance, it participates in the regeneration of our collective historical imagination.

To grasp the substance of the pedagogy that this particular T-shirt attempts to mobilize, consider for a moment the variety of reasons why many people now reject the use of the term "discovery."[2] The most common reason is to assert factually that the lands Columbus visited were quite well known to thousands, if not millions, of people. Thus, to declare his landfall as a discovery is both pompous and absurd. The strongest versions of this position are suitably ironic. Take, for instance, the classic commentary by Roberto Fernandez Retamar (1991).

> Madrid, Paris, Venice, Florence, Rome, Naples and Athens were all discovered by me in 1955 (having already discovered New York in 1947), and in 1956 I also discovered London, Antwerp and Brussels. Nevertheless, outside of a few of my own poems and letters, I have not found any other text which describes these interesting discoveries. I suppose that this clamorous silence has resulted from the fact that when I first arrived in these glamorous cities they were already full of people. A similar line of thought has always stopped me from accepting that the arrival of a few Europeans—soon to be five centuries ago— to the continent where I was born and where I live should be pompously referred to as the "Discovery of America."[3]

In this light, the 500-year-old use of the term discovery is a Eurocentric conceit, which ignores the fact that the history of the peoples of the Americas began long before the arrival of Columbus. In addition, it is argued that the very logic of discovery constituted an acquisitive relationship between the discoverer and the people who met him on the shore. Humans, animals, and plants were collapsed into passive objects, the wonders of both European gaze and desire (Greenblatt, 1991). Hence, discovery denies the possibility of a reciprocal encounter in which human dignity could be acknowledged and affirmed. This denial was not just a historical misfortune but persists as a contemporary concern. It is a legacy that continues and whose disruption requires (as one of the first moments of a counter-commemorative pedagogy) a radical reframing of the story. Thus, narratives of discovery must be rejected and replaced, not simply with the problematic notion of an encounter that initiated reciprocal exchange, but with the realities of what happened from the indigenous point of view.

Recall that the counter-commemorative shirt described above reads: "How could Columbus have discovered America when Native Americans were already here?" Other counter-commemorative shirts proclaimed 500 years of indigenous resistance to European invasion. This shirt, instead, asks a question. It is a question posed from within the North American landscape and is clearly addressed to those responsible for creating and circulating the texts and images proclaiming discovery as well as those of us who have been subject to the truth claims of such representations.

The wearing of this shirt, thus, initiates a double pedagogy. In relation to its membership in the genre of current texts that dismiss European notions of "New World" discovery, the public wearing of such a shirt functions not so much as a question as an assertion of solidarity with indigenous people who are increasingly gaining a wide hearing for a different story. In this sense, the wearing of the shirt is an act of remembrance, which is intended to remind us of that which we previously had not the chance to remember. For centuries, we have missed the "view from the shore"; we have missed "what it is like to be discovered" (Small, 1991). Thus, we are made to be attentive, to recognize that we are being asked to listen. In the first moment of solidarity, we must do so.[4]

What we are asked to hear is that the past is being reclaimed as a site of injustice. Instead of the language of discovery, we are asked to hear the language of invasion, occupation, attempted genocide, and resistance. As indigenous communities in both hemispheres rename the time period since Columbus's arrival as "500 Years of Resistance"—reconstituting communal identities in this moment of historical agency—members of non-indigenous communities are being asked to respond to the question: what does the rectification of past injustice require us to do both in 1992 and beyond?

But, the wearing of the shirt, potentially, does something more. Through challenging those it addresses to question received "truths" and revise the narrative through which we have historically understood the genesis of our collective present, "we" are also being asked to reflect on the status of the people and texts who promulgated these truths in the first place. In other words, the image-text of the shirt also initiates the conditions from which the practice of the uncovering and demythification of power relations takes place. Indeed, this has not been lost on many teachers who are now rethinking the way the history of Columbus's landfall has been taught in schools. Students are now being asked to respond to such questions as: "What other stories in your history texts display similar interpretive biases?" "Why have you used these texts?" "Who has authorized them?" "Whose interests are served by their continued use?" (Bigelow, 1991).

For the above reasons, this T-shirt stands as an example of how specific pedagogies are articulated from within particular modes of constituting the educative relation between the past and the present. The historically pervasive notion of discovery is framed within a practice of ideological hegemony designed to ensure dominant interests. Indeed, the critique of discovery as a hegemonic lie is used pedagogically to call into question the entire apparatus of historical representation that has presented this and other stories central to the formation of the West. New narratives are offered that raise questions of what collectively needs to be done to redress the legacy of colonialism whereas those struggling against current structures and agents of that colonialism are given heart by the rewritten stories of the past.

Yet, I think, if we construct our counter-commemorative pedagogies on these terms alone, we are still missing an important dimension of the educational work that needs to be done. The weakness of a pedagogy of remembrance that discredits the dominant narratives of discovery is the failure to interrogate the basis for their intelligibility in the first place. In words suitable to occasions of history and judgment, Geoffrey Hartman makes clear the issue: "denunciation is not enough; it tends to foster a paranoid style of localizing evil that removes the issues too far from our time" (Hartman, 1989, 55–84) and, I add, ourselves.

Rethinking the Dismissal of the
Language of Discovery

It is for the reason mentioned earlier that I have been spending some time rethinking the importance of *maintaining* the notion of the European discovery of the Americas while simultaneously shifting it out of its mythic abstract encrustation. Instead of dismissing the notion of discovery, it seems to me, it must be made problematic. At stake is the potential of additional insurgent commemorations, pedagogies of remembrance built with a cognizance of how particular ways of apprehending the past might be implicated in our understanding of, and complicity with, current unjust social relations, and the prospects for a personal and communal renewal of identities and the possibilities that structure our everyday lives.

This alternative perspective on the European notion of discovery acknowledges that the word may straightforwardly indicate a revealing of something that was previously unknown. As Mary C. Fuller (1991) points out in English texts about the New World:

> "Discover" frequently carried the sense of revealing, laying open something previously hidden, bringing to light something previously dark . . . Discovery makes what exists at a distance . . . visible, accessible, understood. Discovery is the project of moving what is "in there," the inwardness of the New World, to "out here"—the public space of England—in a simple motion of unveiling. (45)

This perspective makes partially intelligible the use of the term by Europeans who chose to narrate the consequences of Columbus's voyage as a tale of discovery.[5] Columbus did initiate (as others who reached the Americas before him did not) an unveiling of that which was previously unknown to the European world.

In Europe, prior to 1500, the ocean was both a sign signifying the unknown, as well as a physical barrier preventing knowledge. Crossing this barrier initiated a process of revelation; a revealing of a reality not immediately available in experience but requiring mediation through representation. This meant the telling of stories, the description of people, events and places, and the display of artifacts (including people rendered as objects)—all previously outside of European experience. The event of discovery required the symbolic rendering of that which was not previously known into text and image—a practice always limited by existing epistemological frames. Thus was formed through text, picture, and artifact a set of image-landscapes of a New World, ones that entered into the formation of the plans, desires, actions of Europeans both on their own continent and in the "Americas."

This argument does not justify the historically hegemonic narrative of discovery, but rather seeks to interrogate the form and consequences of its associated representational requirements. As Michel de Certeau (1986) has emphasized, at stake here is an inquiry into how a New World was made visible, accessible, and understood by whom, for whom, and with what consequences both for legitimation of action and interest and in concordance with what notions of whose desire?

Such inquiries can form the basis of the remembrance of the European response to what Stephen Greenblatt calls the sensation of "wonder"—"the decisive emotional and intellectual experience in the presence of radical difference" (1991, 14). Undeniably, this response was both *physical and discursive*. While the remembrance of the physical response—what Europeans did—must remain the prime focus, I want to emphasize the pedagogical importance of practices that continue to rearticulate a historical memory of the discursive response. Initially, this may seem arcane; a call for a practice that incorporates the remembrance of a discourse as a discourse. Greenblatt is helpful in clarifying what is at stake.

> If microbes lie altogether beyond the grasp of Renaissance discourse, the other forces that we have cited as brute facts should under no circumstances be naturalized. The possession of weapons and the will

to use them on defenseless people are cultural matters that are intimately bound up with discourse: with the stories that a culture tells itself, its conceptions of personal boundary and liability, its whole collective system of rules. And if gold is a natural phenomenon, the all-consuming craving for gold most assuredly is not. (63–64)

This is not a statement of linguistic omnipotence. The comprehension of events is rarely exhausted in a consideration of their discursive referents. In his focus on discourse, what Greenblatt is emphasizing is the interrelation of the denaturalization of history and the recognition that "the drive to bring experience under discursive control is inseparable from the task of ethical justification and legitimation" (note 37, 170). In other words, a commemoration of the discursive response to the experience of "wonder" is, at root, a remembrance of the presumptions, values, and regulating forms that articulate a constructed moral framework.

This is the decisive point for the cultural work of insurgent remembrance. At stake is a pedagogy that moves away from the exclusive concern with historically isolated discussions of who did what to whom. Such discussions are too easily dismissed by conservative critics as a "pious self serving moralizing . . . of no good whatever to the dead, and of dubious good to us the living, who are, as it is, altogether too prone to think ourselves kinder, wiser, and certainly less infectious" (Mays, 1991, C1). What moves more centrally into focus are the forms through which relationships with those who are other to ourselves are established and negotiated. While this may entail some degree of focus on motives and assumptions of individual historical actors, it is not the chief concern.[6] Instead, such remembrance would ask us to grasp the ways the encounter between indigenous and nonindigenous peoples were structured and continue to be structured and whether one can recognize the discursive continuities and transformations in this continuance. What is at stake is whether or not we can come to a recognition of the ethical relationship between self and other in the narratives we tell.

For this recognition to be possible, it is necessary to find a way to enable non-natives—as individuals who draw meaning from their own cultural identities—to directly engage in the record of European-initiated genocide and colonialism without distancing themselves from this history. In the context of the counter-Quincentenary movement, many people rhetorically asked how Columbus could have claimed to discover America when there were already people living there? But, perhaps, this focus on Columbus the man (repeatedly reinforced by those who insisted on celebrating the Quincentenary) missed a crucial opportunity. More to the point would have been some much needed discussion of the following question: by what right had the crown of Castile occupied and enslaved the inhabitants of territories to which it could make no prior claims based on history?[7] Those who might have focused on this question might have been surprised to learn that 480 years earlier, in fifteenth-century Spain, this was precisely the question that scholarly assemblies were debating.

While historians and journalists have complained about the "revisionist presentism" of the counter-Quincentenary movement, which failed to situate Columbus or the early Spanish colonists as "men of their times," the reality was that these "times" were not simplistically monolithic. It is important to remember that in 1532, at the University of Salamanca, the moral theologian Francisco de Vitoria initiated a series of lectures in which he refuted a number of arguments legitimating title for Spanish ownership of the New World and the consequent subjugation of its inhabitants. In lecture notes documented by his students and published in a text known as *De Indis Relectio Prior,* Vitoria argued:

> . . . there is another title . . . the right of discovery . . . and it was in virtue of this title alone that Columbus the Genoan first set sail . . . Not much, however, need be said about this . . . , because, as proved above, the barbarians were true owners, both from the public and from the private standpoint. Now the rule of law of nations is that what belongs to nobody is granted to the first occupant . . . And so, as the object in question was not without an owner, it does not fall under the title which we are discussing . . . in and by itself it gives no support to a seizure of the aborigines any more that if had been they who discovered us. (138–139)

In bringing attention to Vitoria's natural law discourse, my purpose is not to posit him as a contemporary progressive hero or to simplistically render the totality of this thought as a humane challenge to Spanish claims to sovereignty.[8] Yet, in the first half of the sixteenth century, Vitoria and those who studied and added to his work (men such as Melchor Cano, Bartolome de Carranza, Domingo de Soto, and the most well known today, Bartolome de las Casas) were responsible for initiating a complex and multilayered legal discussion that addressed the legitimacy of European actions in the Americas. Certainly, from the standpoint of the history of the indigenous people of the Americas, these scholarly disquisitions seem to have made little difference. In this view, it matters not at all that Vitoria's work greatly angered the Emperor Charles V and was all but ignored by the mercantile interests controlling daily life in the Spanish colonies. Yet, from the standpoint of how one might remember the actions of Europeans and how this remembrance might effect the way one hears indigenous narration, this "minor event" amid the huge sea of colonial history may be more significant than it might seem. Attending to the materialization of a contentious discourse in a place such as Salamanca puts up for inclusion in the historical imaginary of North America, concrete practices that contest the totalizing narratives that have constructed the mythological trope called "the West." In other words, remembering the discourses of Salamanca means dismembering a mono-dimensional Occidentalism. It also means that there are points of rupture or fissure in the genealogical history of the construction of the figure of the Other that not only would clarify the grounds on which such constructions have been established but would also make clear that such constructions were/are not natural and inevitable. In this light, while listening to the stories of those who have been dominated, subjugated, and exploited, we might create a remembrance of how we have rendered difference, opening anew the question how we might begin to face difference.

Thus, it is a serious mistake when myopic conservatives characterize the remembrance of the genocide and colonialization of indigenous people as an obsessive "detailing of the sins of Europe that has become a perverse form of narcissism" (Miller, 1992, 22). This is anything but narcissism. Assumed here is that we situate ourselves in certain relations to the Other within narratives that orient our actions toward the Other. But also assumed is an agency within which we can initiate the reconstruction of this relation, aided in part by narratives that redefine the basic terms of the relationship between citizens and the fundamental social character of their state. Indeed, at stake here is nothing less than Gomez-Pena's notion of *gringostroika*; a search for the conditions necessary to secure social forms and institutional structures that will initiate a life-sustaining non-subordinate interdependency.

Visual Pedagogies and Discursive Continuities

To illustrate a few of the pedagogical alternatives that exist for re-remembering the meaning and significance of Columbus's landfall and different ways of considering the continuity of the colonial discourses implicated in the intelligibility of this landfall as a discovery, I turn now to three quite different visual images. These images were created as significant contributions to the counter-commemorative pedagogy of remembrance mobilized in 1992. The first of these is a poster for the First Continental Chasky by Rodrigo Betancur and Elizabeth Dante. (See figure 1.1.) As an event integral to indigenous mobilization against the Columbus Quincentenary, this Chasky emphasized the importance of the continuity of indigenous memory and values in the context of a rising up against colonial subjugation. In their poster, Betancur and Dante utilize indigenous imagery and a citation from the Mayan text *Polol Vul* to depict a continuing tradition of resistance to genocide and colonialism, inscribing the theme of struggle as an aspect of historical memory. This imagery is set against the visual citation of a wood cut of Spanish atrocities against "Amerindians" by the Flemish engraver Theodor de Bry. (See figure 1.2.) A Protestant, who was not reticent to imaginatively depict Catholic atrocities, de Bry's graphic engravings illustrated many of the early European books that attempted to provide a history of the discovery and colonialization of the Americas (Conley, 1992). The image Betancur and Dante appropriate was published in 1599 in Bartolomé de Las Casas's *Short Account of the Destruction of the Indies* (1992, 15). Along with other images of Spanish brutality, this image appeared in various New World histories and in seventeenth- and eighteenth-century popular

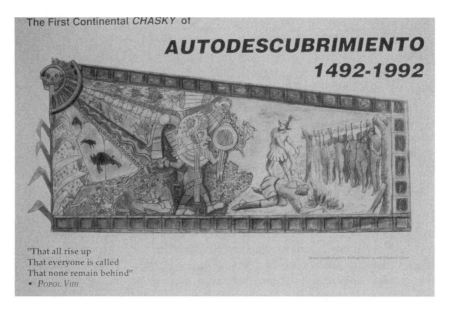

Figure 1.1 Rodrigo Betancur and Elizabeth Dante counter-Columbus Quincentenary poster "Autodescubrimiento."

Figure 1.2 Theodore de Bry, engraving of Spanish atrocities in the context of the New World colonialization. From the James Ford Bell Library, University of Minnesota, Minneapolis, Minnesota.

accounts of Spanish colonial atrocities. These accounts were, in part, intended to generate anti-Spanish sentiment throughout Europe in order to help destabilize Spanish power in the New World and enhance the project of Anglo-Dutch colonialization (Gibson, 1971). Thus, once highly circulated, de Bry's engravings have clearly not had much popular currency in North America for the last 200 years. For their poster, Betancur and Dante appropriated de Bry's image, visually repositioning it within the context of his 1992 counter-commemorative artwork. The result is the juxtaposition of two very different forms of iconography that insists we see, and therefore remember, aspects of the legacy of Columbus that have been too often written out of non-native cultural memory.

The second image is the painting *Columbus Landfall* by Oakland, California, artist William Snyder. (See figure 1.3.) I encountered this image in an exhibit "500 Years Since Columbus" on view at the Triton Museum of Art in Santa Clara, California, in the spring of 1992. The curatorial intent of this exhibit was to present cultural work that challenged viewers' historical imagination regarding Columbus and his legacy. In Synder's attempt to transform historical memory, he gestures toward the historic painting *The Landing of Columbus on San Salvador, Oct. 12, 1492* by John Vanderlyn. (See figure 1.4.) Completed between 1839 and 1846, Vanderlyn's depiction of the Columbus landfall as a noble and heroic accomplishment hangs in the rotunda of the U.S. Capital building in Washington, D.C. It has been reprinted on U.S. currency and stamps, as well as in numerous history textbooks. Recognizing that Vanderlyn's work is well sedimented in the historical imaginary of many citizens of the United States, Synder positions the

Figure 1.3 William Snyder, painting—*Columbus Landfall*. Courtesy of the family of William Snyder.

Figure 1.4 John Vanderlyn, painting—*the Landing of Columbus in San Salvador*, October 12, 1942. United States Capital Historical Society.

narrative gesture of this image as up for reinscription. His work addresses the viewer most powerfully when one can recall at least a partial image of Vanderlyn's painting and, thus, make it available for interrogation. Unlike many works exhibited during 1992, which depicted Columbus as a diabolic figure literally employing skeletal or demonic figures as representational tropes for configuring the European invaders, Synder, with a good deal of humor, reimages Columbus by placing him with a very particular pantheon of North American cinematic imagination. Here, Columbus is metonymically Gene Wilder—or more to the point—the crazed Young Frankenstein who stands surrounded by the likes of the Three Stooges and Disney characters. Using humor (as opposed to horror) to "re-sign" Columbus, Synder produces a remembrance practice that brings the North American past and present in a close dialectical relationship. The intended pedagogical effect is a shift in the interpretive and emotional resonances of the image of Columbus on the beach—a shift produced by an assumed familiarity with the narratives and structure of feeling associated with contemporary figures drawn from American popular culture.

Betancur's and Dante's posters and Synder's painting are, for me, visually compelling attempts to engage the viewer in a way that forces a revision of the living memory of the European discovery of America and its consequent genocide and colonialism. Both works attempt visual pedagogies meant to rupture or displace memories that unproblematically celebrate Columbus and his legacy. As interesting as I think these images are, they do

Figure 1.5 Karen Atkinson, image (I) from installation. *Remapping Tales of Desire*, 1991.

have important pedagogical limitations. Neither imagery addresses the viewer's personal location in the formation of a historical imaginary, nor considers how this imaginary continues to operate in the contemporary world. Even more significant, however, is that these works contain little that might initiate questions as to the origin of our existing memories and the practices that have organized specific forms of collective forgetting as well as remembrance.

Figure 1.6   Karen Atkinson, image (II) from installation. *Remapping Tales of Desire*, 1991.

There is a third pedagogical strategy that appeared in counter-Quincentenary cultural practice that took up the agenda of interrogating the legacy of colonialism in contemporary everyday life, challenging tendencies to distance issues and attempting to provoke a witnessing of their continuing presence. This strategy is well illustrated by the work of Karen Atkinson. Atkinson developed a commemorative practice centered on the issue of how the representation of discovery was relentlessly raced and gendered, what that representational practice legitimated, and how its legacy remains with us today. Her work consists of installations that super-impose contemporary photographs from Caribbean travel brochures with original wood cuts depicting indigenous peoples experiencing the European invasion. (See figures 1.5 and 1.6.) Juxtaposed with these images are texts from tourist magazines, travel brochures, Columbus's diary and letters, as well as from a variety of Renaissance books, which extol the wonders of the New World. What Atkinson's work makes clear is a remarkable continuity in the way in which the Caribbean is textually constituted for a population not indigenous to its islands (Atkinson, 1992). These lands, in the words of promotional tourism, remain "virgin, unspoiled, seductive, refined, laid back . . . they wait just for you." Without collapsing the specificity of different historical eras, what Atkinson is asking us to recognize is the continuity of the colonialist tropes of desire, which organize so much of the North American popular representation of the Caribbean. These are desires that promise fulfillment in a particular form of relationship, where the Other is the exotic, but available and willing, object who is open to being taken.

The insurgent character of the historical images and text employed by Atkinson re-remember the European discovery, but are now reevaluated as a perverse referent that persists in taken-for-granted texts of tourism. From the standpoint of the Other (indigenous/women), Atkinson's work attempts to force a new recognition of a particular colonialist discourse in order to expose its moral frameworks, but in a manner that encourages us to use such a recognition for an interrogation and evaluation of the present and our standpoint in it. In other words, Atkinson has created a visual pedagogy in which remembrance becomes a process by which we are asked—by recognizing our complicity in the continued intelligibility of colonialist discourse—to reconsider the desires and associated assumptions that structure the eros that informs both our human encounters and our ecological interrelation with the environments through which we move.

If one accepts this form of pedagogy as a valuable addition to the notion of insurgent commemoration, a question arises as to how the voices and histories of those who have not been previously heard should be positioned together within a project where the main focus is to "work on ourselves." The answer, I think, is that these two focal themes must proceed in parallel. One emphasis provokes remembrance of invasion, resistance, and survival as an insurgent critique of the idea that any of the nation-states of the Americas should continue to be informed through narratives that propose a common identity linked within a single unifying culture and history. The other emphasizes that past forms of encounter are not to be grasped as inevitable consequences of history—as simply casualties in the early construction of the modern world—but as constituted through the actions of people. On such terms, remembrance is able to take seriously the perspective of those made victim and refuse the obscenity of accepting their suffering in the name of history. Instead of offering the deadening mantle of guilt, it challenges us to act in the name of a collective responsibility to continue the quest for justice and the establishment of new forms of interdependency that honor the dignity and specificity of the other people's lives.

CHAPTER TWO

Pedagogy and the Call to Witnessing
Marc Chagall's White Crucifixion

Should we consider it pathological to burden oneself with the past, while the healthy and realistic person is absorbed in the present and its practical concerns? That would be to appropriate a moral from "And it's as good as if it never happened,"... uttered by the devil at a decisive point in *Faust* to reveal his innermost principle: the destruction of memory.

Theodor Adorno, 1986, 117

Practices of remembrance work on and through us. Understood pedagogically, assertions about the past articulated into images and narratives and deployed in social space do not divest people of their desire or obligations to remember. Rather, the intended function of such practices is to animate and mediate the process of remembering. In this perspective, historical memory is an ensemble of educative acts, not simply aimed at establishing, affirming, or correcting "the record," but most importantly intended as practices that enable a living memory—one that dialectically presses on the sense of one's future purposes and possibilities. The antithesis of a living memory is a frozen one; a form of remembrance in which the past is nothing but the past. In contradistinction, practices of remembrance whose aim is the formation of living memory attempt to evoke the witnessing of historical images and narratives, the consequence of which is a nonsynchronous reconfiguration of past and present.

My primary concern is with historical memories that address events, the remembrance of which incorporate, as one aspect of their particularity, violence perpetrated on persons because of their membership in a larger group conceived of in terms of particular devalued, derided, and/or feared characteristics. Possibilities for such practices have to be considered within the nexus of questions of knowledge (what is a truthful representation), ethics (to what responsibilities must practices of remembrance be accountable), and power (what practices might produce effective forms of remembrance). In response to these concerns, my interest is in pedagogies that might disrupt and transform the complex of logos and desire which has made sensible and justifiable practices within which some people establish relations of exploitation, dominion, or indifference with regard to others.

It is by no means clear, however, how encounters with images and narratives that inscribe versions of past realities might work to form a living memory within which people may trace and transform the social grammars of violence that are manifest in realities such as genocide, colonialism, slavery, racism, and misogynous, gender-directed violence. Such an agenda invokes the difficult, and often painful, task of coming to terms with the past, not in a relation of mastery in which some ultimate repression is possible, but in terms of working-through the materials of remembrance in a way that produces something new (Friedlander, 1992). Rather than being narrowly therapeutic, "working-through" here implies "the possibility of judgement that is not apodictic or ad hominem but argumentative, self-questioning, and related in mediated ways to action" (LaCapra, 1994, 120). As James Young (1993, 13) suggests, the question is not simply of how people are moved by historically referential images and narratives, "but rather, to what end have they been moved, to what historical conclusions, to what understanding and actions in their own lives?" Giving primacy to the pedagogical character of Marc Chagall's *White Crucifixion*, my intention is to clarify how documented engagements with this image exemplify and clarify the importance of this agenda. In these considerations, the boundaries that delimit the historical memory of the Nazi genocide of European Jewry are at stake.

Images and Historical Memory

What is the function of pictures in historical memory? A full discussion of this question would, of course, require a multiform set of considerations not the least of which would be the metonymic burden of pictures to re-temporalize images of people and places so as to bring the absent presence they reference into juxtaposition with everyday concerns. My project, however, moves in a different direction; toward a vision of visioning history, toward an understanding of the terms and conditions on which images enable practices of looking, which intervene in capabilities to perceive, judge, feel, and speak about the past. In other words, my concern is with a visual culture in which the burden of memory is not borne by image-objects but, at least in part, through a reflexive practice of memory work instigated and enriched by expressive imagery. What is stake then is the possibility of a pictorial mediation of historical consciousness and what that consciousness implies regarding future possibilities and the necessary and desirable ways of acting in the present. This leads to a focal consideration; the specific qualities of pictures that may complicate and trouble frameworks of historical certainty and identification, which commonly regulate the dynamics of remembrance.

What is it about pictures, and images they contain, that justifies an extended consideration of how they may inform living memories? The fragmentary elements of historical memory typically consist of highly selected images, anecdotes, dates, and descriptive statistics that are invested with particular significance and emotion with regard to their reference and rendering of specific activities, places, and personalities. Rarely grasped as comprehensive, coherent histories, elements of historical memory do not exist as isolated facts, figures, and stories. Rather, historical memory provides a constellation of representations interrelated to the degree that their interconnections can be proposed (or ignored) through the story-telling practices provoked by one's contemporary desire to produce an intelligible, manageable past. This is not to embrace some normative notion of what it means to "tell" a story, but only to reference remembrance as culturally specific ways of inflecting time through an array of depictions and symbolizations of spatially located events.

Understood within these terms, the central function of pictures with regard to historical memory is the way they precipitate the desire for, and participate in the enactment of, narrative. This said, the interest here is in those images that have the capacity to instigate complex and unruly narrativizations, which are able to secure remembrance as something other than a facile and reproductive gesture. What visual qualities of an image might be implicated in this insurgent agenda? One might begin an answer by attending to the gestus of an image; that visual grammar that helps give form to an imaginative enactment of the actions, emotions, and activity signified and intimated in the image. However, in suggesting that images "gesture" toward narratives (and strategies for suturing image and "text"), it is important to underscore the incommensurabilty of visual and linguistic representation. Clearly, images do enhance and extend language-coded narratives, but they do so in ways that do not completely reduce that enhancement and extension to verbal or written statements. As Mitchell (1994, 152) suggests, linguistic representation cannot make present its object in the same way a visual representation can. "It may refer to an object, describe it, invoke it, but can never bring its visual presence before us in the way that pictures do. Words can 'cite,' but never 'sight' their objects."

What is it then in the visuality of an image (in excess of what can be denotatively inscribed as its referent) that makes certain pictures a rich resource for insurgent commemorative practice? Naming this presence requires at least a double coding. First is the associative potency of an image; a degree of figural ambiguity that encourages the adherence of an array of connotative images, ideas, and feelings. This connotative richness makes room for a range of contradictory associations, which would be disallowed or marginalized by the authority of an overdetermined figural and/or textural denotation. As stressed by Maclear (1995), these connotative or associative aspects of an image transgress attempts of discursive frameworks to fix and "say" what a work is about. When images are not easily tied off with the bonds of a given discursive inscription, there exists a quality that encourages cleaving of memories and bits of knowledge whose polythematic character may prompt and serve an interrogative turn in the dynamics of remembrance.

Second, and equally important to emphasize, is that images with an insurgent commemorative force produce an effusion of unresolved visual concern elicited by discontinuities structured into an image's composition, texture, colors, and use of light. It is beyond my purpose here to assay the full range of discontinuities structured into visual forms within specific media. Given my focus on the *White Crucifixion*, I will simply exemplify the point with John Berger's (1991) observation that many paintings with power to move us are clear as to what is being shown while proposing doubt as to its location, that is, as to where, what is there, is. Berger is referencing spatial discontinuities unresolved by formal perspective. Indeed, with regard to the *White Crucifixion*, I will argue that its commemorative pedagogy begins within its spatial breaks, supplying a jolt of incongruity enhancing the image's interest and extending the visual concern it provokes. This is not a neutral provocation. It demands an accounting of the image's discontinuities; an accounting that threatens historical understanding with unresolved contradictions unless contained within some master framework that settles the problems the painting poses.

Taken together these two qualities, associative potency and an extended visual concern provoked by structured discontinuities, produce "sticky" images. The stickiness of an image is its facility for accumulating associations and questions that not only make an image memorable but also perturbing and inciting. The stickiness of an image enables (but does not decisively secure) a particular way of looking—one that requires a working through the narrative implications of thought-images in which conceptual, material, and pictorial elements remain in a flux that eludes attempts to fix them (Huyssen, 1995). In this context, what makes sticky images particularly fascinating is the fact that their insertion into practices of remembrance, at times, yields yet unsaid or socially and psychically repressed narratives. This is of crucial concern for understanding the potential of images to enter into the formation of historical memory.

In what follows, I will begin to address the *White Crucifixion* and the difficult problems that arise in considering its deployment in practices of remembrance—problems rooted in responses to both its associative potency and spatial discontinuities. What will be at issue throughout this discussion is how and with what consequences for remembrance, historically and institutionally delimited interpretive frameworks structure responses to the instigation of Chagall's sticky image. (See figure 2.1.)

The Testimony of the *White Crucifixion*

As the popular circulation of Chagall's images have been most insistently romantic, I was surprised not only by the possibility of a pedagogical reading of the *White Crucifixion* but by the small plaque placed next to the painting at its site of permanent exhibition at the Art Institute of Chicago. The plaque

Figure 2.1 Marc Chagall, French, B. Belarous, 1887–1985, *White Crucifixion*, 1938, oil on canvas, 154.3 × 139.7 cm, gift of Alfred S. Alschuler, 1946.925. Reproduction, The Art Institute of Chicago, © Estate of Marc Chagall/SODRAC (Montreal) 2004.

contextualizes the painting as Chagall's effort to draw attention to the anti-Jewish Nazi pogroms in Germany during the 1930s and the dangers imminent for European Jewry.[1] The image and text presented at the Art Institute underscores the complications in viewing the painting; it may be seen not only as an expression of Chagall's anxieties and creative vision but—pedagogically speaking—a historical referent with the potential to provoke a dialectical intertwining of the past and the present with decisive insurgent effects.

It was the possibility of an insurgent address that left me with a strong sense of ambivalence about the *White Crucifixion*. How was this address being rendered in the painting and with what effects? Chagall had clearly constructed a dynamic tension between the central image of the crucified Jew Jesus and the depiction of Jewish experience of oppression by Nazis. The painting is dated 1938 providing a visual mark that strengthens its association with the political events and pogroms in Germany during that year. On the central axis of the canvas, Christ is depicted wearing a head covering instead of the traditional crown of thorns. In lieu of a loincloth, Christ is wrapped in a fringed garment which visually gestures to a *tallit* (the Jewish prayer shawl). Above Christ's head appears the traditional INRI (Jesus of Nazareth, King of the Jews) as well as its translation into Aramaic, the vernacular of Jews at the time of Jesus' life. The scenes surrounding Christ on the sides and lower border of the painting are rendered with, for Chagall, an uncharacteristic realism. They function as allusive visual citations of specific events in Nazi Germany. The burning of Jewish books and the public labeling of Jews with large signs hung across their bodies were common practices. Amishai-Maisels (1991) is most explicit about the probable connection of these images to the specifics of Nazi persecution of Jews.

> The latter [images] may also refer to the first Jewish census (May 17, 1938), the registration and marking of Jewish businesses (June 14, 1938), the forced adoption by Jews of the names Abraham and Sarah (August 17, 1938), and the stamping of the letter "J" ("Jude") into Jewish passports (October 5, 1938)—all events that happened while Chagall was working on the painting. Moreover, the burning of the Torah ark and the desecration of the scrolls in the painting were almost certainly inspired by the destruction of the synagogues in Munich and Nuremberg on June 9 and August 10, 1938, while the pogrom on the left side of the painting can be linked with those that occurred throughout the year, reaching their height on *Kristallnacht* (November 9–10, 1938). (142)

The Art Institute plaque referred to above inscribes the *White Crucifixion* as a specific address by Chagall (publically identified as a Jewish painter) to an audience of Christians with regard to a set of actual events of concern to the painter. In these terms, the painting is a form of testimony; a performative engagement between consciousness and history (Felman and Laub, 1992). As a testimonial practice, its function is not just to transmit information about the past but rather to serve in defining a transactional relation in which Christians are being called to bear witness to how Jews[2] had lived and are living history.

In the *White Crucifixion*, Chagall is testifying to the crucifixion of the Jew Jesus and the persecutions of Jews in Germany under Hitler; he is juxtaposing representations of both events in an attempt to provoke a particular mode of apprehending and responding to the entwining of these historical images. The painting tries to state the record while showing a multilayered historical truth.[3] Apprehended as testimony, Chagall's work literally seeks to find a way to keep the image of specific events before Christian eyes, forcing a confrontation with the implications of the image's dialectical tension.

Of course, the painting need not be seen on these terms. Chagall's testimony can be readily viewed through the lens of art connoisseurship or spectacle. Such practices depend on a splitting of the testimonial referents (in this case, substantive and formal aspects of the painting) from the transactional enunciation of a lived engagement with the prior events. Within this splitting, testimony is seen or heard as something to be rendered meaningful within classification and analysis (as in much art history discourse) or used as a source of compulsive fascination (as when the representation of genocide turns into spectacle). Neither of these positions offers much potential for the incorporation of Chagall's testimony as living memory. To do so requires a shift away from problematics of identification (of the image or with the substance of the image) to an acceptance of the responsibilities imposed by the transactional relation of testimony and witnessing.

Accepting the call to witness means accepting the possible insufficiency of the terms of one's own understanding of history. As an ethical practice of apprehension, witnessing implies an openness and reflexivity in one's encounters with testimony accepting that it may initiate a restructuring of one's understanding of the interrelationship among the past, present, and future; establishing possibilities for the alteration of one's priorities, evaluations, and actions. Witnessing, thus, requires formulating judgments as to the substance and significance of what is to be remembered. These judgments are dependent not only on epistemological terms for the apprehension of history but also on the ethical terms that structure witnessing as a transactional task. As such, witnessing also implies the acceptance of very particular obligations. First, it requires one to bear (to support and endure) the weight or psychic burden of historical events, acknowledging that memories of violence and injustice do press down on one's personal and collective sense of humanity and moral equilibrium. Second, it requires one to bear (carry) or transport/translate stories of past injustices beyond their moment of telling by taking these stories to another time and space where they become available to be heard or seen. Third, it requires one to bear the transactional responsibility of showing or telling (to bring forth, to give testimony to) what one has witnessed in the testimony of another to others. This is a carrying forth that, through one's word, images, and/or actions, makes apparent a difference—a difference provoked by what has been borne. This a responsibility referenced by the Hebrew verb "*ta-eh-nah*" (תענה) which has connotations of both providing testimony and answering or responding to a question, a call, or summons to "speak out" (in word or deed), not for others but on behalf of what one has seen or heard. What is at stake is a "bearing witness" that in itself becomes another moment of giving testimony, initiating a chain of possible transactional relations that, if taken to its logical implication, would result in the transformation of a historical imaginary and a revitalization of an ethical public sphere.

If witnessing then can be understood pedagogically as a normative mode of apprehension and response to testimony, how then might the *White Crucifixion* be understood as part of an ensemble of practices with the potential to provoke the witnessing of events connected to the Shoah?

What could initiate the possibility that seeing this painting could make a difference to one's life in the world? This is not a naive question. The painting's figural ambiguity and the extended visual concern provoked by its image function as a deep-seated pedagogical structure rooted not in didacticism or expressions of solidarity, which commonly define the intent of "political art," but in the questioning organized through the design and rendering of the image. From this perspective, the *White Crucifixion* can be understood as a commemorative practice that simultaneously states questions put to history, which demand a response from viewers as well as providing answers to questions viewers have still to ask. Whether, and in what way, viewers respond to this demand will determine much of the insurgent potential in Chagall's painting. My interest here is in exploring the painting's pedagogical power to instantiate both questions and answers.

An Insurgent Commemoration?

To grasp the pedagogical structure of the *White Crucifixion* is not to accede to its efficacy. Chagall's call to witness is not unproblematic. There has been no universal appreciation of the painting as an insurgent image that either indicts those who abandoned the teachings of Jesus in the context of modern abandonment of European Jewry, nor questions the complicity of Christian anti-Judaism and trumphalist theology in the complex determinations of and widespread indifference to Hitler's *Endlösung* (the "Final Solution to the question of the Jews"). Furthermore, the notion of witnessing itself is not an adequate basis for defining an insurgent commemoration. It is certainly possible that one can witness Chagall's crucified Jewish Christ in confirmation that the suffering on the Cross is emblematic for all human suffering throughout history, or that the figure of the Jew on the Cross provides a meaning for Jewish suffering and death. With these important reservations in mind, the rest of this chapter is an attempt to think through the consequences of taking up the *White Crucifixion* as both an aesthetic and pedagogical form; consequences that I believe have a general importance in understanding the terms for a desirable pedagogy of remembrance.

As trite as it may seem, it is necessary to reemphasize the fact that paintings do not remember, people do. Until now, I have presented a rather idealized, acontextual, and (for the most part) de-politicized discussion of the educative potential of the *White Crucifixion* as an element of commemorative practices. Andreas Huyssen (1993) suggests that the success of any practice of remembrance will have to be measured by the extent to which it "hooks up" with multiple discourses of memory. What must be kept firmly in mind is that the possibility of initiating a nonsynchronous witnessing of an account of past events is dependent on the way in which a commemorative element (such as Chagall's painting) hooks into and traverses the multiple discursive networks that provide the conditions of intelligibility of

that representation. In other words, commemorative pedagogies are constituted in the traversal of discursive networks that set the terms not for how
an image is seen, but for how a person will interpret and respond to the
questions and answers that the images evoke.

Responses to the *White Crucifixion*

It is a commonplace to recognize that how people attend to and make
sense of the past is grounded in their investments, identities, experiences,
and aspirations. This does not mean, however, that the public framing of
remembrance is of no consequence. Such framing not only provides
resources for memory work but also for public discourses that validate (or
discourage) particular ways of remembering the past. Furthermore, engagement with and recognition of such discourses may also create communities
of memory, where bonding extends well beyond an individual's own
experience (Irwin-Zarecka, 1994, 56). Here, I want to focus on the *White
Crucifixion* as a form of public framing of historical events and ask in what
ways this painting activates what people bring to it and, in turn, how it
might function in the further articulation of those resources. Comparing
what several people have written about this painting provides a glimpse of
how the *White Crucifixion* "hooks" into existing affective investments and
interpretive resources to produce very different consequences for how the
testimony of the painting might be seen and remembered. Consider then
the following five brief "readings" of the *White Crucifixion* that focus on the
juxtaposition of the contemporary oppression of Jews and the crucified
Jesus.

(1) *Alexandre Benois*: In 1940, *Cahier d'Art* published an abstracted
version of a commentary on the exhibition at La Galerie MAI written by
Chagall's Russian friend Alexandre Benois. Benois's (1940) comments on
the *White Crucifixion* were quoted as follows:

> This painting was undoubtedly conceived in suffering. One feels
> that . . . something woke him (the artist) with a start, that he was
> frightened and revolted by it. It is clear that this vision was provoked
> by the events of the last years, especially by that untranslatable horror
> that has spread itself over Chagall's co-religionists . . . *The painting "Le
> Christ" represents something highly tragic* (It) corresponds entirely to the
> villainy of the epoch in which we live. *It is a document on the spirit of
> our time, a certain cry, a certain call . . .*[4] (emphasis mine)

Clearly, Benois connects the painting to what, at the time, were recent
events in Germany. He does not give a particular interpretation to the juxtaposition but seems to render the image as a tragic expression of evil
times—an image that in manifesting this tragedy calls or cries out.
However, at least in the extract of Benois's writing chosen for publication

in *Cahier d'Art*, what that cry consists of and to whom it is addressed remains unspecified.

(2) *Jean Cassou*: Writing just over a decade after the end of World War II, Jean Cassou was intent on rendering Chagall an ecumenical religious painter. The following are the consequences of Cassou's (1965) apprehension of the *White Crucifixion*.

> Here we have representations of the Jewish people. They are an expression of religious sentiment that goes beyond the differences between Judaism and Christianity, beyond the personalities and the doctrines of the two religions, and expresses rather what unites the two. Chagall takes no account of the differences and distinctions between them, but reduces all to the common denominator of human suffering . . . The concept of suffering with which he identifies leads him to the common ground between religions . . .
>
> As a Jew (Chagall) suffers with the Jews as well as with the King of the Jews—words which appear in Hebrew characters beneath the traditional INRI on the inscription of one of the crucifixions—this King of the Jews who to Christians is the son of God incarnate and who died on the Cross for the salvation of all men after he had taught them to love one another . . . (247–248).

Cassou is more explicit in addressing the juxtaposition directly. He interprets it as expressive of human suffering. While others and I might strenuously object, Cassou comes close to suggesting that Chagall's deployment of the crucified Christ gives Jewish suffering a transcendent meaning.

(3) *Franz Meyer*: Franz Meyer (1964), who was one of the first to document and discuss Chagall's work in a comprehensive manner, saw the *White Crucifixion* this way:

> This Christ is really crucified, stretched in all his immense pain above a world of horror. Men are hunted, persecuted, murdered; a fearful din fills the "vast ivory space" he dominates and permeates as if he wanted to bear it all and give it a meaning. But although Christ is the central figure, this is by no means a Christian picture. The scenes that frame the cross, twined round it like a crown of thorns—from the shattered village to the pillaged, burning synagogue—constitute an exemplary Jewish martyrology . . . But Jewish is not solely this tale of woe: Christ himself is a Jew. Above his head Chagall has clearly written the Biblical "Jesus of Nazareth, King of the Jews" . . . But most important of all, this Christ's relation to the world differs entirely from that in all Christian representations of the Crucifixion . . .
>
> It is not the world that suffers, except in grief for his death on the cross; all suffering is concentrated in Christ, transferred to him in order that he may overcome it by his sacrifice. Here instead, though all the suffering of the world is mirrored in the Crucifixion, suffering remains

man's lasting fate and is not abolished by Christ's death. So Chagall's
Christ figure lacks the Christian concept of salvation. For all his
holiness he is by no means divine. This Christ is a man who suffers
pain in a thousand forms and yet finally always in the same form, a
man who is eternally burned by the fire of the world and yet, being
an archetype, remains indestructible. It is not his divine but his human
nature that Christ's suffering preserves . . .

   The *White Crucifixion* is full of contemporary history, so full of it
indeed that in a mere reproduction every detail thrusts itself too much
upon the beholder's attention. The painting itself makes a totally
different impact; the details lose none of the tragic sharpness one finds
so moving, but in the unity of the picture form they become part of
a timeless, necessary tragedy. In this work Chagall has given the
suffering and distress of the present day the same primordial reality he
gave the Bible story. (415–416)

Meyer rejects any possibility of Christ giving Jewish suffering redemptive meaning, and in doing so, observes that the *White Crucifixion* is not a
Christian picture. In Christian representations of the crucifixion, the
suffering of the world is transferred to Christ so that He can redeem
the world with His suffering. But in the *White Crucifixion*, Meyer suggests
that Jesus' death does nothing to relieve the suffering that spread throughout the world. There is no salvation and suffering remains an everlasting
human fate. Here, then, Christ becomes the archetype not of the divine
presence who saves, but the eternal man who burns but is not consumed.
Meyer, thus, renders the tragedy as not historical but trans-historical and
the Jews—the suffering servants—as the archetype for the unending pain
integral to human existence.

   Although Benois, Cassou, and Meyer differ substantially in their apprehension of the painting, they all seem willing to accept Chagall's figuration
of Christ as an image that repeats the scene at Golgotha. This repetition is
understood as enacting a mimesis within which the iconography of the
Crucifixion writes a narrative of universal (perhaps eternal) suffering
according to which the Jew is positioned and identified. Benois hears the
cry of that suffering but says nothing of its locus in the painting's imagery.
Cassou responds to the specificity of the imagery through an erasure of
Jewish and Christian differences, thus, demonstrating the risk in Chagall's
practice of nonsynchronous juxtaposition. In his response, the Jewish subject is taken over by the Christian Other despite Chagall's emphasis on the
Jewish identity of Jesus. Meyer, too, accepts the repetition but, in grasping
the difference the repetition enacts, seems to suggest a practical solidarity
that could result from a meeting of those who suffer and are not redeemed.

   These engagements with the *White Crucifixion* are full of compassion,
but, as responses of witnessing, they are deeply disturbing in what they
displace. In their compassion, these engagements resolve the ambiguities in
the questions posed and answers given by the painting without troubling

the iconographic authority of the Cross. In doing so, they bear witness to the horror of the Shoah but through a process that unburdens them of any obligation to respond in and to the moment in which they view the realities represented in the painting. There is, however, another genre of response to the *White Crucifixion*. The next two instances exemplify something much more reflexively radical.

(4) *Ziva Amishai-Maisels*: Ziva Amishai-Maisels is the most explicit in viewing the painting as an insurgent image (Amishai-Maisels, 1989). She writes as follows:

> Chagall's choice of subject . . . took his intended audience into account. He did not have to explain to Jews what was happening— they already knew. Instead, he wanted to explain the deeper meaning of events in Germany to Christians, and to do so he decided to address them in their own symbolic language, through the use of the Crucifixion . . . (151)

> Chagall was not trying to depict the Christian Messiah who overcomes all suffering through his sacrifice, but the Jewish martyr who holds out no hope of salvation . . . In the *White Crucifixion* he preached . . . loudly and clearly, stating that what was happening in Germany was a recrucifixion of the Jewish Jesus, an act that only a world forgetful of Christ's teachings could tolerate. He wanted this message to be understood by the Christian world, and to have a positive effect on that world's behavior. (153)

Like Meyer, Amishai-Maisels also interprets the Christ image as something other than a conventional Christian symbol. She recognizes that the *White Crucifixion* is intended for a particular audience (Christians) and sees the painting as addressing this audience through a repetition that draws on Christian symbolic language. To effect this repetition, she reads Chagall as drawing on what, for Jews, has been a dominant alien language and culture, using this language to signal the figuration of a Jewish Christ that emanates from a place outside this master discourse. Given this perspective on the painting's construction, in what sense can the *White Crucifixion* be understood to enact a repetition? Chagall's repetition of the scene at Golgotha here becomes a form of *insurgent* mimicry. The crucified Jesus in the *White Crucifixion* is "almost the same" as in Christian representations but not quite. This difference produces a slippage—a moment of excess of meaning—that constructs a profound ambivalence with regard to Jesus' presence in the painting. What is insurgent in this ambivalence is a challenge to the authenticity of Christian behavior. This challenge is rendered through the ironic assertion that, by forgetting Christ's teachings, Christians were, in effect, nonsynchronously condemning Jesus to death in the gas chambers. Amishai-Maisels brings us to the brink of a very different response to the painting; it is left to Karl Plank to accept the challenge of the abyss beyond that brink.

(5) *Karl Plank*: Plank responds to the painting within the more explicit awareness of the history of the Shoah. He not only grasps what Amishai-Maisels understood about the painting but also takes its implications further. He responds to the Christian address that Amishai-Maisels explicates by making explicit the deep insurgency of the painting. This is an insurgency whose intelligibility is made possible by Plank's familiarity with, and acceptance of, the agenda of post-Shoah Christian theology. Viewed from the vantage point of this discursive formation, the painting poses very troubling questions. For Plank, Chagall's mimicry does not only menace the authenticity of Christian behavior, it challenges the very authority of the central concepts of Christian theology. In the following excerpts, Plank (1987) makes this clear and tries in his own way to formulate a response to that understanding.

> We must not misunderstand Jewish appropriation of the cross in the context of Holocaust art and literature. Where used at all, the cross functions not as an answer to atrocity, but as a question, protest and critique of the assumptions we may have made about profound suffering . . . *White Crucifixion* depicts a world of unleashed terror within which no saving voice can be heard nor any redeeming signs perceived. Separated from the imperiled villagers by only his apparent passivity, Chagall's Messiah, this Jew of the cross, is no rescuer, but himself hangs powerless before the chaotic fire. The portrayal of Messiah as victim threatens to sever the basic continuity we have wanted to maintain between suffering and redemption (or to use Christian imagery, between cross and resurrection). To have redemptive meaning, the cross must answer the victims who whirl here in torment, for, in the Holocaust, the world becomes Golgotha turned on itself . . . Yet precisely here the language of redemption seems trivial, if not obscenely blind to the sufferer's predicament . . .
>
> Crucifixion, be it the cross of Jesus or the nocturnal Golgotha of Auschwitz, breaks the moral continuities by which we have considered ourselves secure and whole. To mend these fragments of human experience lies outside our power. We cannot repair the broken world . . .
>
> We cannot give our victims the cross, for they are already its true bearers. Rather it is they who present the cross to us in the form of an awful scandal. The *White Crucifixion* returns to us the meaning of the cross in its most powerful form. The Jewish testament enables us to see anew what centuries of resurrection enthusiasm have obscured in our won tradition: the fractured bond between God and the world; the lived moment of forsakeness to which we are vulnerable and for which we are responsible in the lives of one another. (966)

In terms of witnessing, Plank's response is of interest precisely because he displays his willingness to wrestle with the ambivalence he sees within the painting. This ambivalence makes clear an "inappropriate" figuration of

Christ, which renders a truth that disturbs the authoritative narratives of the Crucifixion and its aftermath. Antithetically to Cassou, who views the painting through a discourse that represses difference, Plank grasps the repetition in the *White Crucifixion* as the enactment of a resemblance that differs from and defends presence by its partial display. This constructs what Bhabha (1994a) calls a "metonymy of presence," whose insurgent mimicry sets off disruptions to, in this case, a discursive frame that has historically rendered a series of self-confident and self-aggrandizing identity effects.

Of the five interpretations presented herein, the first three do not apprehend the ambivalence in the painting and seem to have no discursive basis for doing so. The other two, written in the shadows of the Shoah, recognize a mimetic slippage whose tensions must be addressed. It is this recognition that activates the painting's insurgent potential. The *White Crucifixion* provides the resources for the reading of a metonymy that alienates the Passion as a trope of universal suffering throwing that discourse into crisis. Seen in this light, the viewer invested in that discourse is obligated to respond to this crisis. Plank does not offer self-serving compassion or any pretense of empathy, but, rather, in his recognition of the specificity of Jewish men, women, and children who were constituted the objects of the *Endlösung*, he seems ready to answer to the legacy of a Christian triumphalism and teaching of contempt whose ultimate consequence is Jesus' nonsynchronous arrival at Auschwitz.

Contemporary Refractions of the *White Crucifixion*: The Renewal of Ambivalence

Some might think that after the war, once the full extent of the destructiveness and horror of the *Endlösung* had become known, the juxtaposition of Golgotha and Auschwitz had become an anachronism and hence Plank's insurgent framework of remembrance interesting, but hardly relevant to contemporary Holocaust commemoration. This is not, however, the case. In a speech at Auschwitz on May 7, 1979, Pope John Paul II declared that Auschwitz had become the "Golgotha of the modern world," and the Jews who had died there, died with Christ's Cross placed over their shoulders. John Paul's statement renewed the image-text of the Jew on the Cross; refracting this renewal through an interpretive turn in which the saving power of Jesus' suffering on the cross is transferred to those martyred in the camps. The similarity between this position and Cassou's interpretation of Chagall's image is quite straightforward. Understandably, for those invested in the traditional discourses of Christian theology, which continue to affirm "victorious power of the cross of Jesus," the image of the Jew on the Cross subsumes Jewish difference into a humankind yet to be redeemed.

This is no metaphysical abstraction without consequence for the dynamics of historical memory. Consider, by way of illustration, the controversy over the beatification of Edith Stein and the ensuing justifications provided. In the 1980s, the Vatican announced the initiation of the beatification process for Stein, a Jewish convert to Roman Catholicism who had entered a Carmelite convent under the name Sister Benedicta of the Cross. For the Germans, however, Sister Benedicta was a Jew who was arrested, transported to Birkenau, and in 1942, killed along with thousands of others in one of the early prototype gas chambers. According to John Paul, she had died the death of a Christian martyr and a daughter of the Jewish people. Cardinal Ratzinger clarified just what this meant:

> Stein . . . once she became a Catholic was saying: "Now I feel myself back to true Judaism" Because not only did she regain the faith in God, but finding the faith in Christ, she entered in the full heritage of Abraham . . . Entering the union with Christ she entered in the heart of Judaism. Following the thought of St. Paul we can say that becoming a Christian, I became a true Jew. (Dwork and van Pelt, 1994, 245)

In other words, Jewish difference is rendered and reiterated as a practice that stands outside the true faith. This position, of course, surprises no one familiar with the long history of supersessionism in Church doctrine and the seeming unwillingness of the Vatican to extend the pluralist positions taken in the decree *Nostre Aetate* issued at the second Vatican council in the mid-60s (Minerbi, 1989).

The legitimacy of the image of Christ at Auschwitz has also been extended outside of the sphere of the Church. The final paragraph of the entry "Shoah" in the 1992 supplement to the encyclopedia *Grand Larousse Universel* contains the following:

> Because of (the Shoah's) unique status, it is not only Judaism which it affects. Whether or not one shares a religious view of the world, it is not excessive to see in it an event of the same nature as the crucifixion of Jesus, on the very horizon of the history of humanity, in all its darkness and with all its enigmas. The Shoah, then, is not only a fracture at the heart of the West which throws the figures of its universality into question, but also a paradigmatic event for all men [sic] since it is the irruption of the radical evil which spares no one. (Vulliet, 1994, 153)

This is quite an unexpected statement for an encyclopedic entry published by *Larousse* and leads to a series of troubling questions. One wonders how the Shoah can be compared to the crucifixion and what such a comparison could mean outside of a specific Christian commitment? What and whose discourses would make intelligible the statement that the Shoah is an event "of the same nature as the crucifixion"? How is *Larousse* contributing to the possibilities of witnessing the contemporary refractions of the Jew on the Cross?

It is not my purpose here to answer such questions; rather, I want to address what seems to me to be centrally at stake in this continued controversy concerning images that juxtapose Golgotha and Auschwitz, a theme I have been discussing throughout this chapter. Bernard Suchecky (1994) perhaps points in the right direction when he asks Jews:

> . . . by proclaiming "Don't put a cross through my memory!" weren't we wrong about the memory in need of protection? Wasn't the memory threatened by the Church primarily that of the non-Jewish world, in other words that of the historical consciousness of our societies? (169)

When Jewish memory is pitted over and against the memory of Poles, Roma, Soviets, homosexuals, and others who died at Auschwitz, what is being lost? If remembrance is solely affirmative (of my pain, my story), displaced may be a serious questioning of how memory is being framed in ways that bypass the possibility of a radical working through of the materials of remembrance. If I follow Suchecky correctly, the point I think is that if one embraces the premise (which I do) that the Shoah must be defined in terms of a specific effort to eradicate Jews simply because they were Jews, then what must become a priority are forms of remembrance that force the question of how such acts as the *Endlösung* are made intelligible. This said, it must in no way undermine *(in fact it must encourage)* the necessity for specific, concrete practices of remembrance that call for a bearing witness to the attempts to eradicate other groups of peoples. There are definite responsibilities here. Not all groups have the social power to shape the historical consciousness of societies.[5] Thus, connections and solidarities must be understood as required political and educational alliances, whose main task is to explore the substance and limits of the interconnections among remembrances in ways that contribute to the interminable journey toward justice.

In the context of this still quite insurgent agenda, perhaps the image of the nonsynchronous arrival of Jesus at Auschwitz remains of contemporary value. In the last two decades, there has developed a lively and hopeful conversation among a diverse group of theologians and biblical scholars willing to face the question of what it means to read scripture and do authentic Christian theology after the Shoah.[6] This exchange is an explicit attempt to work through the recognition that had the Jew Jesus of Nazareth lived in the "right" place and time, he would have been dispatched to the gas chamber. As a working through of remembrance, this effort aspires to (in word and deed) bear witness to the image of the crucified Jew amid bodies of burning Jews.

In bearing witness, such work places a demand on Christian faith that it be accountable to a moral responsibility enacted in a rigorous interrogation of that faith's complicity in the suffering of its victims. This work begins by accepting that Christian scriptures (particularly as they interpret the crucifixion, resurrection, and the truth of revelation of God in Christ) are a causative factor in setting the conditions of possibility for the Shoah through the propagation and maintenance of a doctrinal enmity toward Jews as Jews.[7] These theologians understand the cornerstone of Christian enmity toward Jews as rooted in the concept of supersession and a triumphalism justified in the myth that the mission of the Jewish people was finished with the coming of Jesus Christ. In confronting this, what is required is a radical reworking of the basic concepts of Christology.

The relevance of this theological work to my interests here is how it proceeds from a trope of remembrance, which transposes Auschwitz with Golgotha, in ways that trouble and transform the conditions of possibility for any such correspondence. For example, in their book *Long Day's Journey Into Night*, Roy and Alice Eckardt (1982) stress a specific evil within the present epoch that must be confronted by Christians.

> This is the evil and Godforsakenness of little children witnessing the murder of other little children while knowing that they also are to be murdered in the same way, being aware absolutely that they face the identical fate. Before this kind of event, the death of Jesus upon the cross is lost in relative moral nonsignificance. (135)

Within this understanding of the crucifixion, the metonymy of presence I have traced in this chapter evaporates. If Jesus is to appear at all at Auschwitz, it will have to be without his Cross—as a Jew like all the other Jews who entered the gas chambers without choice. This appearance would not reinscribe old dichotomies of Jewish pain and Christian guilt, but, rather, would create a place of meeting where a more productive conversation may be held as to co-joint responsibilities that might be borne into the future.

Earlier, I said that the *White Crucifixion* could be understood as a commemorative practice that states questions put to history, which demand a response while simultaneously providing answers to questions yet to be asked. The above range of responses to Chagall's painting surely indicate that how these questions and answers will be taken up will depend on which discourses can and will be invoked to mediate such an inquiry. There is an important insight for cultural pedagogy here. The insurgency of any given representational practice does not lie primarily in its message, but in whether and how such a practice develops questions, contradictions, and aporias whose very terms attract additional images and narratives that can admit to a fundamental uncertainty, as to their truth, while still answering to the investigations and reappraisals initiated by these practices.

Currently, our society seems suffused with remembrance; incited to remember. In light of future requirements, we still may find this remembrance deficient. If there is to be any attempt to redress forms of violence that ground their logic in assumptions of the supremacy of one group of people over another, we will require an anamnesis, structured not by our desires for self or collective affirmation, but by an effort to recover the origins and processes within which difference and otherness, exclusion and domination are produced. To be responsive to a hope for the future, such remembrance must rework what is meant by "coming to terms with the past," so that it informs a transformation of the basis on which we relate to others other than ourselves.

CHAPTER THREE

Remembering Obligation: Witnessing Testimonies of Historical Trauma

WITH CLAUDIA EPPERT

> True learning consists in receiving the lesson so deeply that it becomes a necessity to give oneself to the other. The lesson of truth is not held in one . . . consciousness. It explodes toward the other.
>
> Levinas, 1994b, 80

Educators often assume that meaningful encounters with traumatic historical events can be brought about through hearing, reading, or viewing accounts that make apparent personal engagements with history. These accounts variously take the form of diaries or eyewitness statements, documentary photographs or film, novels, poetry, stories, song, fictionalized film, or theatre. The primary purpose of all such accounts is the provision of testimony: to convey through multiple expressive forms the historical substance and significance of prior events and experiences. Testimony, thus, compromises representations either by those who have lived through such events or those who have been told or shown such lived realities, either directly or indirectly, and have been moved to convey to others what has been impressed upon them. Pedagogically, these testimonial accounts are deployed as modes of instruction that attempt to transmit information regarding the past and to keep specific events before one's eyes, thereby instantiating their significance for current and future generations (Wieviorka, 1994). As modes of instruction, such accounts carry the injunction "listen and remember." Yet, how such listening is to be accomplished and what remembrance might mean when mediated through testimony entails pedagogical, ethical, and epistemological considerations.

The Peformative Relation between Testimony and Witnessing

The pedagogical character of testimonial accounts lies in their structure as communicative acts. We view all testimony as produced in anticipation of the educative dynamics of representation and response. In this respect, a testimonial account is a performance intent on carrying forth memories by conveying a person's engagement between consciousness and history (Felman and Laub, 1992). Struggling with the difficulties of communicating experience through symbolic practices, such performances incur a responsibility to convey accurately a tangible sense of prior events in ways that enable their remembrance and the assessment of their significance. This responsibility marks the performativity of testimony as a moment of apprehension and communication in which one testifies to another who, in turn, chooses or is impelled to represent what was seen or heard, thus continuing the process with someone else. As Brinkley and Youra suggest, "To receive the words of a witness is to find that one has also become a witness, that one's responses are there for others to witness as well. Once the transmission begins, one cannot stand outside its address" (1996, 123). Hence, the first-order witness initiates a chain of testimony-witnessing held together by the bonds of an ethics forged in a relationship of responsibility and respect. Testimony is thus always directed toward another. It places the one who receives it under the obligation of response to an embodied singular experience not recognizable as one's own.

Focusing on the particular character of the demands of testimony of historical trauma, we use the term "historical trauma" to refer to human-initiated, catastrophic events, which, when witnessed, often evoke a specific set of experiential dynamics (Caruth, 1996). Most importantly, historically traumatic events summon forgetting and remembrance simultaneously. In their shock and extremity of horror, such events impel a forgetfulness or displacement at the same time that they repeatedly return on emotional and ethical terms for private and public consideration. This return is encouraged by the way in which such events resist assimilation into coherent and articulated explanatory frameworks. The incessant and insistent re-arrival of the past indicates how such events can and do possess their witnesses, commanding an attention fraught with complex emotion. This return of the past—this traumatization—is experienced not just by the primary witness (the survivor or eyewitness), but can occur for those who hear or read accounts of what others have experienced.

Testimony of historical trauma is, obviously, not intended to foster either repression or immobilization in the face of history. Rather, it is often understood as a vital personal supplement to impersonal documentary evidence. Pedagogically, it encompasses a means for "making history come alive". Overturning the anonymity that is often the fate of victims of historical trauma, testimony is treasured to the extent that it saves the shards of catastrophic experience from oblivion. Thus, as Carey-Webb notes, testimony may serve as an expression of survivance and loss, simultaneously aspiring to "human continuity, the establishment of justice, and the making of the future" (1996, 7). The moment when memory and history are brought together within these aspirations, testimony imposes particular obligations on those called to receive it—obligations imbued with the exigencies of justice, compassion, and hope that define the horizon for a world yet to be realized. These obligations are premised on the recognition that

> justice . . . is not an abstraction, a value. Justice exists in relation to a person, and is something done by a person. An act of injustice is condemned, not because the law is broken, but because a person has been hurt. (Heschel, 1962, 216)

An often quoted phrase from Benjamin's (1969) "Theses on the Philosophy of History" asserts:

> There is a secret agreement between past generations and the present one. Our coming was expected on earth. Like every generation that preceded us, we have been endowed with a *weak* Messianic power, a power to which the past has claim. That claim cannot be settled cheaply. (254)

We see this claim of past generations as one made on present capacities to act in ways that relieve the conditions under which injustice prevails. This claim is not just a matter of enacting some form of retribution or providing material redress as compensation for an oppressive and deadly violence inflicted on families and communities; nor is it an empty nostalgia or mourning for a lost portion of one's own identity. The claim of past generations made through the call to remembrance requires something more than an egoism that predefines remembrance as that which confirms who one is and what one knows. More radically, what is required is an ethics of remembrance that acknowledges and assesses the indexical character of testimonial practices, while referencing the people and events indexed as in excess of their narration and thematization. Such an ethics responds to the alterity, the singularity and noncomparability, of what is given in testimony, thus, opening the possibility that remembrance of historical trauma will place previously unacknowledged claims on one's identifications, plans, and actions. This ethics considers how and on what terms one can admit testimonial accounts into a contemporary moral community so that they make an active claim on one's present and future actions in ways that do not simply reduce the terms of this admittance to projections of one's own identities and desires. Finkielkraut emphasizes this concern when he polemically writes: "Memory does not consist in subordinating the past to the needs of the present . . . If the future is for all things the measure of value, memory has no ground: for he who looks to gather the materials of memory places himself at the service of the dead, and not the other way around" (1994, 54).

If witnessing is to be understood as one possible response to the "power to which the past has a claim," determining the specific obligations of witnessing that constitute a just and compassionate response to testimony becomes a vital concern. We argue that "bearing witness" to historical trauma demands (but does not necessarily secure) *acknowledgment, remembrance,* and some indication that the provision of the testimony has been of *consequence.* One must bear (support and endure) the weight or the psychic burden of a traumatic history, acknowledging that memories of violence and injustice do press down on one's sense of humanity and moral equilibrium; also, one must bear (carry) and, thus, transport and translate stories of past injustices beyond their moment of telling by taking these stories to another time and space where they become available to be heard or seen. Finally, through words, images, or actions, one must indicate to others not only why what one has seen or heard is worthy of remembrance but also how such a remembrance may inform one's contemporary perceptions and actions. Thus, witnessing is a practice that is completed not only by enduring the apprehension of difficult stories, but by transporting and translating these stories beyond their moment of enunciation. Central to witnessing is either the re-presentation to others of what one has heard or seen, or the enactment of one's relationship with others so as to make evident that one's practice has been informed by the living memory of prior testimony.

By invoking these obligations as central to witnessing, we assert that witnessing is first and foremost an ethical concept. In other words, witnessing is to be defined through a normative structure that sets the conditions of possibility for testimony's participation in just remembrance. Hence, in our view, witnessing can and should be distinguished from other possible responses to testimony; such as mimicry, voyeurism, or spectatorship.[1]

Meeting the obligations of witnessing testimonies of historical trauma requires a double attentiveness to intertwined ethical and epistemological responsibilities. Each form of this attentiveness bears upon the obligations of witnessing in different ways. That is, acknowledgment, remembrance, and consequence are accomplished on very different terms within these complementary modes of attention. The first form of double attentiveness involves judgments as to the accuracy and historical significance of testimony; it requires carefully attending to what is said in a testamentary account. The terms of this attentiveness are methodologically prescribed. To determine the significance and truth value of testimony, witnesses must accept their obligations as members of discourse communities that have normalized rules for making valid assertions about the past and present character of one's life-world. Those who engage testimony and then seek to bear witness to what they have heard, must—in practice—establish their allegiance to structures of evidence and theorization, which make possible just judgment. This engagement requires attending to the specific procedures for defining, legitimating, and validating information—procedures that make possible thematic statements as to the significance of any given testimony and that permit coherent and publicly justifiable statements about people, events, and objects. Eventually, such assertions may take the form of "histories," provisional narratives dependent on the codeterminative judgments as to what is regarded as factual evidence and how such evidence should be interpreted.

The second form of attentiveness inherent in the obligations of witnessing is a consignment of oneself as an apprentice to the provision of testimony. As an apprentice, one's obligation is to attend to the particular ways in which any testimony attempts to translate what is singular—a person's experience in or of the past—into an idiom through which witnesses can be addressed. To the extent that testimony burdens witnesses with considerations of judgment and apprenticeship, it is a doubled teaching; doubled through what Emmanuel Levinas (1991) terms, a "saying" and a "said." Contemplating the accuracy and historical significance of testimony is a response to its said. Attending to the translative, performative moment of testimony is a response to its saying.

Levinas asserts that "a saying states and thematizes the said, but signifies it to the other with a signification that has to be distinguished from that borne by words in the said" (1981, 46). The saying is irreducible to the ontological language of the said. It is "the non-thematizable ethical residue of language that escapes comprehension within the conceptual framing of thought" (Critchley, 1992, 24). This residue insistently invokes an undoing of the said, an interruption that marks the said's insufficiency and, hence, becomes a point for further approach and attunement to the fundamental alterity of a given testimony. The saying of testimony initiates a communicative encounter in which one may be seized in the performative moment of testimony by the transitive "facing" of the other and as a consequence, compelled to submit to a responsibility for that other. It requires an attentiveness that can be accomplished only by greeting the embodied call to witness with a binding allegiance: "Here I am." Here I am to learn and *attempt* to exceed the limits of my knowledge. In my approach as apprentice, I submit myself to learn the limits of myself and, in doing so, bare myself to a wounding—a trauma inflicted by the other's story.

To learn the limits of what one can and needs to say as a witness and try to respond to what lies beyond what is thematized within what one already knows, the task is to acknowledge and remember the person, while not always speaking *about* her or his testimony but *to* that testimony. One must accomplish this task while being open to the way in which one's structures of knowing cause one to stumble and fall short of what needs to, but cannot be spoken. The ambiguity here is not an indifferent linguistic self-reflexivity, but the opening to an other (Handelman, 1991, 250). Speaking *to* testimony (not always *about* it) means that testimony is no longer grasped only as a datum—an empirical referent to be assessed on the terms of what one already knows. It also means attending to the limits displayed when the recognition of another's experience lies in the mis-recognition of that experience as something one already knows. It is the confrontation with such limits wherein lies the possibility of experiencing what Levinas (1969, 73) refers to as the "traumatism of astonishment"—the experience of something absolutely foreign, which may call what I know and how I know into question. To accept the obligations of witnessing on these terms, thus, invokes a difficult and, at times, painful task of coming to terms with a past always in excess of its possible narration. This "coming to terms" might best be thought of as a "working through" of the materials of remembrance in a way that produces something new (Friedlander, 1992). Rather than being narrowly therapeutic, "working through" here implies "the possibility of judgement that is not apodictic or ad hominem but argumentative (*and*) self-questioning, related in mediated ways to action" (LaCapra, 1994, 120).

These two fundamental forms of attentiveness—judgment and apprenticeship—are co-implicated in the fulfillment of the demands of acknowledgment, remembrance, and consequence imposed on witnesses of historical trauma. The tensions between them are well illustrated by the following incident, which exemplifies the complexities of responding to a testamentary account.

Listening Otherwise: Divergent Responses to a Testimony

In *Testimony: The Crisis of Witnessing in Literature, Psychoanalysis, and History* (Felman and Laub, 1992), Dori Laub, a Professor of Psychiatry at Yale, provides an extended conceptual meditation on his experiences interviewing survivors of the Nazi genocide of European Jewry for the Yale Video Archives for Holocaust Testimonies. On one occasion, he and other interviewers were receiving the testimony of a woman in her late sixties narrating her experience at Auschwitz. Laub describes her as slight, self-effacing, speaking almost in whispers, her presence overshadowed by the magnitude of the event she was describing. At one point in her narration (and just for a brief instance), Laub tells his readers that she burst into a passionate and intense depiction—a virtual remembrance—what Langer (1991) (following Charlotte Delbo) calls a deep memory in which the past is reexperienced as if it were immediately present. Her narration was as follows: ". . . we saw four chimneys going up in flames, exploding. The flames shot into the sky, the people were running. It was unbelievable" (Felman and Laub, 1992, 59). Writing of his experience of witnessing this testimony, Laub says that, at that moment, there was a silence in the room against which the woman's words reverberated loudly. It seemed to him that this silence carried a trace of the sounds of a stampede of people breaking loose from behind barbed wires, screaming and shouting jubilantly. Laub reports that after completing this segment of her testimony, just as suddenly as she had begun her outburst, the women fell back into her distant and colorless speaking mode, adopting a subdued and uneventful tone. The incident the woman narrated was the planned revolt, and the subsequently failed escape attempt, at Auschwitz in October 1944.

Later, at a conference on the relation of education to the Holocaust, a tape of this women's testimony was shown. The historians at the conference claimed that the testimony was not accurate and, therefore, not credible; historical research on this incident was clear, only one chimney had been blown up, not all four. This was not pedantry on their part. Viewing history as an ongoing trial in which evidence is weighed in the search for the truth, the historians at this conference were insistent that for testimony to judged as credible, it must be factually accurate, lest Holocaust revisionists discredit everything.[2] Besides, they concluded that the woman had misrepresented the historical significance of the event. The revolt was a disaster; no one escaped, the Jewish underground had been betrayed by the Polish resistance, and those involved in the incident, if they were not killed while trying to escape, were executed soon thereafter.

Laub disagreed with this response. In his view, the woman's testimony bespoke neither the precise number of chimneys blown up nor the fallacy of a successful revolt, but rather the "reality of an unimaginable occurrence" (Felman and Laub, 1992, 60). The unimaginable occurrence was not just an event thought impossible (i.e., a revolt), but also, what Laub calls, a "breakage of the frame of Auschwitz," where Jewish armed revolts just did not happen. In other words, Laub is attending to the woman's testimony in an attempt to hear what he ultimately could not—what the woman's testimony signified about her totalizing experience of Auschwitz and that moment when the totalization was broken.

One way to grasp the distinction between Laub's hearing of the testimony and what he reports as having heard by the historians at the conference is to view Laub and the historians as differently positioned with respect to the obligations of witnessing another's testimony. The historians reasonably responded within the frame of professionally organized ethical and epistemological obligations. They were interested in the determination of the historical significance of the woman's testimony given justified presumptions about the fallibility of memory and in light of established evidentiary knowledge regarding the revolt at Auschwitz.[3] It was on these terms that they attempted to work through how to respond to the obligations of acknowledgement, remembrance, and consequence. Because the historians interpreted the woman's testimony according to the methodological and interpretative dictates of their discourse community, they concluded, according to Laub, that it was incomplete and historically invalid, and hence that it needed to be characterized as such within practices of historical argumentation and Holocaust education.

In contrast, Laub's response was an acknowledgment of and attunement to a textured excess mediating the women's attempt to evoke the palpable presence of a prior traumatic event. Such an excess, an inherent structural feature of trauma testimonies, marks something rendered beyond the limits of what can be spoken through available discourses for articulating incomprehensible violence and human loss. Including, but not defined by, the erosion of memory or the dynamics of repression, excess infiltrates those moments when one who testifies seeks to be accountable to, and not occlude the proximity of, those no longer able to testify. Excess is encountered in the multidimensional texture of testimony, in its emphatic marks as well as its silences, in its outbursts as well as its hesitations, in its pronouncements as well as its uncertainties, in its narrative elisions as well as its exaggerations.

Through this textured excess, testimony accomplishes something more than the provision of information. This excess makes evident a material, embodied, and contextualized human presence whose practices of retelling are infused with trauma, loss, and desire. In this intricate testimonial weave, the said of testimony is made present while gesturing toward its inevitable failure to say enough (or to say what needs to be said well enough). To witness the excess of testimony, one must be prepared not only to judge the significance of what is said but also situate the said within the relational encounter marking it as something beyond the merely said. This relation marked as a saying undoes the instrumental certainty of the said. For Laub, the textured speech and silences that bore witness to the woman's experiences of resistance and survival were more significant than the event's empirical facts. The woman's narration was organized through a historical sensibility that testified to the breakage of the frame of the concentration camp universe wherein such events were unbelievable. By attending to the saying of her testimony, a saying that disrupts any straightforward thematization of her said, Laub opened a path to another way of rendering the obligations of acknowledgment, remembrance, and consequence.

Paradoxically, the woman's testimony conveyed a compelling statement of historical significance in a report within which its factual details were questionable. This paradox suggests that, rather than attending to testimony as simply a conveyance of observed events, one must also attend to how a person translates her or his experience of historical trauma across time and space. This requires a moment wherein a witness adjourns the trial in which the speaker's testimony is judged with regard to the elision between what the testifier claims to know and what that person does not, or could not, know. This adjournment acknowledges the limits of what can be said, while opening up what might be heard in testimony to a referent beyond what is fully masterable by cognition (Caruth, 1995). It allows for truths to emerge from a plane on which testimonial reference cannot be recognized and adjudicated as discursively organized knowledge.

Listening in this way does not, however, mean abandoning judgment in relation to testimony. Rather, it signals what we earlier called the need for a doubled attentiveness when one attempts to witness the translation of a person's grasp of a past event as it is transactionally presented and still hold the substance of that testimony accountable for the multiple truth claims it may reinforce or initiate. Laub remains correct in criticizing the historians for their reductive, positivist apprehension of the woman's story, while the historians remain correct in assessing the limitations of her story with reference to the truth effects it attempts to circulate. At issue here is not simply that there are two different responses to the women's testimony, but rather that witnessing her testimony gives rise to serious and incommensurate claims integral to the instantiation of her testimony within the formation of historical memory. This incommensurability is an irresoluble conflict as there is no rule of judgment applicable to both arguments; rather, it is a difference (or *differend*) (Lyotard, 1988) that marks the topography of obligation required to witness testimonies of historical trauma.

Shadow Texts and the Paradox of Betrayal

As a response to testimonies of historical trauma, witnessing is neither natural or inevitable. Rather, it is a practice of commemorative ethics that requires a particular *kavannah*[4]—a particular embodied cognizance within which one becomes aware of, self-present to, and responsive toward something/someone beyond oneself. This embodied cognizance enables one to listen with dual attentiveness and to respond with acts of acknowledgment, remembrance, and an indication that hearing another's testimony has been consequential. Presuming that such a practice is desirable, pedagogical commitments require that one ask how it might be possible to nurture such a cognizance, and hence support an ethical practice of witnessing.

To begin this consideration, recall that testimonies are understood as communicative practices intent on conveying to others a palpable sense of prior events. As such, testimonies of historical trauma attempt to translate the tangibility of occurrences across time and space. As translations, however, testimonies are indelibly marked by their own insufficiency. These marks—inscribed within the texts themselves—are the scars testimonies bear to their discursive inadequacy to render fully the realities of human cruelty and suffering. Consequently, testimonies of historical trauma always enact a degree of betrayal. Betrayed is the obligation to convey thoroughly "what happened," both to those who survived and to those whose deaths negated the possibility of their witness. Paradoxically, however, this very betrayal establishes the condition for witnessing testimony through double attentiveness (i.e., attending to what is said while hearing how the saying of testimony undoes the discursive grasp one has of the other's story). Through testimony's betrayal, the unspoken is "heard," "so that listening remains a way of thinking" (Levinas, 1994b, 80).

The inevitable translational betrayal of the testimonial act means that narratives and images of historical trauma are commonly shot through with absences that, in their silence, solicit or "ask" questions. To remember such testimonies actively entails not only repeating them but also posing difficult and often unanswerable questions that nonetheless press for responses that could help decipher what is to be heard when listening to a testimonial account. The explanations sought in such questions typically are not attached to something within the text but rather to something missing from the text. When spoken, these interrogative emotions enact the recognition that scars of traumatic testimony break the "in-order" and "well-ordered" frame that bounds the possibility of a just and compassionate communal life. When not overtly spoken, such questions lie close to the surface of a historically contingent, public articulation of contemporary moral idealizations. In North America, for example, testimonies of the Nazi genocide of European

Jewry commonly evoke questions such as: How could anyone do this to other human beings? How could such horror really happen? Why the Jews? Didn't the Jews realize what was going on? Why didn't more Jewish people take action to protect themselves? Why did people in the rest of the world let these events happen? Could it happen again, could it happen to me? What would have happened to me? Would I have survived? Collaborated? Resisted?[5]

The importance of such questions cannot be overestimated. They are symptomatic, returning again and again as answers to them fail to resolve the difficult concerns that trauma testimony continually evokes. Such questions, although irresolvable, are insistent and demand a response. One significant response is the attempt to write "shadow texts" (Mitchell, 1994; Simon and Armitage-Simon, 1995), secondary narratives a reader or listener "writes" (but does not necessarily write down) in response to the unresolved questions a primary narrative elicits. Shadow texts seek in the text something apart from its contents. Attempts to write shadow texts are an "asking after" something that has not been satisfied. Within the *kavannah* required for a commemorative ethics, shadow texts respond to a saying that goes beyond the intention of a testimonial text. The listener is impelled to search and forage for that which has yet to be said, which—as it is written— slips away yet again.[6] The writing of shadow texts, on these terms, expresses a desire that refuses fulfillment in either thematization or enigma. In commemorative ethics, shadow texts are neither juvenile nor narcissistic; they are cultivated precisely because they fuel an unrest—a movement without definitive end—which is the only possible way of sustaining the pursuit of justice.

Yet, the writing of shadow texts may proceed on very different terms. Drawing on taken-for-granted knowledge and beliefs in order to provide workable interpretations that make traumatic events and experiences more comprehensible, shadow texts may be written not only with partial historical knowledge but also with misconceptions, misinformation, myths, projections, and prejudice. Reflecting an inability or unwillingness to sustain interminable work on irresoluble questions, shadow texts may become simplistic (or worse, racist or sexist) rationalizations that short-circuit one's capacity to witness testimony. Alternatively, this inability or unwillingness may simply lead to an indifference to the history of mass systemic violence, a precondition for its forgetting. The work of writing shadow texts—of attempting to provide at least a partial explanation or rationalization that might stabilize our understanding of what happened in the past—is an effort to establish a basis on which the memory of a testimony might be claimed. Such work is always both personal and communal, but it is the communal aspects we stress here, because it is within communal structures that the *kavannah* necessary for witnessing can be nurtured.

It is not surprising that testimonial accounts, in their attempts to convey a tangible sense of prior catastrophic events, often carry a surreal quality.

This surreal aspect provokes a disorientation that displaces the terms upon which one seeks to define oneself and one's relationship with others. Such testimonies are limited in their capacity to become part of the traditions of remembrance that confirm the terms of a hopeful existence. In this sense, the remembrance of testimonies of historical trauma is always partially transgressive. As the compulsion to write shadow texts illustrates, remembering genocidal events may bring into question the central stories and propositional schemata that order one's life. When one faces a testamentary texture that unhinges such faith, stories lose both their ability to translate past events and articulate discourses in which to articulate one's singular and communal significance. As Terrance Des Pres (1977) suggests,

> the survivor (of the Shoah) is a disturber of the peace . . . a runner of the blockade . . . erect[ed] against knowledge of "unspeakable" things. About these [the survivor] aims to speak, and in so doing . . . undermines, without intending to, the validity of existing norms. [The survivor] is a genuine transgressor . . . .(42–43)

In this respect, to evoke through testimony the memory of genocide is to be caught in a potential disruption to our understanding of human possibility, a disruption that may frighten us "insofar as [it] bears witness to our own historical disfiguration" (Felman and Laub, 1992, 73–74).

How does one retain and retell testimonies that themselves bear witness to death, degradation, and "our own historical disfiguration?" This question is not merely one of an individual's readiness or ability to hear a testimony. Remembrance can proceed without the loss of significance of everyday meaning and inform new codes of behavior only when testimonies of dehumanizing experience become part of a community's history and its shared narratives of self-representation. To remember in this manner, a community must claim, appropriate, and react to testimonial accounts, *but not on terms already in place.* As Avni (1995) suggests,

> the historical imperative today is not to sort out but to find a way of taking in the reality of industrialized killing, knowing fully that this reality contradicts every aspect of our historical project, everything we would like to believe about ourselves.(216)

This view implies that the cognizance needed to witness must be nurtured and encouraged by a communally mediated consideration of why (and which) memories matter. This consideration in turn requires attention to both the saying and the said of testimony in a way that incorporates testimony within an intelligible past while recognizing that such remembrance may unsay this intelligibility and disrupt the basis on which one communally grounds everyday affairs.

Communities of Memory

To consider communal structures within which the cognizance needed to witness may be nurtured, it is important to attend to those opportunities in which two or more people are able not only to share their responses to testimonial practices but also to consider the importance of what they have just apprehended. The contexts for such exchanges include school and university classrooms, but also reference informal adult study groups as well as more intimate gatherings. Within the perspective of the formation of collective remembrance, such occasions may engender *communities of memory*, moments of social life wherein practices of remembrance are contested, shaped, and deepened by the consideration of the possible shared significance of what has been heard, seen, or read.

Communities of memory, thus, designate structured sets of relationships through which people engage representations of past events and put forth shared, complementary, or competing versions of what should be remembered and how. Within these relationships, people make topical the significance of their understanding of past events, arguing over the reworking of narratives and images that embody and elicit living memories. What binds people within such relationships is the promissory relation of memory to redemption. At root is the question (and the possibility) of remembrance,[7] of what could and should be preserved (or rescued) in view of the transience of life. This concern is addressed, not by denying the reality of death, but by establishing temporal relations whose significance transcends the ego-framing of one's momentary existence (Gibbs, 1992, 108).

To participate in a community of memory is to struggle with the possibility of witnessing, a practice quite different from a passive attention to legalized interventions seeking to arrest time by prescribing and regulating what are to count as the significant memories of a community's past. Rather than accept such ossifications, members of a community of memory pursue a redemptive course in the interminable return to and renewal of their understanding and assessment of past events. This return and renewal is accomplished by argument and deliberations that inform performative retellings of what members deem significant to pass-on. In this context, one commits to historical narrations by performing (teaching) them. This is a poetic that must be done in ways that involve all members. The quotation marks surrounding "involve" signal the recognition that not every participant is positioned to take part on equal terms. Such deliberative moments are not free of historically formed material and cultural disparities. There should be no pretension that communities of memory are necessarily harmonious spaces, free of relations of power and insurgency. The greater the diversity of social identities, the greater the likelihood that commitments to remembrance (and the identities implicated in such remembrance) will conflict. Such conflicts cannot be worked through without taking into account the realization that historical knowledge often reflects the perspective of those whose histories have prevailed. Thus, for any practice of just recollection, at least for commemorative practices performed in public time or space, the redemption toward which they point includes the formation of a community able to possess the ability to say "we" while hearing difference and recognizing disparity[8] through which these commemorations are engaged.

Toward a Pedagogy of Remembrance: Witnessing through Retelling

As we have argued, an ethical practice of witnessing includes the obligation to bear witness—to re-testify, to somehow convey what one has heard and thinks important to remember. Communities of memory are locations where such obligations can be worked out. More specifically, they are productive spaces in which to name, distribute, produce, and practice those expressive resources that enable a witnessing that establishes living memories and admits the dead into one's moral community. In this sense, communities of memory are locations within which one can (1) work through the difficulties of responding to the symptomatic questions elicited by testimonies of historical trauma, and (2) decide which testimonies, and what aspects of them, should be retold to whom and in what ways. As a conclusion, and by way of illustrating the implications of these concepts for a pedagogy of remembrance, we consider here how one might begin to work through the obligations of ethical witnessing in the context of schools and universities.

In classrooms, a community of memory is set in motion by the practical questions of how, and for what purposes, a teacher and a group of students are to engage testimonial narratives and consider what of (and about) these testimonies should be remembered, why, and in what way. Decisions as to which testimonies a teacher or students choose to present, what preparation teachers and students should have before engaging testimonies, and what evidence of students' engagements teachers will demand, no doubt affect how remembrance is mediated. However, being pedagogically mindful of the opportunity presented in the practical tasks of remembrance also requires time and a conversational structure in which to explore and work through responses to specific testimonies with regard both to questions of comprehension and the demands of witnessing. In other words, the activities that structure a community of memory must also include not only support for struggling with the symptomatic questions testimony elicits, but also the provision of a structure within which it is possible to meet the obligations to bear witness to the testimonies one has encountered.

Thus, working with communities of memory means finding ways of helping students articulate the (often unspoken) questions that compel the writing of testimonial shadow texts, while, simultaneously, opening to collective investigation the possibilities and limitations inherent in different ways of responding to these questions. The writing of shadow texts affects what people hear in testimony and this writing must be pedagogically acknowledged as an attempt to respond to excesses in testimonial accounts. Actively working through both the desire and the attempt to write shadow texts can become a method for dealing with, and at times altering, the cultural and personal premises[9] on which testimonies are comprehended.

Classroom-based communities of memory require that their members take on the practical responsibilities to name a story as important to pass-on, and re-present that story in concrete form to others. This means encouraging and facilitating a dialog through which students work out an interpretive, multidimensional idiom with which to witness what they have read or heard. Through this dialog, a nuanced vocabulary of witnessing is built, enacted, and borne out in the practice of living memory. The idiom of a retelling need not be constrained by any group's linguistic facility, since retelling testimony could include dramatic and visual modes as well as written or oral ones. Here, a teacher's task is to create the conditions and means for moving beyond attempts to speak that falter into silence or regress into familiar and potentially debilitating frames of reference.

By retelling, a group initiates its own testimonial address to another. Pedagogically, retelling is anything but an abstract or arbitrary exercise. It must be accomplished concretely as students consider if, why, to whom (and crucially), how, when, and where a testimony would be retold. Thus, students would have to decide what aspects of a testimony would have to be emphasized and what could be left out. In the context of these deliberations, they would need to explain why they have chosen to re-present (and remember) the testimony on those specific terms and clarify how precisely this re-presentation is to be communicated (via words, images, gesture, song, etc.). In such considerations, students would have to make clear how their re-presentations take into account the persons to whom they would address their witness; they would also have to consider whether there were particular times during which it was most appropriate to re-present a given testimony, and which spaces or spatial arrangements were most appropriate to their re-presentation.

Dealing with such concerns not only clarifies the comprehension of a testimonial account but also grounds one's witnessing in commemorative ethics. These ethics must be open to the claims of past generations on practices of remembrance and the imbrication of these claims within the texture of our current daily commitments. These claims cannot be fulfilled by establishing a single, definitive historical narrative. An ethical commemoration must always take place in full awareness that what can be said never exhausts that to which it refers. Such an ethical practice necessarily recognizes the ceaseless struggle to capture the ambiguities and paradoxes of an always incomplete testimony that initiates fissures or breaks in what can be said. As witnesses struggle beyond cliches and aspire to something not yet said, an engagement with the "unsayable" is precisely where the practices of living memory are reformed and renewed. Every retelling undoes a prior said through a saying, which attempts to find new idioms that welcome the proximity of the past in interminable dialectical tension with the horizon of a just future.

Fulfilling the obligations of witnessing means enabling practices of "re-memory" (Morrison, 1987), practices that concretely encourage people to hold onto an affirmation of life in the face of death, to feelings of both connection and disconnection and, to stay wide awake enough to attend to the requirements of just recollection and the work of transforming the future. These are not tasks that can be accomplished alone but concretely define the dialogic grounds for a community that remembers. We certainly acknowledge that bearing witness to traumatic history can be a difficult and risky venture. This risk leads some to justify silence as a preferred ethical and pedagogical response. But, such a position fails in a necessary vigilance—a vigilance embodying the courage to witness, to remember justly, and to recognize the impossibility of its successful completion.

A story is told of the people of Chelm, among whom it was rumored that the Messiah was about to appear. Fearing the Messiah might bypass their town, the Chelmites hired a watchman to be on the lookout for the divine guest. The watchman, after a while, started thinking that the ten kopecks he received as weekly salary was mighty little to support a wife and child. So he went to the town's Rabbi to ask for a raise. The Rabbi turned him down, arguing that: true enough, ten kopecks was an inadequate salary, but that one must, after all, take into account that this was a permanent job. Settling the past's claim on the present is an interminable task. Much like the watchman, those who bear its burden are not likely to be richly rewarded. Yet, they too, like the watchman, must struggle not to fall asleep and miss the Messiah as she passes the edge of town.

CHAPTER FOUR

Beyond the Logic of Emblemization: Remembering and Learning from the Montréal Massacre

WITH SHARON ROSENBERG

Fifteen years ago, fourteen women were murdered at l'École polytechnique (the School of Engineering) at the University of Montréal in Québec, Canada. For those who lived in proximity to these murders, the details do not need to be recalled (for it is likely that they never left us). For others, this recollection alone will be insufficient to the substance of memory. So, in brief: in the early evening of December 6, 1989, Marc Lepine, a twenty-five-year-old white man, entered a university building in the city of Montréal, armed with a semiautomatic rifle. He walked into a fourth year Mechanical Engineering class of some 60 students, ordered the men to leave—which they all did—and shot the remaining six women to death, screaming the accusation that they were a "bunch of feminists" (Rathjen and Monpetit, 1999, 10). He then walked through hallways and entered other classrooms, murdering eight more women and injuring thirteen others (nine women and four men, men who were shot presumably because they attempted to impede his rampage). Then, he killed himself. In the three-page note found on his body, but not released into public circulation for a year, he described the murders as a political act and blamed feminism for ruining his life.[1] These murders received widespread public attention across Canada. From grocery store lineups, to public memorial services, to campus classrooms, much was spoken and written about the killings and their significance, bringing to the fore debates about issues of violence against women in a manner that was unprecedented. One result of this attention was the 1991 declaration by the Canadian Federal Government to commemorate December 6 as an annual National Day of Remembrance and Action on Violence against Women. While controversial debate about the murders has waned in the ensuing years, each anniversary continues to be marked by a range of memorial activities (including vigils, televised panel discussions, art shows, and video documentaries) attempting to sustain the memory of the killings and come to terms with their legacy.

Marked, narrated, and widely commemorated in the first five years after the murders, the remembrance of these killings was thus, at first, difficult to avoid. Those of us who were subjects of—and subject to—the public inscriptions of the Massacre were inevitably positioned as coming after the event, as falling into its shadow. For us, the memory of the Massacre lingers, supported by public remembrances that were not only expressions of grief and mourning, but insistent pedagogical acts, deliberate attempts to prompt and engage people in the development of a historical consciousness that might affect their perceptions, judgments, and actions. Yet, a decade later, the future of this socially sustained memory remains unclear. As we move further from the immediate aftermath of the loss and grief provoked by the murders, attention to the Massacre and its legacy is fading into sedimented symbolization. The markers of remembrance that had circulated widely in previous years—candles, roses, ribbons, and vigils of silence—seem increasingly inadequate.[2] This sense of inadequacy is not simply explained by references to the short attention span of a public memory seeking its next spectacle. Rather, at issue, we suggest, is the question of remembrance itself.

One central argument of this essay is for a much-needed consideration of remembrance as a set of historically situated material and discursive practices, practices that bind cognition and affect in attempts to secure a memorial legacy. In putting forward an understanding of remembrance on these terms, we are foregrounding a recognition that any remembrance of the Montréal Massacre necessarily includes a pedagogical intent to bequeath a memorial legacy to those it addresses. That is, practices of remembrance always incorporate an intent to initiate various learnings, learnings that may include: the significance of and methods for keeping present-to-mind details of specific events, providing information previously unknown, fastening or contesting meanings assigned to signs and symbols, and/or creating attachments to and investments in certain formulations of historical narrative. What these dimensions of remembrance emphasize is its social quality. Not singularly achieved, remembrance is formed within communicative practices that always require another. Indeed, that remembrance cannot be formed alone underscores its pedagogical character. Thus, considering how a set of remembrance practices structure their pedagogical project is crucial to understanding remembrance and its effects.

For this reason, we consider the prevailing remembrance practices with regard to the Massacre, addressing what has contributed to their normative form, what problems have resulted from these formations, and what new memorial possibilities there might be. Specifically, we first propose an argument for understanding "the event" as including not only the killings per se, but also, crucially, the memorial formations that have been forged in its wake. One such memorial form, indeed the one that has principally organized remembrance practices in Canada, is emblemization.

Emblematic memory, thus, provides the focus for a second layer of consideration in the essay, in which we argue that "reading" the Massacre as symbolic of mass systemic violence against women by men has, on the one hand, been vital in efforts to develop a public awareness of such violences, but, on the other, is a limited (and limiting) remembrance practice that requires critical attention. Our thinking about these limitations is grounded in a small-scale study we conducted with a class of B.Ed. students, to whom we posed the task of thinking through remembrance of the Massacre in a school setting. In contemplating individual and group responses to this task, it becomes evident that emblematic memory—as a memory formed on the basis of resemblance/substitution—calls both women and men into restrictive remembrance identifications, identifications that limit what, and how, we may learn from the event of the Massacre.

On the basis of these arguments, we put forward a fundamental rethinking of "remembrance pedagogy" (Simon et al., 2000) in response to these murders and their memory. In the final sections of the chapter, we consider again the question of "resemblance," arguing that an emblematic, identity-based emphasis on the resemblance between the Massacre and more everyday violence against women has displaced attention to a *traumatic resemblance* that was initiated by the killings. On these terms, we return to data collected from our study, considering, in particular, the repeated practice of splitting off of the emotional weight of the Massacre (traced, e.g., in expressions of student distress) from the educative importance presumed inherent in memorial activities. While such splitting is consistent with prevailing notions of teaching about difficult social issues (recognizable in the common phrase "first mourn, then organize"), we argue that learning to develop and sustain pedagogical attention to the deep unsettlement of remembrance of the Massacre is necessary if one is to take in its traumatic inheritance.

Event Remembrance

The marking of the murders in Montréal as *an event* in and for mainstream living memory in Canada (a marking that began with the immediate naming of the killings as the "Montréal Massacre") can be understood, in de Certeau's terms, as delimiting, and, as such, establishing the necessary conditions of possibility for grasping what has transpired. As he explains, "[t]he event is the means thanks to which disorder is turned into order. The event does not explain, but permits an intelligibility. It is the postulate and the point of departure . . . of comprehension" (1988, 96). As the years pass, the killings, ordered under a proper name, have provided the terms on which their substance and significance have begun to be remembered. What is significant to stress is that the event of the Montréal Massacre has come to include not just the fact of the murders, but also the public responses and ongoing efforts made to sustain or contest the value of their memory. From this perspective, as long as people are moved to document their practices of memory,[3] the event of the Massacre can be understood as interminably in formation; an event whose boundaries are neither static nor stable. Thus, conceptual considerations of the Massacre *now*, more than a decade after its occurrence, cannot simply turn to the killings per se, but must necessarily include its memorial aftermath.

On these terms, the memorial legacy of the Massacre is, at its very root, indeterminate, because it presumes a difficult, challenging, and personally confrontational question: how will you live after the event; how will you live with the images and narration of the Massacre? Hence, to embrace the legacy of the Massacre requires that its event structure (itself continually evolving) be engaged and read—for it is how the event is read that will constitute its inheritance, what of the event will touch one's life. This is a question not only of what might be learned through any given form of remembrance of the Massacre, but also how such memories will be taken into account in one's actions.

Obviously, people confronted by the questions posed by remembrance do not all stand in the same relation to the event. This difference is not simply an issue of what and how much a person knows of what happened (although this does matter). It also concerns how what is known of the event resonates or is discordant with one's own memories and contemporary realities in regard to living with(in) violence; the invested identifications through which people attempt to secure a stable sense of self-understanding; and past patterns of relationship that might be imposed through transference on the event structure of the Massacre. Thus, whereas for some the Massacre may seem increasingly distant, for others what is remembered may be deeply imbued with the private, the body, that site where the impacts of violence and violation are lived in the pulse of blood, under tissue, scarred in flesh. While such differences are inevitable, the memorial legacy of the Massacre (what constitutes its inheritance) must not be understood as idiosyncratic. Quite simply, structures of remembrance matter. How its event structure is articulated (in various texts, images, songs, monuments, and rituals) offers bounded sets of symbolizations and emotional textures, structuring what can be understood by the remembrance of the Massacre and what it is that may be learned from such practices. It is to a prevailing formation of memory that we now turn.

Emblemization of Memory

If we are to deepen our understanding of what is at stake in practices of remembrance and how and why they matter, there is a need to look carefully at what organizes historical memory. Structuring much of the complexity, passion, and, at times, ambivalence with regard to the remembrance of the Massacre (which includes its social and psychological aftermath) has been the controversy regarding its emblemization. By emblemization, we refer to the practice of choosing/producing a specific act as standing for a range of other acts that are understood to be constituted on similar terms.

As a family of resemblances, these acts are assumed to share certain characteristics, and the remembrance of one, hence, gestures to the remembrance of all. When one specific event is chosen on the terms of resemblance, it is chosen to function emblematically. The most dominant feature of the emblemization of the Massacre has been to read it as standing for, as symbolic of, mass systemic violence by men against women. Indeed, one of the central effects of emblemizing the Massacre on these terms has been to bring acts of male violence against women into historical memory. That is, ongoing attention to the Massacre has given such violence a concrete eventness, a specific space/time location that demands remembrance and understanding.[4]

We might note however, that this reading of the Montréal murders as emblematic has only been stabilized in mainstream living memory in more recent years. It initially appeared as a strategic response to the interpretation circulating widely in the media within hours of the killings—an interpretation that constructed the murders as "incomprehensible" (Lakeman, 1992, 94), "one man's act of madness" (Nelson-McDermott, 1991, 125), in which "the victims just happened to be women" (Schmidt, 1990, 7). This is a reading that individualized and pathologized the perpetrator, Lepine, and, if it worried about the women at all, refused them a gendered identification. As Jennifer Scanlon explains, "feminists were accused of taking advantage of the situation by talking about misogyny. The killer was crazy, many argued; his actions had nothing to do with women and everything to do with psychosis" (1994, 77). Critical response was largely mobilized through the urgency of contesting this reading, arguing, instead, that Lepine's actions were supported by normative constructs of masculinity in a society in which violence against women remain highly commonplace.[5] Julie Brickman argues, for example: "[i]f they [the fourteen women murdered] did not live as feminists, they certainly died as them. The nature and circumstances of their deaths has shaped the meaning of their individual lives, transforming these fourteen women into symbols, tragic representatives of the injustice against women that has been built into the fabric of the society in which we live" (1992, 129).

While a response that emphasizes the systemic character of the killings has been absolutely necessary—and will no doubt continue to be so—we want to argue that it bears further consideration as a pedagogy of remembrance. We suggest that interpretations articulated *in response to* those that positioned the murders as the result of individual pathology were already "caught up" by this reading. Pulled by a need to negate the frame of individualization, critical responses necessarily constituted the *resemblance* between the murders at l'École polytechnique and systemic male violence against women on the basis of the wide repetition of the narrative structure of Lepine's act (male [subject]—violence [verb]—women [object]). As noted earlier, this reading of the event of the Massacre has gained prominence in public memory, effectively displacing the "madman" interpretation that first prevailed. At first glance, this may appear surprising, particularly given the not insignificant efforts in the early aftermath of the killings to discredit any reading that insisted on a gendered dimension. Statements such as the following give texture to this position: "The act of a madman or a tragedy sparked by society's pervasive sexism? That is still the question being asked today, exactly one year after Marc Lepine killed 14 women students."[6] And, "Surely this is a crime against humanity, not women."[7] However, we suggest that it would have been untenable to sustain memory of the event of the Massacre on the terms of Lepine's individualized idiosyncrasy. It is the very structuring of the Massacre as emblematic—possible to be read as standing for other acts—that created its memorial force.

One deeply concerning effect of this memorial structure, however, is that it creates, within its regime, the identity/substitutability of all women for each other. Emblemization of the Massacre on these terms contains two mutually problematic effects. On the one hand, if the fourteen women who were killed in Montréal come to stand for all women subject(ed) to violence at the hands of men, then the specifics of the lives and deaths of other women encompassed within this event become inconspicuous. If, on the other hand, the murder of the fourteen women slips out of symbolic significance and is replaced by other particular acts of violence against women, then the tragedy of the loss of the lives of the women in Montréal is minimized.[8]

Counter to this reading, some feminist writers and activists have argued for an understanding that recognizes resemblance *and* difference.[9] In this interpretation, there is an effort to recognize that the women at l'École polytechnique were shot explicitly because they were women, because they were presumed to be feminists, *and* that they were relatively privileged as women (within contemporary race and class relations) to be attending and participating in a university. From this perspective, it is unlikely that their deaths would have become a site of remembrance investment—not only by the state apparatus, but also a range of women's groups—had they not been perceived to be in a position associated with innocence and opportunity. While this reading is important for how it complicates a view that traces a singular line of connection between the Massacre and "violence against women," it nevertheless faces an irresolvable contradiction in remembrance. The reading of resemblance and difference simultaneously accepts and refuses the Massacre as emblematic. That is, it is a position that argues for recognition of the Massacre's partiality in a structure that depends, for its intelligibility, on seamless symbolic substitutability.

It is clear from these instances that the historical remembrance of the Massacre, as currently conceived and practised, cannot escape the dilemmas of emblemization. Left open to question is whether arguing either for or against emblemization on *symbolic terms*—terms that structure representations of substitutability—misses something urgent and deeply pedagogical in the memorial legacy of the Massacre. What is missed in such arguments becomes apparent when we recognize that the dilemmas of emblemization are not only about the terms of substitutability among the dead, but also about how the living are positioned and struggle to position themselves in relation to the dead. This is a recognition that we will consider in some detail in the remainder of this chapter, as we contemplate the responses of a specific group of students asked to confront the task of devising plans for the public remembrance of the event of the Massacre.

Posing the Task of Remembrance

In the summer of 1996, under the auspices of the Testimony and Historical Memory Project at the University of Toronto, we began discussions with one of our colleagues to work with a class of her students enrolled in the university's B.Ed. program. The professor we approached had addressed remembrance of the Massacre in earlier years of her Foundations in Education course, within a concern regarding violence against girls and women in schools. She was interested in working with us to the extent that we could help her students to think about remembrances of the Massacre as a "teaching event." This met with our interests in learning more about the ways in which various groups of people (may) read the legacy of the Massacre; thus, we devised a short study for her class in which students might be engaged by, and engage others in, remembrance and learning.

While largely receptive to our approach, the professor was concerned that our teaching work should be inclusive and, particularly, that we not alienate the men students from practices of remembrance. This concern anticipates, indeed begins from an awareness of, the possible effect of what we have earlier identified as the normative structure of emblemization, in which the figure of Lepine comes to be substitutable for "all men." By insisting on a task structure that would not alienate male students on these terms, we understood our colleague to be requesting the possibility for men, as men, to address the remembrance of the event of the Massacre. As we will observe here, this request paralleled the concerns of many of the students in the class, once they began to engage in the task of remembrance that we put forward.

In the context of the concerns mentioned earlier, we agreed to generate a two-period unit in December 1996 in which the students would develop, in small groups, plans for school-wide events that would "remember the Massacre." To facilitate and help focus their planning, our project team created a series of resource rooms containing materials memorializing the Massacre. We filled the spaces with videos, slides of artwork, audio renderings of songs and poetry, and various written texts including personal responses, newspaper articles, and journal essays. While the memorial materials were diverse in terms of form, they were fairly consistent in content, repeating the (by this time) dominant emblematic reading of the event of the Massacre.[10] This consistency was not a matter of our lack of interest in different readings, but a result of the degree to which the outpouring of memorial response, from 1990 to 1996 in English Canada, had been focused on efforts to work through connections to and resemblances between the Massacre and other specific acts of violence against women. This is a repetition that became problematic for many of the students, as we will discuss here.

The students were asked to spend one period of their class (about two hours) engaging the resource material in preparation for developing their "remembrance plans." These plans were to detail the content and method through which the memory and legacy of the Massacre might be addressed in school settings. As such, they were to be guided by the following series of curriculum-oriented questions. To whom would you direct remembrance in a school setting? How would you present your remembrance of the Massacre (using words, images, gestures, songs, e.g.)? Given the resources available to you, what aspects of the Massacre would you want to emphasize and what would you leave out? In what ways, if any, do your assumptions about whom this remembrance event is directed to influence your thinking about what is to be remembered? How do you envision the space in which this event would occur? When would the event take place? And how would people be asked to participate in the remembrance event? Additionally, we emphasized to the students that if—after considering these questions—they decided that public remembrance of the Massacre in the school was not a good idea, this was a legitimate response as long as they were able to provide their professor with a justification for this position. We further underscored in our preparatory remarks to students that remembrance is a contested site, and, thus, we recognized they were being asked to grapple collectively in a process that would likely be marked by significant and pressing differences amongst them with regard to the priority, significance, and weight that should be given to remembrance of the Massacre. To meet their course requirements, all students were asked to participate in small groups to work out the details for a remembrance plan.

Groups were required to submit the plans to their professor as part of their grade component. While they were asked to provide us with copies and allow one of our observer–recorders to be present during their planning discussions, these were not requirements. Of seven small groups, all but one agreed to have a recorder present and all agreed to allow us to have copies of their plans. Given the gendered character of the Massacre, we held the expectation that there might have been students in the class who would have found mixed gender discussions troubling. Thus, we created the option for students to sign up for same-gender or mixed-gender small groups. One women-only group was formed; each of the six others included either one or two men, and each group had a total of five to six members.[11]

Gender, Identification, and Remembrance

Through contemplation of the responses produced in the small groups, we return again to the issue of emblemization. We have already indicated that the professor of the course anticipated difficulties associated with the now-normalized emblematic character of the Massacre. In a moment, we will discuss how students echoed this concern. But, first, we want to signal our conceptual orientation to the issues raised by the students. As we mentioned earlier, we have come to understand that the pedagogy of emblemization raises the question not only of how the dead are (being) remembered, but also how the living—women and men—are (being) positioned in relation to those dead. This positioning seems to be of enormous consequence in *setting the terms* on which people are prepared, encouraged, or constrained to read the event structure of the Massacre. An inscriptive positioning, the memory formation of emblemization, writes people into positions that they may be willing to embrace, but also, at times, refuse as simply too inconsistent or contradictory with their own deeply held identifications.

One of the most striking features of the data collected was the degree to which the women members in the mixed-gender groups (but not in the women-only group, to whom we will return) were concerned with how the remembrance of the event of the Massacre might impact on men. There is an emphasis across the recorders' notes on students' desires to enact a remembrance pedagogy that "educates" but does not "upset," "offend," or "alienate" male students and teachers. These comments are typical: "The thing I was worried about, as a woman, a lot of the male population in the school is going to feel bashed." "I got the sense that men are bad, cruel, that all men are violent . . . if I were a man my back would [be] up." This issue was also raised in the justification provided by the group that decided not to hold public commemorations of the Massacre. As part of their written comments for this decision, they state: "it is impossible to teach non-violence in an atmosphere where one person or group feels threatened or attacked."

Taking these concerns seriously means, we would argue, not reading them as simply indicators of an unfamiliarity with or distance from feminism. Rather, we suggest that, in contemporary gender relations, how individual women are positioned by, and position themselves in relation to, the emblematic structure of the event of the Massacre is indeed complex. As the details of any given account of male violence against women are suppressed in the reductive narrative of male perpetrator/female victim, men and women both are solicited to read the Massacre through practices of dichotomized gender identifications. Thus, it is not uncommon for women to anticipate men responding to the narrative of the Massacre as if that narrative always accuses them of actual or potential perpetration.

Taking up these interpretations on Foucauldian terms, one might anticipate that they follow the internal logic of the discourse of emblemization, in which men will be summoned to read the structure of the event through an identification with Lepine. This is an identificatory dynamic that unfolds on the terms of a historically specific discursive formation (emblemization), through which recall of Lepine's actions inevitably bleeds over to themselves and other men as figures of violence—figures that necessarily put women at risk. This logic of emblemization structures further problematics of identification; for example, if women do not accept the "worry" regarding the impacts of the emblematic structure of the Massacre on men, then they risk being understood as "feminist" on the terms of Lepine's accusation—that is, as women whose interests are always and explicitly aligned and enacted over and against the interests of men, a position that then has the potential to elicit the rage of "a Lepine." A further interpretation of the consequence of the memorial discourse of emblemization is that the women students may feel impelled to embrace this stance of not upsetting and offending men in order to sustain an invested set of self identifications within which they may maintain close ties with husbands, partners, sons, fathers, or friends.

In contrast to the women in the mixed-gender groups who spoke quite extensively about the impact of a discourse of emblematization on men (and, inadvertently, thus, the impact on themselves), the men in these same groups spoke very little on this issue. There are some indicators of men students beginning to gesture in this direction, but they leave sentences unfinished, are interrupted, or are met with silence. For example, in reference to a scene in Maureen Bradley's video *Reframing the Montréal Massacre*, one of the male students remarks: "The only part . . . that disturbed me [referring to Bradley's criticism regarding the dominance of male figures leading a memorial service for the fourteen women murdered], maybe because I'm a man . . . that pushed it too far . . . I think it hurt me as a . . . ." He is interrupted by a woman in the group, who jumps in with: "We have to be careful about men in the audience. I have heard about men being ashamed . . . it is tough and we have to be careful about that." In another instance, a male student asks, in relation to his group's discussion about a school memorial service, "What about the guy who is quiet and says to himself I'm not violent?" But this question is met with a pause and then a change in direction in the group discussion. What such comments may indicate is a substantial anxiety on the part of the male students as they attempt to grapple with a memorial positioning in which they desire and attempt to articulate terms for a connection with the women murdered, yet, still recognize that remembrance through emblemization discursively requires, and hence makes intelligible, their being identified with the killer. We read such a struggle again in the comments of a male student in a different group, who states:

> "[there was] lots of blaming, generalizing of how men are raised . . . instantly excluding a whole sex . . . I could listen to it and say to myself it's about uniting women . . . I said that is not what they intend to do, to exclude, to exclude me . . . any man would feel in part responsible . . . it is a very tricky topic to get a hold of . . . I felt isolated and blamed."

As this student begins to grapple with the terms on which to understand his anguished relationship with the Massacre *as a man*, it is noteworthy that his recourse seems to be to forego questions of obligation or accountability in the context of ongoing structured relations of power between men and women, turning instead to a presumed necessary pedagogical a priori of victimhood. He states, "I think we have to reach the males and that is only possible [if] men see themselves as potential victims not the perpetrators." What might this student be asking us to understand men as victims of? To read his statement simply as an attempt to refigure the terms of the emblematic narrative, such that men too are victims of Lepine's violence, misses a fundamental consequence of remembering the Massacre on emblematic terms alone. Perhaps, what this student is gesturing toward is some sense of feeling *subject to* a memorial formation that reduces masculinity to the perpetration of violence. While we would not intend, for our interpretation, to be read as minimizing the deaths of the women in Montréal, this student's comments can be understood as trying to come to terms with a position for men in which they can be identified (and identify themselves) as separate from Lepine's actions, thus, circumventing alienation and shame in relation to Lepine's gendered act of murder. This raises a set of issues to which we will return.

Although such dynamics of self-identification for the women in these mixed-gender groups received less explicit attention, there was evidence of a concern regarding the problematic character of an emblematic structure that positions them as (inevitably) victims. In the majority of the groups, there were women specifically insistent that any memorial event include a component in which women were encouraged to take an active stance with regard to male violence. These women wanted practices of remembrance that carried the message of hope and change, not simply of victimization. Thus, it was common to hear women speak of focusing not only on "what's sad, but also on prevention." This concern was elaborated and reinforced continually in comments such as:

> ". . . we need to make sure in the planning that girls don't end up at the end of the session feeling victimized . . . I was told by my associate teacher that if you are going to do something negative then you need to do something positive so the kids get the message of hope."
>
> "The Massacre came from somewhere . . . it's negative we have to explain this . . . but not focus and harp on that . . . [another person notes in response] yes [we need to do something] empowering."
>
> ". . . a remembrance event should take place in a context of some ongoing form of activity . . . that would provide a place to go to do action."

What this insistence on a turn from memory to action signals is a struggle to create and mark a place of identification for women that recognizes *but is not limited to* their (potential) victimization as objects of Lepine's anti-woman, antifeminist act. Where the women students could concur with the notion that "it could have been me,"[12] they refuse this memorial structure of identification as too all-encompassing and passive. This is a stance that has also been common in feminist memorial responses, which have endeavoured to turn Lepine's accusation—"Feminist"—into a proclamation of solidarity with the women murdered. As Marusia Bociurkiw has noted: "[t]he only way to avenge Lepine's hateful, terrorist act is to prove him right . . . to organize" (1990, 10).

The import of Bociurkiw's insight appears to resonate with the substance and tone of the discussion in the women-only group. Overall, these students appeared to support the emblemization of the Massacre as it shores up a feminist narrative regarding the realities of violence against women. Presenting themselves to us as an already formed group, there was little doubt that the prior relationships among these women enabled an in-class, joint affirmation of the unproblematic character of emblemization. Overall, the women in this group seemed, in their discussions, to not only acknowledge the vulnerabilities for women that students in the mixed-gender groups made topical, but also to pose the pedagogical complexities of facing these vulnerabilities. As one woman expressed: "my problem with this whole thing is that we're still in the middle of the Montréal Massacre, and then we're trying to invoke its memory? We're living in it! It would be different if we were already beyond it." Contrast the tone and substance of this statement to those in the previous paragraph, in which the students rather quickly displace the anxieties associated with the emblematic recognition of the significance of the Massacre with a turn to "positive" pedagogical scenarios. We might speculate that what helps the students in the women-only group to stay focused on the anxieties foregrounded by an emblematic rendering of the Massacre is the deployment of this narrative on already articulated feminist terms, such that feminist becomes an identity that always excludes identifying oneself as victim within the terms of a gendered binary. This is a position that also allows the students, as teachers in-training, to conceive of a discursive space in which they "instruct" their male students to reject positions of gender dominance. As one of the members noted, "[I] want to make sure that [my] male students do not say, 'Hey, this isn't me; I'm not doing this.' " Whereas the actual substance of such instruction remains unclear in this student's remark (this was not necessarily to be a direct "telling" to male students of how they might think and act), at least the pedagogical desire spoken of here is one that opens up the possibility of a discursive practice within which men could recognize and accept themselves as conceptually inhabiting the position of perpetration, while concretely disavowing any desire or intention to act within this position.

The women in this group appear to find a historical significance, shared sensibility, and collective pedagogical project in the discursive terms of emblemization. Indeed, such terms have been historically and politically imperative given a broader social context in which the Massacre and violence against women are marginalized. However, as we have argued, what such adherence to the emblematic structure risks foreclosing is attentiveness to the limits of this structure with regard to remembering and learning from the legacy of the Massacre. Such limitations are twofold; first, they prevent a full grappling with the contested nature of emblemizing the Massacre on gender terms alone, terms that obscure the raced and classed dimensions of these killings and their remembrance. As noted previously, this is one of the most significant consequences of emblemization and an area of substantial debate in feminist communities. Second, prioritizing a gendered binary misses addressing the positioning of women and men and the identificatory struggles such positionings initiate.

A direct attack on and rejection of the emblematic structure of the Massacre was, in fact, provided by the group that chose not to plan a public remembrance. They were highly critical of the way the Massacre had been singled out as that event which had become, in their words, "the most newsworthy, the most worthy of national recognition, mourning and com-memoration," thus, obliterating coverage and consideration of "diverse experiences [of violence] among a heterogeneous population of women," including the "countless instances of daily violence which, while sometimes less dramatic, are no less significant in the lives of women who experience them." The difficulties articulated by this group are echoed by all the students who are either ambivalent toward or disavow the singular signifi-cance of an emblemized Massacre. What they recognize is the risk of the collapse of self into an other—a collapse organized on terms requiring structures of resemblance that depend on a symbolic equivalence inviting identifications via the potential for substitution. Because such dynamics of identification depend upon and are put into play by the semiotic logic of emblemization itself, it is crucial to imagine more complex terms for work-ing through what it means for women and men to remember and live after Montréal.

Until now, we have been concerned with making clear the limits of this pedagogy of remembrance; now, we want to explore the terms on which practices of remembrance might be reconsidered. We are not suggesting that historical remembrance can fully escape the dilemmas of emblemiza-tion and identification, nor are we dismissing the symbolic importance of memorial emblems in mobilizing and organizing support for social struggles. However, we do want to point to a different direction for the importance of remembrance, one that emphasizes its potential to evoke more than awareness, comprehension, or anamnesis. We pose the possibil-ity of a remembrance that might accomplish a reframing of the substance and limits of both how and what we learn and know.

Awakening and Pedagogy

We have come to believe that emphasis on identity-based connections between the Massacre and the repetition of violence against women refuses and displaces a deep structure of traumatic resemblance that lies in the sense of shock and incomprehensibility first expressed in the hours and days after December 6, 1989. In other words, what we are suggesting here is that—for those who experience the Massacre as a compelling memorial inheritance that elicits their attentiveness—resemblance must be rethought, not in terms of signifying equivalences, but in terms of formations or "bundles" of affect. Hence, this resemblance does not come from outside the event as an interpretation that provides a symbolic equivalence; rather, a resemblance is forged *by way of the event itself.* What is fashioned is a decisive linkage between the traumatic impact of two distinct loci of emotion, both constituted as the experience of rupture. The first of these is the rupture of what is expected and anticipated for women attending an institution of higher learning in late-twentieth-century North America; that they/we are safe, welcome, and, therefore, can attend classes without experiencing violence and violation.[13] The second is a rupture of the necessary and everyday systemic refusals to attend to the horrors that pass as normal. In other words, the Massacre may be considered "emblematic" in that it enacts a return of the repressed, in which one is confronted with horrors revealed in the realization that one's "I can't believe it" is a veneer. This is a realization that makes evident one's defences as just that—defences against the unthinkable amid a consciousness of the "shock of the known" (Guillaumin, 1991, 13).

On such terms, the resemblance that remembrance of the Massacre initiates may be likened to Freud's notion of a traumatic awakening. Here, the remembrance of the Massacre takes the form of a dream, specifically a nightmare, from which one is constantly awakening into a heightened sensibility, variously experienced as anxiety, fright, anger, or vigilance. That is, remembrance of this event might be likened to an awakening where the experience of trauma does not simply consist of "the experience within the dream, but the experience of waking from it" (Caruth, 1996, 64). Thought on these terms, remembrance takes on a considerably different cast. Hence, we might ask: what if remembrance of the Massacre was refocused here, as practices that attend to the replay and relay of traumatic awakenings? Of what significance might be the deliberate attempt to organize public remembrance on such terms? What learning might be staged in and through such remembrances?[14]

To think through these questions, we first put forward the quite striking and palpable differences we have noted between the students' responses to the memorial materials we prepared for them to engage and the remembrance plans they subsequently developed. During their engagement with the materials, student responses—particularly on the part of many women— were visceral and clearly marked by distress. One of our recorders noted:

> I remember wandering in and out of the resource rooms, the installation spaces, we have created. I come across women students huddled in small groups, tears pouring from their faces; I see women curled up, tucked away from what, I am later told, feels like an onslaught; women leave—literally and psychically—removing themselves from the space.

What is striking to us is the *difference* between the palpability of these types of responses and the remembrance plans that were produced and submitted by the groups. With the exception of the group that argued that the Massacre should not be given a formal commemorative focus in schools, the majority of the plans proceed as if deep unsettlement within remembrance *disrupts* the learning inherent in memorial activities, evoking pain that would be best avoided, and, therefore, is in need of containment.

That there might be something pedagogically important in a shared, public expression of traumatic experiences of remembrance is not acknowledged. Thus, the scope and sequence of the student plans focus unproblematically on two quite common features of memorial activities. First, they gesture to a ritual marking of the Massacre (such as an all-school assembly where candles are lit and the names of the women murdered are read); second, they call for information about the Massacre and suggest the initiation of gender equity awareness through such activities as providing violence statistics, asking men to wear white ribbons, and bringing in speakers in nontraditional occupations. When concerns were raised by the students regarding the potential for emotional distress within memorial events, this was understood on individualized terms and as a condition that required rapid amelioration. For example, remembrance plans included suggestions that distressed students remove themselves from memorial activities and possibly talk with professionals trained in helping people to deal with emotional anguish.

The difference between the logic of the planned memorializations and the traumatic responses experienced within remembrance reflects the pedagogic intent to minimize the distress that accompanied the ruptures initiated by remembrances of the Massacre. Within the students' remembrance plans (and, more broadly, in Massacre remembrance practices deployed commonly across Canada), such anguish appears to be understood as unproductive, anti-pedagogical, and, when it does occur, specifically an individual problem in need of therapeutic intervention. Comments such as the following were expressed in the group planning meetings:

> "We really have to think about the emotional part of this thing. I knew I'd be sad, but I was surprised at how much." "I wouldn't even want to be part of a process [referring to the resource rooms] that brings up all this emotion . . . the event needs healing activities . . . [I] walked around like an 'open wound' all weekend and wouldn't want to be involved in making other people feel that way." "I don't want a remembrance event; I want an awareness event."

This approach to remembrance suggests a need to restrict the emotional weight of the material engaged, intimating an antipathy between learning and unsettlement. Such containment of the distress of remembrance is consistent with conventional notions of teaching and learning about difficult social issues that stress comprehension, consciousness-raising, and the rational working for change. These most commonly depend on the cultivation of sympathy and the provision of information. Since planning a memorial enterprise is an instance of what we have previously identified as remembrance pedagogy and, thus, constitutes a practice of initiating an event to be experienced by others, we also suspect that the student–teacher comments and plans evince a serious concern with the pedagogical and ethical appropriateness of initiating events that might be emotionally troubling. Certainly, this is an important concern, one which we do not at all dismiss.

Within contemporary practices of schooling (particularly in public education), it is profoundly unsettling for teachers and administrators to think of teaching and curricular practices that might acknowledge and attempt to work with felt responses to historical events that provoke forms of traumatic awakening. The basic issue here is often articulated through the questions: what right does a teacher have to initiate pedagogies that might acknowledge, make topical, and, hence, draw out anxieties and fears that are often repressed and thought by various stakeholders to be better left alone? Furthermore, what qualifications might teachers need to undertake such efforts?[15] An in-depth response to these questions would require a genealogy of the limits of the recognition of affect admitted into the institutional practices of public schooling, as well as a discussion of the changes in curriculum and teacher education that might be required to admit the pedagogical import of the classroom recognition of traumatic awakenings. Such a response is beyond the purposes of this chapter; rather, what we wish to stress is that existing pedagogical and ethical conventions may too quickly displace what might be learned in contending with "not just the response to difficult knowledge on the outside but also the response to difficult knowledge within" (Britzman, 1998, 133). It is in this spirit that we wish to open up the educational conventions that are oblivious to what might be achieved in situations of pedagogical risk. Indeed, it is the limit of these conventions that points us in another direction—toward the educational significance of accepting that remembrances of the Massacre have initiated and may continue to initiate traumatic awakenings that, if admitted, may reopen the very conjunction of learning and remembrance.

Within the "shock of the known" that the Massacre awakens, there is the encounter of a memorial responsibility that binds the one who remembers with both those who were killed *and* those who subsequently have testified to the impact of the killings on their everyday lives. This is a traumatic binding, not locatable in one moment alone, but in the successive relationships among the initiating event of Lepine's multiple murders at the l'École polytechnique, and the iterative registration of this act in the consciousness of those who learn and remember its occurrence. Conceived of on these terms, this is an event that does not diminish and recede into the past, but rather feeds on itself and grows in magnitude with each successive public recording of moments of remembrance. It is on these terms that we find the significance of taking up the Massacre as an event structure that includes not only the killings, but also the history of public responses to these murders. This is a monstrous public memory, obviously grotesque in its ability to feed on itself and extend the traumatic relation across time. But, perhaps ironically, at the root of this grotesqueness lies the very pedagogical importance of traumatic awakening.

What is the meaning of this awakening? What is it an awakening to, and for whom? If, as we have suggested earlier, the remembrance of the Massacre can be likened to a nightmare from which one may be constantly awakening, what is to be emphasized is that the trauma does not simply exist in the experience of "the event," but also in the experience of waking from it. It is the experience of waking into consciousness that, peculiarly, is identified with the reliving of the trauma (Caruth, 1996, 64). It is not the event/nightmare itself that is solely surprising, but the waking that constitutes the shock—a shock of awakening to the terms of one's own survival. What this puts into play within memorial repetition is the demand that one acknowledge and claim one's own survival in the wake of the Massacre. At the heart of this understanding of what it means to survive (the dead) is a question of responsibility, namely of one's responsibility to the gap between the other's death and one's own life. This places the one compelled to awaken in a position of enacting the impact of the very difference between life and death.

We cannot, of course, elaborate these terms of understanding without an immediate and crucial attention to the difference that social positionings may make to the meanings of this awakening. Before considering this, however, we first note that both women and men may be compelled into a traumatic awakening not through their own identificatory relation to the event of the Massacre, but through their intimate relationship with others who they mark as subject to the grammar of this event. For example, both fathers and mothers may experience a traumatic awakening into the recognition that their daughters are not safe in a university, regardless of whether those daughters themselves "admit" this. Similarly, men and/or women may awaken to the recognition of the fragile acceptance of women in the university through their erotic and/or intimate relationships with other women. The meanings of such traumatic awakenings are likely to mean differently depending on one's indentificatory positionings through other social relations, that is, as fathers, mothers, lovers, partners, and siblings of women in a university.

Women, for whom there is an identificatory traumatic awakening, may awaken to survival, not simply to their survival in the wake of the Massacre, but also to survival in a continuing patriarchy, albeit one not articulated monolithically. For such women to awake to survival may be to awaken to an astonishment that the assumptions of civility and safety are, at best, tenuous—veneers that cover the varying fragilities of daily existence. What is distinctive and memorable in this awakening is not necessarily the recognition of patriarchy's violence, but the astonishment that one has known (of) this violence all along and yet is still surprised by its enactment. For other women, the shock may be one of awakening to a survival that must contend with the structured inequality attributed to the value of different women's lives, such that some women's deaths become an occasion for remembrance while others slip from social memory altogether. In either case, one's awakening to survival is the recognition that who one is, is founded on the differences between the dead and the living. Awakening to survival is thus an awakening to difference as the very condition that constitutes one's existence. This condition demands recognition of the continuities and discontinuities between the living and the dead.

If the first responsibility spawned by the awakening to survival is not to collapse the differences between those who are still the living and those who are now dead, the second lies in the demand posed by the unbreach-able gap of this difference. This is a demand that one confront the question of what one has and has not done, and is yet to do, as a woman awakened to the recognition that other women's deaths are caught up in her/our own existence. This may be understood as an awakening into feminism—a feminism founded on a question of what one is to do when one's living, now, is framed through the acceptance of oneself as a "survivor,"[16] a term the only meaning of which, in the context of this chapter's argument, lies in the very fact of an indissoluble relationship to the dead. We underscore, here, that in arguing for remembrances outside of the logic of emblemization, we are arguing that survivorship is not to be equated with victimization.[17] Rather, survivorship constitutes a structure of recognition, responsibility, and learning. While it is beyond the scope of this chapter to speculate on the details of a feminist practice and theory on such terms, we are won-dering if it is not precisely the task of this contemporary feminism to accept and respond to the question: how am I singularly, and with others, to enact a responsibility to the gap between the living and the dead?

Clearly, traumatic awakenings evoked by the Massacre are not limited to women. In moments of remembrance, men may awaken to their survival of and in a continuing patriarchy—a survival fundamentally formed through their privileged immunity *as men* from the repetitive and normalized struc-ture of male violence against women. Furthermore, this awakening may also consist of the recognition that one's survival is enhanced by a passivity in the face of such violence—an understanding that one's survival might be compromised if one risks that passivity through challenging other men's violence. These awakenings constitute a very specific notion of male priv-ilege, which, baldly stated, would enable a man to say "thank God I am not a woman." Awakening to the strange aberration of this gratitude is the crucial consequence of men's traumatic relationship to the remembrance of the Massacre. Such an awakening is particularly fraught with problems for men enmeshed in social/historical relationships that make it difficult to admit this mix of horror and relief. It is against this backdrop that we recall many early attempts to read the Massacre as an act against humanity, not women; a discursive shift that perhaps gestures to possible terms on which men might secure an unconscious protection against the anxieties of awakening to the "shock of knowing" the pervasive character of male violence—a protection that nevertheless allows for an expression of a deep affective response to the Massacre. What this protection deflects, however, is an awakening to the abhorrent terms of men's survival, which demands that each confront the question of what he has and has not done, and is yet to do as a man awakened to the recognition that the violent deaths of women (known and unknown to him) are caught up in his own existence. The responsibility accrued in this recognition can neither be relinquished nor wholly determined in advance.

All of this presumes, however, men who are compelled to awaken to the traumatic remembrance of the Massacre. This may not be so for men whose enactment of violence against women inhibits their awakening. For, in these instances, there may be no "shock of the known," or perhaps this shock cannot be known. On these terms, men may either celebrate their enactment of dominance or dissociate from their own violence or passivity, alternatives that are not without opportunities for social legitimation in, for example, family and friendship networks. For either, the remembrance of the Massacre may be of little consequence.

Traumatic Awakening and
Performative Practice

On the presumption that there is an infrangible connection between remembrance and learning, and that "traumatic awakening" can profoundly shape the texture of that connection, on what terms might we reconsider the educative importance of "remembering the Massacre?" The student who wants an awareness event, not a remembrance event, is acutely perceptive. For women, the risks of remembrance are substantial if memorialization means reexperiencing a traumatic awakening in which the potential fragility of one's own or another woman's survival is sensed. For men, too, the risks of remembrance are substantial if remembrance means awakening to a reality in which one's survival as a man depends on the displacement and disavowal of one's responsibility in the face of violence enacted on women. Thus, if a "remembrance event" means that those participating awake to their own survival, it is no wonder we ought to think twice about memorial stagings that may leave men feeling a little less certain, women a little less secure and trustful, and both a little less open in an unredeemed world in which violence is an everyday fact, and "death" is the moment for which there is no preparation.

Clearly, the anxiety signaled here sketches the contours of the pedagogical risk inherent in remembrance practices that attempt to hold an attentiveness to traumatic awakening. Deeply felt, such anxiety can lead to a feeling of fragmentation, a sense of being cutoff from a previously stable, coherent world (Felman and Laub, 1992, 49–50). On such terms, one might experience a degree of disorientation and disconnection—a feeling of suspension of one's knowledge of how to negotiate one's daily relationships. Drawing on Felman's insights, we anticipate that such suspension may also include a loss of language, that is, a loss of a discourse that enables a predictable, understandable, and at times controllable, relation to the terms of social life. Given that such losses may indeed accompany traumatic awakening, it is not surprising that remembrance on these terms would have little space in schools as they are currently configured.

Yet, to simply try to avoid remembrance on such terms is itself an inadequate response—in part, because it misses the reality that the Massacre has already initiated, and will likely continue to continue to initiate, traumatic awakening, especially (yet singularly) in the lives of women. Ignoring this, or presuming that what is raised can be settled in a counselor's office, is an understandable, but severe, limitation on the learning embedded in remembrance. Moreover, as important as it is to deploy the remembrance of the Massacre as a semiotic sign—through which practical efforts to mitigate the provocation and consequences of violence against women are organized—this too stands as a limit on the learning embedded in remembrance. In contradistinction, what we are attempting to open up here is at least a consideration of a form of remembrance and, hence, learning, that might take us to new understandings about ourselves, our commitments to others—both dead and living, and the relationships between remembrance and activism. To recast the oft-circulated feminist response to the Massacre ("*first* mourn, *then* work for change"): at issue is imaging a relationship between "mourning" and "working for change" that could offer something very different if it was enacted on other than linear terms. If remembrance as traumatic awakening entails experiences of loss—losses not only of people, but also of ideals, frames of understanding, notions of self and community—confronting this loss must be understood as requiring something more than the melancholic expression of insignificance, grief, and rage. Required then is a form of mourning wherein what is brought to the fore are the insights of recognition and responsibility that begin to reset the terms for the structure and substance of one's activism, and, more broadly, one's living in the world. This is an enactment staged, of course, not only on the terms of the present, but also in awakening to a future—to opportunities still open, choices not yet made.

These concomitants of a remembrance that makes space for traumatic awakenings are not yet the stuff of social transformation, but it is hard to fathom transformation without such antecedents. Certainly, what traumatic awakening requires us to acknowledge is that social change cannot be simply legislated and administered. What transformation requires, then, is not simply becoming aware of or learning about events such as the Massacre, posed as both a warning and a moral object lesson. The practice of remembrance as warning and object lesson is formed within the assumption that others (beyond oneself) need to attend to the historical reality of specific events and their implications, and that such attention itself will be the compelling condition for a change in one's relationships with others. On such terms, initiating and participating in remembrance defines one's responsibility as one of educating others (since one already knows about the events in question), a practice that too often and too easily slides into a postponement of what one needs to do oneself.

Adjourning this postponement would require more than a "learning about"; it would require a "learning from" (Britzman, 1998). This is a learning from memorialization that allows one to recognize one's responsibility to the gap between the other's death and one's own living—between one's living and another's trauma. Such learning from requires event structures that can hold an ongoing attentiveness to the rupturing impacts of traumatic awakening and, thus, provide terms on which to work through the responsibilities that survivorship entails. Any pedagogy of remembrance that attempts to meet the challenges of such possible learning, clearly, cannot foreclose the anxiety and loss associated with engaging with the event of the Massacre; nor, however, can it ignore the importance of structures that work to contain such unsettlement—structures whose core concerns must be a turning to consider one's responsibilities as a member of the communities that live on after the event.

To conclude, we would like to briefly contemplate one instance of what might be implied by this shift in the logic of remembrance. Consider the practice of naming the dead at memorial events—a practice that encompasses not only the naming of the fourteen women killed in Montréal in 1989, but also women murdered in other communities, and during broader time frames. Such voicing of the naming of the dead may be understood as a practice of "bringing them to mind" (Roth, 1995, 222), of making the past present, as a learning *about* who has gone and that they have gone violently. Naming on these terms is most often presented as a spectral procession, an attempt to individuate the dead, which, in its enunciation, becomes, instead, a practice that tends to massify. In arguing this, we are not at all dismissing the practice of naming. Instead, we point to Judith Butler's observation that, "language cannot restore life, but it can reveal the historical ground of the speaker's own life, and, in the case of recollective naming, the historical lineage of one's own sociality" (1988, 69). What is crucial in Butler's observation is the performative power of naming: a practice that calls on those who speak to attend to the gap between their ongoing survival and the death of so many others. Calling out the names of the dead can be understood, then, as both a challenge and an address to those gathered, to find a way of "living with the dead as the past in the present" (Roth, 1995, 226). It is this performativity that shifts the practice of learning: from one of learning about to one of learning from.

Thus, we have begun to wonder about the remembrance effects of moving away from the more usual practice of a preestablished list of names to be read at events, and creating, instead, a space for those gathered to call out (as they feel it is timely) the names of dead women to whom they feel called to bear witness. Perhaps, if names were called out across a site, marked by uneven spaces between one calling and the next (because the names would be spoken according to a sense of being in the moment), voiced at different sound levels (perhaps some will whisper, some will scream), then they may be more readily distinguished than if they were read by one or two women (the more usual practice in our experience). The sounds of these voices building and faltering may bring about visceral reverberations as those standing beside each other call out names differently. But, most important of all, this is remembrance as performative practice, a voicing from a speaker's own emotional, visceral relationship to traumatic awakening. Such awakenings instantiate openings to others who are gathered to attend to that traumatic awakening and repeat a name called out as it touches one who listens. This repetition is *not simply the repetition of a name*; it is, instead, an attempt to acknowledge and re-say the traumatic dimensions of the saying that one has just heard—at layers beyond comprehension.[18] It is in such instances that the monstrous and pedagogical character of the Massacre comes home. It is in this practice of calling out, being touched, and calling out in turn that the gap between one's own survival and those who are the dead might be enacted, remembered, and constituted as an encounter with learning.

CHAPTER FIVE

The Touch of the Past: The Pedagogical Significance of a Transactional Sphere of Public Memory

I remember when the people were brought to Churchill, my husband and I watched them being unloaded off the plane at the shores of Hudson Bay. "This is a bad, bad thing for our people," we said. "Somebody's making a great mistake. From here on, they will be suffering. They are not prepared for this." There were no houses for them anywhere. The winter was closing in. I was very saddened by what was happening. I felt, from now on, there'll be nothing but disaster for our people.

Betsy Anderson

I also remember the time we were moved to Churchill. When our elders say that the people where dumped on the shores of Hudson Bay, they are telling the truth. Some families didn't have tents for shelter, and they had young children, but they were left like that. As the winter set in we had no other way but to live in a canvas tent for the whole winter. My dad eventually built a shack with scrap lumber across the Churchill River where some people were living. We would live there in the winter and come across to the town and summer at the point, Cape Merry. We had a home-made stove made out of a forty-five gallon gas tank. People didn't own proper woodstoves in those days.

Mary Yassie

We were working at the airport. We were outside, doing casual labour, when the plan landed and the people were unloaded. The plane was a huge aircraft with a round belly. It landed and the people came out one by one. I remember the children crying and the few dogs yelping to get free. Eventually everything and everyone was unloaded and put on a big truck and driven down into town. They were all taken to the point at Cape Merry. There, the people were dumped to fend for

themselves on the shores of Hudson Bay. Winter was closing in. Some
of the people set up their tents, and some made makeshift shelters for
themselves. One of the tents stood out because you could see the
shadows of the people who were sitting inside. Already, the feeling of
hopelessness was in the air. There was no laughter, no joy, only dead
silence. Even the dogs were not moving. The feeling just hung over
the people like death.

Charlie Kithithee

All the quotes are from *Night Spirits: The Story of the Relocation of the
Sayisi Dene* Ila Bussidor and Üstün Bilgen-Reinart (1997, 47–48).

What might it mean to live our lives as if the lives of others truly mattered?
One aspect of such a prospect would be our ability to take the stories of
others seriously, as not only evocations of responsibility but also as matters
of "counsel." Walter Benjamin referred to counsel as, "less an answer to a
question than a proposal concerning the continuation of a story which is
just unfolding" (1969, 86). For Benjamin, in order to seek and receive
counsel, one would first have to be able to tell this unfolding story. On such
terms, for the lives of others to truly matter—beyond what they demand in
the way of an immediate practical solidarity—they must be encountered
as counsel, stories that actually might shift our own unfolding stories, particularly in ways that might be unanticipated and not easily accepted.
In what way then might the stories such as those of Betsy Anderson,
Mary Yassie, and Charlie Kithithee be encountered as counsel? In order
to explore the possible terms of such an encounter, I will address here the
importance of a sphere of public memory as a transactional space, not for
the consolidation of national memory, but for mobilizing practices of
remembrance-learning (Eppert, 1999) in which one's stories might be
shifted by the stories of others.

The notion of public memory moves remembrance beyond the boundaries of the singular corporal body. Whereas autobiographical memory
references the ability to recall previous states of consciousness (including
thoughts, images, feelings, and experiences), public historical memory is
grounded in a shared pedagogy of "re-memory" (Morrison, 1987)—a
decidedly social repetition, or better a re-articulation of past events suffused
with demands of remembrance and learning across generations, across
boundaries of time, space, and identifications. As Michael Roth points out:
"talk about memory has become the language through which we address
some of our more pressing concerns. This is because in modernity, memory is the key to personal and collective identity. . . . [However] the
psychologization of memory makes it extremely difficult for people to
share the past, for them to have confidence that they have a collective connection to what has gone before" (1995, 8). In stressing this point, Roth is
keenly aware that memory is not just that which contributes to knowledge
of the past and/or underwrites a claim to group or communal membership,
but, quite divergently, memory may become *transactional*, enacting a claim

on us, providing accounts of the past that may wound, or haunt—that may interrupt one's self-sufficiency claiming an attentiveness to an otherness that cannot be reduced to a version of our own stories. Such an interruption underscores the potential radical pedagogical authority of memory in that it may make apparent the insufficiency of the present, its (and our own) incompleteness, the inadequacy of our experience, the requirement that we revise not only our own stories but the very presumptions that regulate their coherence and intelligibility. On such terms, a transactive memory has the potential to expand that ensemble of people who count for us, who we encounter not merely as strangers (perhaps deserving pity and compassion, but, in the end, having little or nothing to do with us), but as "teachers," people who in telling their stories change our own.

As I will argue, the substance of such a transactive public memory is informed by the reflexive attentiveness to the retelling or re-presentation of a complex of emotionally evocative narratives and images, which define, not necessarily agreement, but *points of connection* between people in regard to a past that they both might acknowledge the touch of.[1] Certainly, such acknowledgments will always be marked with the contemporary and historical specificities, inequities, and power relations that shape the terms of various everyday lives. But, for the moment, what I wish to emphasize here is that the practice of a transactive public memory evokes a persistent sense—*not of belonging, but of being in relation to*—of being claimed in relation to the experiences of others. It is thus that a transactive public memory proposes a connection between oneself and what has gone before—a connection that may be other to one's identificatory investments. As Roth stresses "the psychologization of memory and the doubts about the possibilities for objective history have combined to create an attitude that lets each person have his or her own history. What may appear to be a benign pluralism (or multiculturalism), however, can actually be another symptom of the continuing privatization (or ghettoization) of our relationship with the past. This form of social amnesia depends on a superficial relativism in which one has no investment in the past that one might share with another" (15).

A transactive public memory places one in relation to the past in its otherness and in its potential connection to oneself as coming after (perhaps, emerging out of or against) the past. In this sense, public memory invokes a "kinship" beyond that rendered by biology, tribal traditions, or national histories. Thus, such a form of public memory should be in a position to raise the questions: who counts as our ancestors? Whose and what memories matter—not abstractly—but to me, to you? To what practices of memory am I obligated, what memories require my attention and vigilance, viscerally implicating me—touching me—so that I must respond, rethinking my present?

Boundary Work

The boundary of historical memories is often defined in reference to experiences within sets of social relations regulated under the regime of "nation" or "tribe"—whether that national or tribal entity be coincident with the terrain of state sovereignty or a diasporic cultural formation.[2] It is not accidental that the historical traces that continue to touch me in significant ways include the 1905 Kishnev pogrom, the mass slaughter at Babi Yar, the genocidal concentration camp universe now recognized by the designation "Auschwitz," the founding of the State of Israel, Baruch Goldstein's slaughter of Muslims at prayer in the Cave of the Makhpela in Hebron, and the murder of Yitzhak Rabin. My education and ongoing communal attachments have created identifications that are bound to these and other specific memories; memories with profound implications for how I face reality and live and work with others whose routines and material circumstances provoke memories with very different substances.

However, if the limits of historical memory are fully constrained by notions of identity and identification, the possibilities for transactive public memory are clearly limited. For in such identity-based affiliations begins the refusal to take other people's memories seriously, as of no concern, as having nothing to do with you, as not your responsibility, unless perhaps, one can forge an identification between one's own troubles and traumas and those of others. It is not difficult to hear a condescending indifference in this refusal of the touch of the past as when, for example, native land claims are dismissed as the views of "those who wish to impose their memories on us, to have us re-live the past and wallow in what has be done rather than live in the present." This refusal is also heard in the studied rage and resentment of those subject to the legacies of imperialism. "You ask us to suffer with you, but your memories are not ours, and your narcissistic lamentations do not bring tears to our eyes" (cited in Finkielkraut, 1992). In these words spoken by the defense at the trial of former SS officer Klaus Barbie, one encounters a refusal of the connection between the Nazi genocide of European Jewry and the lives of those subjected to centuries of racist and imperial exploitation (a refusal that falls into an attempt to read the practice of Holocaust memory as an expression of Western racism rather than a supplement to attempts to rupture its continuing presence).

The point here is not that we must transcend our historical specificities and identifications; rather, it is to recognize that a transactive sphere of public memory is a space cross-cut with boundaries that serve both as limit and resource for one's capacity to be responsive to the touch of the past and, thus, hear the counsel in the memories of others. These boundaries mark my distance from that undergone and spoken of by others. They estrange me from various pasts to which I always arrive too late, reminding me that the time of other people's memories is not my time. Yet, these boundaries are not simply the limit of my social imagination condemning me to indifference, voyeurism, or an epistemological violence that can only render the experience of others in terms I recognize or imagine as my own. Rather, these boundaries initiate the terms for the reconstruction of my historical memory (Simon 2000); that is, on these boundaries I can begin to enact my memorial kinship to the memory of another with the recognition of my distance from these memories. And I can accomplish this practice when, as a witness to other people's memories, I attempt to hear and respond to the stories of others in a way that takes cognizance of the strangeness of these stories, their foreignness. This is a form of re-memory in which memories of "that which were never my fault or deed" (Levinas, 1987) begin to touch, to interrupt my taken-for-granted performance of the present.

Given the increasingly heterogenous space of the nation-state and the increased human stake in an interdependent global future, national and diasporic formations cannot remain the limit of our concern. Our lives together may indeed depend on questions such as: how, in what sense, and under what conditions might events such as the recent slaughter of Tutsis in Rwanda or the Mohawk uprising in Oka, Quebec, or less immediately, the Irish Great Hunger, or the events of the Middle Passage, which instituted slavery in the Americas, become "personal" for me? What might be the substance of a point of connection at which I am touched to respond to the memories of others, not in the sense of some meaningless sentiment, a too easy empathy, or the false nostalgia of a late imperialism, but rather as a means of experiencing certain events as part of ongoing relations of power and privilege, the legacy of which I participate in and I am called to transform?

No doubt, the institutionalized practices of historical memory that organize and regulate our encounters with histories "which are not our own" severely restrict the terms on which people may hear and learn something of each other's lives. Even when there is interest and responsiveness, these restrictions often diminish the power of the seen and heard to rupture one's performance of the present. Rarely do we engage other people's memories "faced" by others (to cite a concept central to the thought of Levinas); responsible to and claimed by their unthematizable difference in ways that we cannot expect. Thus, if the terms of public memory are to shift, increased attention must be given to practices that confront us, claim us to a memorial kinship because they reside beyond the bounds of the histories that give substance to one's attachments, affirmations, and expectations, confirming who we are and what we know. What might such practices be?

Testimony and Public Memory

Consider for a moment the practice of testimony. The primary purpose of testimony is to convey through multiple expressive forms the historical substance and significance of prior events and experiences. Testimony consists of representations either by those who have lived through specific events or, alternatively, by those who have been told of such lived realities, either directly or indirectly, and have been moved to convey to others that which has been impressed upon them. What I wish to emphasize most about testimony is that it is a multilayered communicative act—a performance intent on carrying forth memories through the conveyance of a person's engagement between consciousness and history (Felman and Laub, 1992). Thus, whether across generations or cultures, testimony is always directed toward another, attempting to place the one who receives it under the obligation of response to an embodied singular experience not recognizable as one's own.

If one listens to testimony receptive to this transactive address, one finds oneself at a point of connection, commanded by a persistent sense of belonging to something or someone that is other to oneself. To be present to testimony, to be responsive as a requested witness (not as spectator, voyeur, analyst, or student), is to be claimed to an another in ways that are not reducible to practices of identification or humanistic assertions of empathy. To clarify this position, I shall briefly describe two quite different sensibilities: the *spectatorial* and the *summoned*. The notion of sensibility I refer to here is a particular way of opening oneself to another—of approaching another through a particular embodied cognizance.

A spectatorial sensibility concerns the construction of an observer—one who listens and watches. Limited to neither one's visual nor auditory sense, spectatorial sensibility references a larger, pervasive organization of perceptual engagement; a particular management of the way one attends to another. This sensibility embodies and enacts a capacity to grasp a given testimony within frames of understanding that render it intelligible and meaningful in ways that evoke thought, feeling, and judgment. But, a spectatorial sensibility is not limited to abstract and objectified forms of historical interpretation. In a spectatorial sensibility, one might expect to be informed but also, inspired, delighted, disgusted, saddened, and horrified. What is not expected is that one may become obligated[3] and called into question by the summons of another, consigned and challenged by the substance and substantiality of that one who now holds my regard. Thus, quite otherwise, experiencing testimony on the terms of a summoned sensibility requires a very different embodied cognizance—one incarnated in notions of touch rather than sight or sound. This is a sensibility that instantiates the proximity of self and another; an other who calls, who summons me, and who, thus, puts me under an encumbrance in which I must consider my response-ability.

These two forms of sensibility lead to very different ways of discussing one's response to testimony. They also align themselves quite differently in relation to various forms of public memory. Within a spectatorial sensibility, testimony is generally framed as a document. One might regard this document as partial evidence supporting or refuting a historical argument and/or a display of the constructed character of memory, particularly in relation to traumatic events. In either case, its characterizations are of the order of an observer in relation to a "text." Testimony is apprehended, read, or heard as a document of memory being remembered; but, it is not only a document; it is a very specifically textured performative act. To repeat an earlier foreshadowed argument, in bearing witness, one always bears witness to someone, so that in speaking, the witness who speaks summons another to witness this speaking. If one accepts this summons, accepts co-ownership of the testimony–witness relationship, and the burden of being obligated to testimony beyond one's a priori instrumental concerns, then one may be said to approach testimony within a summoned sensibility. The contrast between spectatorial and summoned sensibilities suggests not merely that there are different ways of reading or listening to testimony but that there are different ways of living historically, each with contrasting assumptions regarding the relationship between remembrance and learning. It is not a matter of attempting to adjudicate which among differing forms of engagement is the superior, reducing remembrance to one correct form. Indeed, one might choose or find oneself impelled to participate at different times in each of these sensibilities. What is important to underscore, however, is that for a public memory to enact its most radical pedagogical potential, it must include both these sensibilities. Why is this so?

In being summoned as a witness, one remains open to the possibility of unforeseen memory, the possibility of unfamiliar or uncanny connections; connections that may disrupt attempts to comprehend events and their implications on the lives of people affected by them. While this disruption leaves one less secure in negotiating daily life within an assured "history of the present," it also brings forth the possibility of time, the possibility of futurity. Following Levinas's on time, the future is *what comes toward the self, ungraspable, outside its possibilities* (Cohen, 1994, 142). In this sense, a community desirous of hope requires a transactive public memory, a sphere of memorial practice that includes the summons to witness past events that are beyond one's memory and in which one has not been directly implicated. More boldly stated, there is no future without such transactive memorial claims, without responsibilities to memories other than one's own, to memories you have no responsibility for, but which claim you to a memorial kinship. As Levinas suggests, in this responsibility "I am thrown back toward what has never been my fault or my deed, toward what has never been in my power or my freedom, toward what has never been in my presence, and has never come into memory" (1987, 111). Hope and an ethical pragmatics mix in this responsibility "to a past that concerns me, that "regards me," and is "my business" outside of all reminiscence, retention, re-presentation, or reference to a remembered present" (111–112). This mix of hope and ethics depends on a responsiveness to others, which recognizes that the meeting of testimony and witness does not take place "at the same time"; that one does not witness the other as a contemporary. Witnessing, then, is an event of two disjunctive temporalities, an event in which the other's time disrupts mine. Thus, *it is a new time*, an extraordinary disjuncture of other and I, an experience of proximity that initiates an "infinite distance without distance" (Cohen, 147). It is a moral time, a time of non-indifference of one person to another, of obligation and responsibility to, and for, the other (Cohen, 149).

It should be clear by now that I am proposing a transactional sphere of public memory as an educative space, a crucial set of actual practices for

encountering historical memories on terms that might teach us anew
how to live in the present. As an educational space, a transactional sphere of
public memory must be instilled with practices that help us attend to the
alterity of the lives of others. What might such practices be, practices that
could encourage the disruptive touch of memories not mine? What pedagogies can we initiate that might shift the sensibilities through which
we listen to the stories of others? With these questions, I want to bring
these reflections home—in this case—to Canada. Returning to stories of
the Sayisi Dene with which I began, I will further consider what is at stake
in memories of that which has "never been my fault or deed."

Listening as a Mode only of Thought

The 1996 Royal Commission on Aboriginal People (RCAP) suggested
that Canadians are simply unaware of the history of the Aboriginal presence in what is now Canada and that there is little understanding of the
origins and evolution of the relationship between Aboriginal and non-
Aboriginal people that have led us to the present moment. In an address to
launch the Royal Commission, Georges Erasmus, the cochair of RCAP
and a former chief of the Assembly of First Nations, stated "The roots of
injustice lie in history and it is there where the key to the regeneration
of Aboriginal society and a new and better relationship with the rest of
Canada can be found" (Erasmus, 1996). It is in regard to this latter prospect,
new and better relations between the people of the First Nations and
Canadians, that I now wish to address the possibilities inherent in a transactional sphere of public memory.

No doubt what is currently remembered/forgotten of the histories of
Aboriginal–Canadian relations is implicated in permitting (indeed encouraging) Canadians to distance themselves from, and abdicate their responsibility with regard to, the ongoing conditions of injustice that are part of the
day-to-day lived experiences of Aboriginal people in Canada. Certainly,
there is the need for much increased public attention to the history of
Aborginal–Canadian post-contact relationships, an attention whose hope is
a renewed historical consciousness that would impact on how Canadians
enact their current relations with native communities. However, what
remains unclear is the necessary substance of such a historical consciousness
and how it might be established? While one surely must start by supporting
the inclusion of "post-contact" histories in educational sites such as schools,
cinema, broadcast televison, and the internet, one must also recognize the
limits to the provision of history as "information," as if historical narratives
were a neutral form of reportage that encouraged the measurement of
historical awareness in terms of how many "facts" someone knows about
particular past events, personalities, and communal/societal structures.

The publication and distribution of various forms of written and oral
testimony has been an attempt by Aboriginal communities to contribute to
the development of historical awareness and understanding of the history

of Aboriginal–Canadian relations and its impact on the lives lived in its wake. The testimonial record produced in Canada is consistent with efforts by Aboriginal communities worldwide to speak of their own histories and the histories of their subjugation by, and resistance to, colonial regimes. One aspect of this history has been government-initiated removal of peoples from land they had being living on for centuries. The RCAP published report emphasized that much of the shared history between native people and Canadians is one of dispossession and displacement of Aboriginal people from their traditional homelands; homelands crucial to their physical and cultural survival. One compelling chronicle of such a forced dispossession and displacement is Ila Bussidor's (1997) *Night Spirits: The Story of the Relocation of the Sayisi Dene* (written with the collaboration of Üstün Bilgen-Reinart). In *Night Spirits*, Bussidor provides an account of her peoples forced removal by the Canadian government from their traditional home-lands and hunting grounds in Northwestern Manitoba to the barren shores of Hudson Bay near Churchill. Bussidor not only writes the story of her family as they experienced the relocation but also provides interview excerpts from various Sayisi Dene who bear witness to particulars of this shameful event and its tragic and traumatic consequences. The reports by Betsy Anderson, Mary Yassie, and Charlie Kithithee cited at the beginning of this chapter are a component of this witness. So is the following account by John Solomon of the events of August 17, 1956 when a government chartered transport plane arrived at Little Duck Lake, Manitoba, to remove the people living there.

> The plane came with three white people plus the pilot. They said they came to move the people. The people never replied. We took whatever we could with us, we left behind our traps, our toboggans, our cabins, and we got into that plane. When we got out in Churchill, there were no trees. The wind was blowing sand on everything. We didn't know what to do next. We couldn't do anything there. We couldn't go trap-ping. We couldn't set a net. There was nothing to hunt. We were in a desperate state. We had nothing to live on. (*Night Spirits*, 46)

Testimonial accounts such as this one have the potential to make a transac-tive claim on Canadian public memory, one with the possibility of shifting the stories non-Aboriginals tell of themselves and, hence, possibly renewing the terms on which to build a redefined relationship between First Nation peoples and Canadians. But, what could it mean to listen to such testimonies in order to open oneself to the radical pedagogical and political potential of such memories?

While accounts such as those of Anderson, Yassie, Kithithee, and Solomon seem straightforward enough, they can place difficult and serious demands on readers who recognize that they are being called to listen to a bearing witness directed toward themselves, a "telling," a "speaking to" of traumatic events, which will always exceed the words spoken. In this sense, no matter how many words we might read of Sayisi Dene accounts, their testimonies will manifest the marks of insufficiency. These marks—inscribed within the texts themselves—are the scars that bear the difficulties of fully rendering the realities of human cruelty and suffering. It is in this limit condition of testimony that the unspoken may be heard, and it is in the practice of attuning to what is not spoken that the possibility for listening to become a way of thinking exists.

The inevitable limits of the testimonial act mean that narratives and images of historical trauma such as those reported by Anderson, Yassie, Kithithee, and Solomon, are shot through with absences that, in their silence, solicit questions. Actively attending to transactive claims of such testimonies includes more than their simple comprehension, more than registering a few shocking facts that one did not know, more than chalking up more evidence of a history of injustice. Such listening requires an attentiveness to the questions one feels such accounts solicit, that is, an attentiveness to one's compulsion to pose difficult and, at times, unanswerable questions, which nonetheless impulsively press for responses that *seemingly* (from within one's own entanglement of history and epistemology) promise help in deciphering what is to be heard in a testimonial account. What is sought in such questions, typically, is not attached to something within the text but rather to something missing from the text. Rooted in one's own insufficiencies, these are not necessarily polite questions. Indeed, it may be troubling to those bearing witness to hear them spoken, particularly so when such bearing witness is self-understood as an attempt to heal the wounds of a traumatic past. Nevertheless, what is crucial to stress is that such questions are emotional interrogatives on the part of the listener, marks that the testimony heard is breaking the well-ordered frame that regulates our everyday sense of how human relationships take place. Thus, it is that more than one non-Aboriginal reader of *Night Spirits* has asked the question (minimally, to themselves): given the lack of information the Sayisi Dene had as to why they should move, the sudden unexpected arrival of the plane, the short time they were given to collect belongings, the fact that only four White people arrived to initiate the move, and the absence of reports of people being threatened if they resisted being removed, why did the Sayisi Dene get on the plane? Why didn't the people simply refuse to comply with the government agents who told them to do so?

Now, we may, indeed, render this question as not simply impolite or even cruel, but violent and obscene. This is particularly so to the extent that the question initiates a process of revictimization of the Sayisi Dene and works to alleviate government responsibility for the forced removal and its devastating consequences. Arrogantly judgmental, the question more than hints that the Sayisi Dene were passive victims whose passivity is implicated in their own fate. Indeed, in my view, when the genesis of a question such as this is left unexamined, there is little to redeem this form of "curiosity." Alternatively, one may take the pedagogical position that, no question is inappropriate and that, indeed, such a question can be taken as a teachable moment for the provision of information regarding the long history of the development of British and Canadian state structured authority as it imposed itself on, and became entwined with, the lives of aboriginal peoples. However, the provision of information rarely addresses the generative basis of such a question. If information is provided as authoritative history that cancels the question, it may, in fact, short-circuit the pedagogical process that takes as problematic one's practice of listening to others.

It is the possibility of a critical, transformative learning that offers listeners the chance to redeem their obscene questions. This learning begins when we view such questions as *symptomatic* of the difficult knowledge (Britzman, 1998) contained in the testimony of the Sayisi Dene, knowledge that places a claim on its non-Aboriginal listener and requires a degree of self-reflexivity in order to be responsive and responsible to that claim. Testimonies such as those of Anderson, Yassie, Kithithee, and Solomon carry a surreal quality for those of us who find such experiences unimaginable. In this sense, they lead to the query: how can this be so? How could this have happened? These are questions that can never be totally resolved by historical narrative. In seeking to find some stable frame for undoing the surreal character of what has been heard, further questions are posed in an attempt to make some sense of the events under description. What is crucial to recognize in this is that when attempting to listen responsibly, one may find testimony, such as that provided by the Sayisi Dene, disrupting one's taken-for-granted sense-making practices. On such terms, testimonies of historical trauma are always at least partially transgressive bringing into question the central stories and propositional schema that order one's life. Faced by a testimony whose texture unhinges one's sense of "what and how things happen," one seeks a "shadow text" (Simon and Armitage-Simon, 1995; Simon and Eppert, 1997) that may recover and reinscribe a lost sense to a testimonial account. Drawing on taken-for-granted knowledge and beliefs in order to provide workable interpretations that make traumatic events and experiences less incomprehensible, shadow texts may be written not only with partial knowledge but also with misconceptions, misinformation, myths, projections, and prejudice. Thus, whether and how the writing of shadow texts are attempted implies much in regard to how the obligations of witnessing are enacted. The work of writing shadow texts, of attempting to provide at least some partial explanation or rationalization that might stabilize our understanding of what happened in the past, is an effort to establish a basis on which the memory of a testimony might be claimed. Yet, to evoke through testimony the memory of an injustice that has initiated a traumatic legacy of death and misery is to be caught in a potential disruption of one's understanding of the human possibility inherent in configuration of our present social order—a disruption that may frighten us insofar as participants in that social order it "bears witness to our own historical disfiguration" (Felman and Laub, 73–74).

Thus, a responsible listening to the testimony of the Sayisi Dene may require that we face up to the question of how we are to hear accounts of

Aboriginal–Canadian history, which bear witness to displacement, death, degradation, and "our own historical disfiguration." This is not a matter of merely of an individual's readiness or interest to hear such accounts. Certainly, most Canadians will read Bussidor's book without experiencing a loss of significance of their own sense of the social arrangements that inscribe their everyday lives. Perhaps, they will be shocked, perhaps they will "weep" (as a promotional statement for *Night Spirits* suggests), and perhaps they may demand that the government atone for its actions through symbolic and material means. But, much more radically, we are still left with the question of how we are to hear and remember the stories of the Sayisi Dene in ways that incorporate them into an intelligible past while recognizing that there is an insistence in their stories which require reopening the present to reconsideration; in other words, reopening the very historically constituted terms on which we live and that provide for our understanding history. Beyond the usual rhetoric that testimony renders historical abstractions personal and emotional—characteristics that often fail to lift testimony beyond the entrapment of spectacle—testimonial witness does have the potential to break through one's spectatorial notions regarding what constitutes comprehendible narratives of suffering, survival, and resistance. While such notions enable a certain comprehension of stories of colonialization, to the degree that testimonial address astonishes, disturbs, transgresses those it addresses, it provides much more than information previously unknown. It initiates a summons that is simultaneously a possibility for a learning with the potential to radically reorient what is required to face history anew, a learning rooted in what Levinas (1969) refers to as the "traumatism of astonishment"—calling what I know and how I know into question.

It is for this reason that symptomatic obscene questions asked in the face of testimony hold enormous pedagogical potential. To actualize this potential means recognizing that such questions arise from the transactive claim on the listener that testimony initiates and that, in order to respond responsibly to this claim, we must re-think how to accomplish the act of listening. A responsible listening, thus, may require a double attentiveness—a listening to the testimony of the one who is speaking and, at the same time, listening to the questions we find ourselves asking when faced by this testimony. It is then that we might ask ourselves, in hearing a testimonial account: why are we asking the questions we do? Why do we need to know this? In other words, rather than setting our questions aside or simply posing the questions to, for example, the Sayisi Dene, in order to work through a responsible listening, one must pose to ourselves questions about our questions, interrogating why the information and explanations we seek are important and necessary to us.

Here, then, is a critical moment of learning. Without prescribing what this learning might be, let us consider a few possibilities. The first consequence of this reflexive turn to consider the grounds of our own questions may be the realization of our own insufficiency to hear Sayisi Dene testimony, our own inexperience and our own historical ignorance. Surely, an initial response to this insufficiency would be a responsibility to learn more about what happened to the Sayisi Dene, collecting as much information as one can regarding the relocation and its consequences. To this, reasonably, would be added further study of the history of Aboriginal–Canadian relations and how this history is implicated in the event and consequences of the relocation. However, as I have been suggesting, simply acquiring more information will never suffice if one is to respond to the force of a testimonial address—a force that, if acknowledged, puts ourselves into question. Thus, we would not only have to try to alleviate our own ignorance but transform the very grounds for its existence in the first place. Crucial here would be the recognition that our insufficiency to hear the testimony of another is a *historical* insufficiency, one with structural conditions that hold it in place. Thus, too, we are challenged to study our own education and limits, beginning to understand how the social arrangements of our lives and the investments that they inculcate are not only incomplete, but deficient at least in terms of what we need to know to reconstruct the substance of Aboriginal–Canadian relations. But, such a formulation of the learning inherent in questioning our questions is far too limited. Ignorance is not simply a rationally organized state of affairs, but is also a dynamic, unconscious structure that fosters resistance to knowledge. Thus, an exploration of our own insufficiencies means attending to what presumptions and defences Sayisi Dene testimony elicits. This would be an attempt to learn not only about this testimony, but to learn from it by working through the vaguely felt and little understood psychic projections and culturally invested frameworks that order our attention to narratives that speak to "the past in Canada."

The recognition of insufficiency, however, sets only one half of the learning agenda. The other half requires yet another turn in the practice of critical reflection. This is an openness to the possibility that our questions are not really questions at all, but rather rhetorical statements based on the premise that we really are able to understand what we are being told, that, indeed, we have heard of similar things happening before and that we can understand (and judge) Sayisi Dene testimony on these terms.[4] Thus, is set another learning task defined as a response to the following questions: what other histories are elicited (perhaps free associated) by us when hearing Sayisi Dene testimony? How does this displacement of the relocation of Dene on to other histories condense what, in fact, are separate realities? What knowledge and understanding is subjugated in this process of displacement and what perspective might be gained in it? And what is our relation to these "other" histories, and how is comprehension of Sayisi Dene testimony filtered through our struggles to understand these other instances, particularly those including forced population removal, for example, the Nazi attempt to make Europe *Judenrein*, or the recent Serbian attempt at "ethnic cleansing" in Kosovo?

While such explorations might help unravel the grounds of our own questioning further, critically examining the rhetorical tenor of these questions requires one further step. This would be an attending to the particular historically and culturally structured forms of narrative coherence and reason that have become a precondition for our attention to, and making sense of, the stories we are told. We might note how in listening to certain testimony that is "hard to follow" our attention wanders, contrasting this with the narrative structures of an account that seem riveting, holding our attention throughout. Also, we might note to what degree the "sense of an account" devolves to a judgment as to the persuasiveness and reliability of the practice of witness. It is not that one can ever completely eliminate the practice of judgment in hearing the stories of another (nor would such an elimination be desirable), but rather what is at issue is taking full measure of how and why the terms of our judgments are invoked in the practice of listening, and what this prevents us from hearing.[5]

In holding together the doubled moments of attentiveness to testimony—one informational, the other reflexive—there is a practice of binding together remembering and learning. If such a practice is brought to a sphere of public memory, learning in such a space could be more than knowledge acquisition and remembering more than the retrieval, recollection, or recall of something past but now forgotten. It may be objected that the reflexivity I suggest necessary to a transactive public memory is a perverse narcissism that turns an engagement with history toward a concern with oneself rather than the concerns of the other. After all, what is important about the Sayisi Dene testimony is that it makes claims on us to learn of events hidden to most Canadians, to hear stories of people who suffered and died unnecessarily and as a result of government action, and to work in solidarity with those Sayisi Dene who are still living the legacy of this event attempting to recover a viable and dynamic communal life. The fundamental issue is to recognize an injustice within a demand for justice and take the measure of what changes must accrue as a result. However, what must accrue as a result is not only retributive justice for the Sayisi Dene, but as Bussidor and other Dene recognize, a change in the way non-Aboriginals view their shared history with native peoples. For this change to happen, we will have to learn to listen differently, to take the measure of our ignorance, and reassess the terms on which we are prepared to hear stories that might trouble the social arrangements on which, as Canadians, we presume a collective future. In Benjamin's idiom, we have to learn to take the counsel in stories of a shared past as told by Aboriginal people.

Education and Canadian Public Memory

That which is being given in and through the testimony collected in *Night Spirits* is a memorial inheritance whose importance exceeds the immediacy of one's own personal engagement with these memories. Bussidor's own testimony and the testimonies collected by her make a claim on

Canadian public memory. This is particularly so if we take Canadian public memory as a sphere for developing a historical consciousness, not as an individual awareness and attitude but as a commitment to, and participation in, an organized practice of remembrance and learning. Certainly, this would be a form of public memory quite different from the reiteration of valued stories that attempt to secure the permanence of collective affiliations and identifications in stable notions of a meaningful past. Rather, I prefer to think of public memory as a sphere of interminable and exacting learning where one is not just informed through remembrance but where one learns to remember anew. What needs to be offered within a practice of public memory is not the sameness of common memory but the discontinuities of an always incomplete remembrance. On such terms, memory would not be simply a private act, but rather a social gesture—a gesture that bears responsibility for the past to the present, reopening the present in terms demanded by a fair hearing of the past. With regard to such a notion of public memory, an educator's responsibility is not only to support the inclusion of forgotten or unknown histories that pertain to our contemporary problems and relationships, but to help constitute public memory as a pedagogical space by making evident and supporting the critical exploration of the questions, uncertainties, ambiguities, and failures that arise in the process of trying to hear testimonies that speak to these forgotten or unknown histories. That is, in order for Canadian public memory to foster a renewed historical consciousness, which would impact on how Canadians enact their current relations with Aboriginal communities, as educators, we must try to find ways to define memory-spaces (in schools, in media, in art practice, in internet-based exchanges) in which stories of speaking and hearing, remembering and learning are exchanged, examined, and understood as the grounds for a critical pedagogical practice of remembrance.

The insistence on the importance of a "public" memory at this moment in Canadian history is a self-conscious response to contemporary inclination toward the privatization of memory. Such an insistence affirms the need for a collective space of remembering and learning quite different from the construction of memory strictly defined on individual terms. One cannot, of course, minimize the importance of personal, local memories. But, when we are asked to attend to the testimony of witnesses speaking about experiences that bear on the possibilities of new and better relationships among diverse members of the geographical-based political economy we find ourselves within (and may still, acting in concert, at least partially restructure), it is necessary to affirm one's commitment to a public dialogue in which the transactive character of memory is seen as an opportunity for a necessary learning. This would be a learning founded on an a priori commitment to attend to the concerns of those who are here, facing us; who in speaking to us of a shared history, draw near demanding something of our time, energy, and thought. It is also a learning that recognizes the witness as a "genuine transgressor" (DesPres, 1977) whose words refuse to be reduced to the terms of prevailing categories and, indeed, are necessary for the invention of new forms of social life.

Sayisi Dene Testimony and Public Memory

One might argue that the little known story of the Sayisi Dene must be recovered because it is emblematic of systemic structures of violence enacted within Canadian colonial relations. Indeed, Ila Bussidor herself asks that the story not be heard as unique to the Sayisi Dene. Undoubtedly, the Sayisi Dene testimony references a larger picture of the Canadian colonialization of Aboriginal peoples. No doubt, the death and suffering of the Sayisi Dene must be related to millions of other instances of Aboriginal death and suffering over the last five centuries. But, within a renewed Canadian public memory, a story need not satisfy the criteria of being emblematic or exemplary in order to be worthy of remembrance. No one's pain should be diminished by saying it is less emblematic, less historically important than anyone else's. Certainly, a public memory ought to acknowledge that if remembrance is required for justice to be pursued, then remembrance is required when people have been injured. But it is not simply the fact of victimization that is the force of obligation to remember and attend to Sayisi Dene testimony, it is also that they are here, now, addressing us, summoning us to listen to and learn not just about their story but from their story, teaching us, in turn, how it is that the story they tell is not just about them but about us as well.

The Sayisi Dene live in the present with the ongoing consequences of injustice that has resulted from policies and decisions made by the Canadian and Manitoba governments on behalf of their constituents. To witness the stories of the forced removal of the Dene in 1956, one has to hear about traumatic deaths and sufferings of specific people. The loss and grief, both personal and collective, remain deeply experienced. Amid the lives of real people, justice is no abstraction; it exists in relation to people who have been hurt, and requires that something be done to support the repair of this hurt. While remembrance does not ensure anything, least of all justice, it can concretize human aspirations to make present a world yet to be realized, thus presenting us with claims of justice and the requirements of compassion.

However, for remembrance to be truly hopeful, something more must be put into play than human aspirations for a better future. This requires attending to practices of remembrance as a difficult learning—a learning that can hold open the present to its insufficiency. To do this, remembrance requires attuning oneself to the power of the Sayisi Dene testimony to rupture our invested understanding of ourselves, our government and the regulating political, economic, and technological frameworks we unconsciously use to negotiate our world. The trauma that the Dene experienced and the compelling nature of Bussidor's and others' testimonies are such that they refuse to remain assimilated to the terms of dominant historical understanding. Rather, this testimony keeps returning, provoking deep questions about what it means for us to understand the lives of others. It calls again and again to attend, hear, and respond responsibly, attempting to recognize what of ourselves is tied up with our understanding of the history and contemporary substance of Aboriginal-Canadian relations. While the roots of injustice lie in history, we have yet to realize a historical consciousness, as a mode of learning and practice of instantiating living communal memories, that might be capable of supporting the regeneration of new and better relations between native peoples and Canadians. This then is the time and the task.

CHAPTER SIX

Witness as Study: The Difficult
Inheritance of Testimony

WITH CLAUDIA EPPERT, MARK CLAMEN,
AND LAURA BERES

I am trying to remember something I couldn't possibly know. I am
trying, as I was two days ago in Lithuania, to move by feel, to know
when I was close to where they had been. At first I just walked in the
Jew's town without anyone helping me, without anyone telling me.
I walked until I remembered.
    Myra Sklarew, *Lithuania: New and Selected Poems* (1995, 34)

Not to find one's way about in a city is of little interest. But to lose
one's way in a city, as one loses one's way in a forest, requires practice.
For this the street names must speak to one like the snapping of dry
twigs, and the narrow streets of the city center must reflect the time
of day as clearly as a mountain valley.
    Walter Benjamin, *A Berlin Childhood Around 1900*
    (Szondi, 1978, 491)

Geoffrey Hartman notes "there is no lack of serious attention to the Shoah;
after a slow start, after a stunned reaction, historians, philosophers, psycho-
analysts, and artists have entered what has been characterized as a period of
obsession" (1996, 1). What is not at issue—at least in the midterm—is
whether or not the Shoah will be forgotten. However, what is very much
a practical and urgent concern, a matter of considerable debate and
controversy, is how and what of the Shoah will be remembered through
contemporary practices of Holocaust history, memorialization, and education. No doubt it would be best if this question remained interminably
current. If one takes seriously Walter Benjamin's (1969, 255) warning that
each generation must beware the conformism that is about to overwhelm
its traditions,[1] one must persist in reopening the question of how one is to
face the historical period known as the Holocaust. It is the necessity of this

persistence that animates the memory work put forth in this chapter. Without pretense that Holocaust remembrance could or should be reduced to fixed terms and methods, we address what it might mean to renew practices of public remembrance of the Shoah. This renewal takes place in the recognition of the human need for hope and the obligation not just to learn about the past, but to learn from attempts to face the traces of lives lived in times and places other than one's own. The attempt to construct a linkage between hope and remembrance in the context of the Shoah is no trivial matter. Too often, efforts to find a redemptive dimension within the events that subsume the Nazi genocide of European Jewry seem self-serving and forgetful. If such a linkage is possible, it will require rethinking the very substance and purpose of remembrance.

A useful place to begin a reconsideration of formation of public memory is with the recognition that varying practices of remembrance embody differing assumptions about time, historical memory, and pedagogy. While considerable attention has been given to the various "uses of the past" and conceptions of time (and space) implicit in practices of remembrance, little concern has been given to the notions of teaching and learning inherent in the presumptions and organization of different forms of remembrance. Indeed, the centrality of questions of pedagogy to notions of remembrance is often missed, eviscerating discussions of how and why public memory matters. There are two dominant modes through which these questions of the purpose and practice of remembrance are most often addressed: history and memorialization.[2] History, in this context, refers to the writing and interpretation of narratives that attempt to organize a reasoned understanding of past events through attention to detail, document, and argument. Public memory addressed through practices of historical narrative and interpretation most commonly presupposes pedagogy as the provision of information and insight. The intent of this provision is to develop historical awareness and understanding with the consequent reduction of historical ignorance and innocence, enabling one to discover the degree to which one did not know about or fully grasp the significance of prior events. As a critical enterprise, history matters to the degree that it informs a constant reappraisal of current presumptions about the past and its inheritance.

Quite differently, memorialization as public memory presumes a pedagogy of anamnesis, a practice that seeks the recovery of what has been lost, neglected, or misplaced. Thus, memorialization is a reminder of that which has previously been known, but now must be told of again. This "telling again" is first and foremost a reminder and a warning of what threatens to be forgotten or has already been forgotten. This is no idle admonition, for the forgetting that memorialization acts against, if actualized, risks dissolving the very grounds on which notions of self and community are built. In this sense, memorialization is premised on the moral injunction, "one must not forget." Pedagogically understood, the telling again of memorialization is a performative practice that attempts to bring past lives and places into presence. To accomplish this task, memorialization must transform modern conceptions of time as a spatial continuum through which we move. Within memorialization, there is an attempt to hold the past, the present, and the future as co-terminus; most importantly, the past is not really past at all, but eternally present. Hence, within practices of memorial remembrance, the desire for a manifest continuity is made apparent; oblivion is refused. The pedagogy of memorial remembrance relies on historiographic detail, reminiscence, vignette, and symbolization to remind and announce that "this has occurred," "this person lived." What has been lost must be brought into view not only so that one might "know" what happened but so that we might attach ourselves to this remembrance. Thus, memorial practices often include pedagogical structures designed to bond emotions and processes of identification with historical narrative and symbol in ways that reinforce the significance of specific memories for the identities and commitments of specific groups, be they families, communities, or nations.

Our interest in the renewal of practices of remembrance is not intended to dismiss or devalue the importance of pedagogies of historical narrativization or memorialization. Both obviously offer forms of learning central to life in human communities. There is, however, a troubling conservatism endemic to both pedagogies that stems from a limited conception of what constitutes the substance and significance of learning about the past. The root of this conservatism lies in a shared, social, hermeneutic project; that is, both history and memorialization are practices that attempt to transmit to others an awareness and interpretation of past events/lives in order to assert, affirm, confirm, or revise communal narratives and symbols. In this regard, it is rare that practices of history or memorialization examine the pedagogical terms on which both are founded. Both practices are motivated by the attempt to bring "news" as new (or re-remembered) sets of facts and interpretations. Thus, as a consequence of engaging history or participating in memorialization, one might be able to add to a previously accumulated "store of knowledge," reactivate what is already known, or mobilize historical referents for inclusion within one's specific set of identifications. However, any given history or memorialization may also be viewed as providing redundant, irrelevant, and insignificant information and, thus, deserving but cursory attention. Neither practice, however, supports the possibility of an anagnorisis,[3] a learning from "the past" that is a critical recognition or discovery that unsettles the very terms on which our understandings of ourselves and our world is based.

As we shall argue throughout this chapter, binding hope to the public memory of the Shoah requires forms of learning that unsettle the present, opening one to new ways of perceiving, thinking, and acting. More specifically, we elaborate a practice that attempts to secure not only some measure of understanding of past events, but also sustains an open and potentially radical relation between the texts of a historical archive and the readers who such texts address. To this end, we engage in the citation of testamentary records and present accompanying commentary written as both an argument for, and an act of, pedagogical witness; a bearing witness to our readers that can itself constitute an act of study. In making such study public, we do not offer our comments over and against discourses of historical and literary interpretation, but rather as an invitation to a quite different form of historical thought, a thinking together as to how to live in relation to the past.

We offer here, then, a justification and display of an alternative practice of remembrance. This is a practice of remembrance that is also a practice of learning—a practice aimed at reopening the certitude of our frames of reference for understanding (separately and relationally) the traces of the past and our contemporary relationships. We advance this approach to remembrance concretely, in regard to our attempts to face the traces of a specific historical geography—the Vilna Ghetto. Engaging the surviving testament of the ghetto—the texts, audiovisual testimony, images, and music that speak of and attempt to convey what happened there—we argue for a public staging, a pedagogical witness, of one's practices of reading, viewing, and listening that make evident how witnessing may become an event in which an other's time may disrupt my own.[4]

Why Vilna?

The Shoah cannot and should not be compressed into any one account, any one time, and place (Roskies, 1984). To some extent, we were drawn to the ghettos of Eastern Europe as a counter-response to the contemporary metonymic emphasis on Auschwitz as the reductive center of the Shoah. The ghettos were geographies far more porous than the concentration camps; where the leakage of life back and forth through the walls of forced incarceration served not only as a constant reminder of the specificity of the violence—who was doing what to whom—but also as a reminder that this violence took place within a more inclusive urban geography where many were aware of the existence of a ghetto and what was happening to its inhabitants (Ezrahi, 1996, 132). Of course, this does not account for the singular choice of the Vilna Ghetto. There certainly are historical arguments for underscoring Vilna's uniqueness as an important center of Jewish culture and learning.[5] Also, it may be argued that Vilna was the first major Jewish community to experience the genocidal devastation of "the Final Solution."

However, historiographic argument is not what brought us to Vilna. Our responsibilities begin quite differently. Searching broadly for testaments of everyday life in a ghetto, we came upon the diary of Yitskhok Rudashevski (1973). Rudashevski was fourteen years old when the German army entered Vilna on June 24, 1941. At the time, there were nearly 70,000 Jews living in the city. During July and August, approximately 30,000 Jews were murdered, most shot at the killing fields at Ponar by Germans and their Lithuanian accomplices. On September 6, 1941, Vilna Jewry was driven into a ghetto. Mass *aktions* against the Jews continued until late December 1941. By that time, another 20,000 Jewish people had been murdered. During the first months of 1942, a period of relative stability was established for the remaining ghetto population, most of whom worked in factories in support of the German war effort.[6]

The diary Rudashevski secretly kept records his experiences of ghetto life. What compelled us about the diary was not its personal poignancy—Rudashevski, in fact, writes little about himself—but rather the historical sensitivity and commitment Rudashevski shows in vividly attending to the life around him. It was this sensitivity and commitment that initially claimed our attention and concern. Rudashevski attempted to report what he saw, creating depictions that embodied the complex texture of the ghetto without relieving it of its unrelenting cruelty, depressiveness, and horror. But what impressed us most was his clear sense of the burdens of witness.

In the fall of 1942, Rudashevski writes of his participation in an organized effort to write the history of the ghetto:

> Thursday the 22nd [October 1942]
> I got a taste of a historian's task. I sit at the table and ask questions and record the greatest sufferings with cold objectivity. I write, I probe into details, and I do not realize at all that I am probing into wounds, and the one who answers me—indifferent to it: two sons and a husband taken away—the sons Monday, the husband Thursday. . . . And this horror, this tragedy is formulated by me in three words, coldly and dryly. I become absorbed in thought, and the words stare out of the paper crimson with blood. (73)

A few days later, in the midst of his "field work," Rudashevski was confronted with the moral ambiguity of such remembrance. He reflects on a hostile reception he received when attempting to interview a ghetto resident:

> Thursday the 5th [November 1942]
> Today we also went to Shavier 4 with the questionnaire for investigating the ghetto. We did not get a good reception. And I must sadly admit that they were right. We were reproached for having calm heads. "You must not probe into another person's wounds, our lives are self-evident." She is right, but I am not at fault either because I consider everything should be recorded and noted down, even the most gory, because *everything will be taken into account*. [emphasis ours] (84)

For us, reading Rudashevski's diary was not a voyeuristic access to private confession. The diary—understood as testimony—stands very much as "a telling," addressed to us (his readers), predicting a time to come when "everything will be taken into account." However, from our standpoint, this

prediction has lost its force as forecast. In the present, it becomes an illocutionary statement putting us under an impossible obligation, *that we are the
ones responsible for taking everything into account.* Hence, reading Rudashevski
was unsettling. What could this requirement, "to take everything into
account," mean for us? We began with more study. Needing to learn more
about life and death in Vilna under the occupation, we went in search of
other testimonial traces of daily existence in the ghetto.

Clearly, the surviving diaries, memoirs, war trial transcripts, documentary
ephemera, audiovisual testimony, memorial books, poems, and songs that
indexically reference the history of the Vilna Ghetto all have different
details to convey and stories to tell. However, our current, ongoing efforts
to engage these traces have not been circumscribed by the intent to reach
a plausible historiographic understanding of "how it was" that would
render a more accurate, complete history of ghetto life.[7] Nor do we seek
to corroborate Rudashevski's account with various alternative forms of
historical evidence; rather, as we will elaborate, we read Rudashevski's
prediction-cum-injunction as a demand, an insistence that one re-face the
problem of how to live on "after the event." That is, how could and should
I live on, while living with images and narratives of the Vilna Ghetto informed
and sustained through contemporary practices of public remembrance?

Facing anew the problem of how to live on after the ghetto meant
grappling with the difficulties of returning to the ghetto-in-ruins. Over
fifty years ago, Yiddish writer and poet Chaim Grade confronted this
problem on very concrete terms. In his memoirs he described his return to
Vilna after its liberation by the Soviet armed forces (Grade, 1986). Grade,
through a measure of intent, circumstance, and fate, managed to survive the
war years as a refugee in central Russia. His wife and mother, however,
became victims of the Nazi genocide. In his memoirs, he describes a
conversation amid Vilna's ruins with Anna Itkin, a pediatrician who had
worked with his wife in the children's ward of the ghetto hospital. Itkin
lived through the experience of the Ghetto while her husband and one of
her two sons was murdered. Now, after liberation, she is focusing her
memories on her life with her husband as it was before the Germans
entered Vilna. She says to Grade, "Now I even avoid walking through the
ghetto, but, I noticed, you wander about there for days on end." Of this
moment, Grade writes:

> It is true, I answer, that I spend whole days wandering around amid
> the ruins and there seek to comprehend that which she, Anna Itkin,
> terms the normal days, the normal moments, in the Ghetto. I know
> the exact dimensions of the Ghetto, which courtyards were part of it,
> and have even crawled down into some of the underground *malinas* in
> which Jews hid. I know as well the sequence of the massacres, the
> chronology of the slaughters. But what I do not understand is this:
> how did people live from one massacre to the next, singing songs,
> attending concerts, getting married, celebrating the Festivals? How

people perished in the Ghetto—that I understand; what I cannot understand is how they lived there . . . I don't want to understand! That is, I do want to understand, but I do not want to accept it . . . I don't want to accept what you call the normal times in the Ghetto, nor the return now to a so-called normal life. Before I again enter into harness, before I begin to live this accursed life, I must find a way to make my peace with what happened here. . . . (357)

Grade wants to understand but not accept, but he also wants to make peace. In his view, to confront this contradiction between nonacceptance and making peace with the past requires either forgetting or a form of retributive justice. Thus he writes:

. . . . to go on living, it can only be in one of two ways: either I forget everything, or I and every other survivor must kill at least one of the murderers. Perhaps then it might be possible both to remember and to go on living. To have settled accounts! But as long as all the murderers are still alive and neither I nor anyone like me has grabbed a hatchet and gone hunting for them, and since I certainly can't forget all that's happened, I shall roam day in and day out about the Vilna Ghetto, even if Fate carries me off to the farthest corner of the earth, even if not one stone of the Ghetto is left standing on another! I have not the slightest wish to leave it, here is my place!" (358)

Fifty years later, we too find ourselves returning to the Vilna Ghetto, spending whole days wandering through its testimonial fragments, its semiotic ruins. By refusing to circumvent this topography of remembrance, we not only resist forgetting but open ourselves to a memorial insistence that confounds and defies attempts to secure the memory of lives, places, and events within reported narratives and found images. We have come to understand that our task is not to make peace with what happened in Vilna. Neither vengeance, prosecution, nor compensation will settle accounts and provide permission to forget.[8] For us, to live on after the event is not to live in peace. It is to confront head-on the difficult matter of why the interminable remembrance of specific lived moments within space/times such as the Vilna Ghetto are necessary.

Hope as a Condition of the Present

In spite of our aspirations that public remembrance support practices of justice, compassion, and tolerance, there is good reason to remain ambivalent with regard to the capacity of remembrance to serve the yearning for a better, less violent world. The pervasiveness of public remembrance in a century as violent and destructive as our own, would seem to give us little cause for hope. Remembrance does not ensure anything, least of all justice and compassion. Yet, our moral and pedagogical commitments demand that we remain hopeful, demand that we see the present as incomplete, and, thus, open to the challenge of what is not yet present. On what grounds might this difficult linkage between hope and remembrance be brought about?

First of all, we hold to the important—if indeterminate—place of historical consciousness within human communities. By historical consciousness, we refer not to "a state of mind" (e.g., what historical knowledge one holds), but to a social praxis—a very determinate set of commitments to and actions that define practices of remembrance among members of a particular community. This praxeological historical consciousness is situated in that series of interlinked performances through which members of a community "pass-on" and revisit something of the substance and significance of past events. In this view, the locus of "knowing" is social rather than solitary. "To know about a past event" is not something fulfilled by the recall and understanding of what one sees, reads, or hears. Rather, knowing requires a communicative act that re-cites and re-sites what one has learned—not only about what happened to others at/in a different space/time but also (and this is key) what one has learned of and within the disturbances and disruptions inherent in comprehending the substance and significance of these events. This is the communicative act we have called "pedagogical witnessing." As a practice, such witnessing always has a moral force, but what we wish to emphasize here is its educational structure. On these terms, to witness means not only to learn, but also to teach, precisely to teach how one learns (Handelman, 1996). In our view, a hopeful historical consciousness is enacted through this specific performance of witnessing. It is for this reason, then, that much of our current thinking is addressed to exploring how such witnessing may sustain the connection between remembrance and hope.

At first glance, hope would seem necessarily directed toward the future, more a wish for a desirable "not yet" still to come rather than a form of thinking that might help us address the problems of thinking and acting in the present. Yet, if hope remains conceived of on these terms, it may rightly be criticized as bankrupt in its unending delay in ever thinking the present and its concerns. Thus, as Andrew Benjamin suggests: "Rather than allowing the present to remain unthought . . . [we might ask] what happens to hope once it is stripped of its utopian garb by locating it in the present? In what sense may hope become a way of naming the present's inherent incompleteness. . . . functioning as a structural force . . . holding the present open and thus as being unfinished" (1997, 10)? If remembrance is to participate in "holding the present open," it will have to take on a form of memoration other than one that serves to preserve a continuity among the present, past, and future.[9] In a quite different move, we see hope sustained by a rending, a tearing of continuity in the recognition that existing traditions are unable to provide the terms for a hopeful remembrance. This rending, however, is not meant to shock one to attention, setting in motion a trauma that arrests thought. On the contrary, hope is only present when learning is affirmed as a radical necessity, when tradition is recognized as that which must be rethought, and when remembrance embodies this rethinking as a praxis. Thus, hope and remembrance are linked when remembrance exists as the reworking of memory and in the reworking of memory (Benjamin, 71). It is in this spirit that we find ourselves seeking new practices of public historical memory; practices of historiography in a very different key.

The necessity of such a remembrance requires returning to testament as a locus of teaching. In this moment of return, we recognize Rudashevski's testimony as an utterance that bestows on its readers a most difficult inheritance. More precisely, we read (or better, hear) Rudashevski as addressing us with a behest, one that both accuses and enjoins us to acknowledge a debt the present owes to the past. We can do no less than acknowledge this debt as the requirement of hope; hope neither as rational optimism nor eschatological promise of a new beginning, but as an openness to the past in which something new might still be learned, hence ensuring the very possibility of a future. That this debt is a difficult inheritance there is no doubt, for it obligates us to a vigilant, wakeful, incalculable attending to a testament hard to bear and impossible to cancel. Understood pragmatically, as a sign that binds remembrance and learning, testimony enjoins us in the perpetual work of settling this debt and learning hope. Payments, however, cannot be made cheaply, but only in the form of a particular attentiveness. Settling this difficult claim made upon the present requires consideration of the present not as a site or spatial location, but as modality—a particular structure of attending.

A hopeful present requires a continual reopening of the past, for only such an opening persists as a teaching. Reopening the past enables a reopening of the present as something yet to be completed. To take up one's responsibility to "learn hope" requires practices of remembrance, of reading, seeing, and listening, of facing testament that open onto a past that exceeds its idea in the present (in me). This is a crucial pedagogical point. It is only within such practices that the past can *still* teach, can persistently and insistently teach. The past, then, in its relation as "teacher," comes to me, comes to the present, from outside—for only that which "I am not" (which I think not, which I am not already capable of speaking of) can teach me. The separateness and alterity of the past, this distance across "that which was never my fault or deed . . . [that which] has never been my presence, has never come into memory," is what *faces* me (Levinas, 1987). In this tensive demand of facing, there is a momentary shattering of the hermeneutic horizon on which past and present meet and within which historical interpretation becomes possible. This shattering interrupts the givenness of the present, opening the possibility of learning not just *about*, but *from* the past. In the past, thus, there inheres the possibility of an unforeseeability, a *futurity* without predetermined direction. The past approached on such terms opens the present not merely to gaps in its knowledge, but to a radical reframing of historical remembrance where it accomplishes more than awareness, comprehension, and/or anamnesis.

Taking Details into Account

So we begin, charged with a remarkable debt inherited within our intent to witness the testament of the Vilna Ghetto. As witnesses, we stand in a transitive relation with the traces of those who continue to speak through the material existence of testamentary documents. Thus, at minimum, to bear witness to the traces of Vilna, we must in some medium—whether print, electronic, or performance—cite and point to specific texts or documents. In citing testamentary texts (be they diaries, memoirs, video interviews, poems, art, or song), we stage a necessary indexicality. Testamentary documents are signs that, first and foremost, are determined historically by the events that produced them (Brinkley and Youra, 1996, 121–122). Thus, in citation, attention is called not only to the presence of testimony but also to testimony's gesture beyond itself to past events. In this sense, the citation of testimony does—importantly—"bring news," returning to attention that which has been missed, or misplaced.

The citation of testimonial detail is not a simple privileging of the authority of the "eye-witness." It does not presume that such testimony can bring one closer to the truth. Rather, we emphasize here that citation is an act in which what is given, is given again. Memoration or quotation is not simply repetition, but an iterative reworking in the site of the present (Benjamin, 50), a reworking that in its very work may unsettle the invested frameworks that help one grasp and negotiate present realities. The unsettlement citation may provoke lies in the substance and method by which citation provides details. It is our premise that through the confrontation with detail, one can begin to regard one's own facility for attending to testimony, for learning what it has to teach, and for helping formulate a responsible response not only to what is said but to its persistent moment of saying. Thus, for us, the importance of citation lies in the confluence of its indexical and delineative dimensions.

But on what terms may citational detail unsettle and provoke, binding remembrance, learning, and hope? Details in and of themselves would seem problematic in this regard. As a discursive device that in the depiction of an event, evokes a figurative singularity, details differentiate, marking the specifics of a moment and calling us to attend to these specifics. Details also render a physical, material texture to action, often signifying a transitivity, a doing rather than a statement that something was done. However, disaggregated and tightly framed by the terms of certain traditions, details may be narrowly understood to fill in a picture that is already recognized. They may be accepted as details, because we recognize them a priori as part of a picture; on these terms, they can be graphically shocking, vividly memorable, but they can neither surprise nor teach. On such reductive terms, details individuate narrative, inviting identification or introjection while becoming metonymic candidates for a broad range of experiences. Framed this way, details may be said to invite a continuity between our personal experience and those of the other to which we attend, blind to the limits of representation and, at times, offering a false sense of "knowing how it was."

Clearly, the practice of the citation of detail, while central to the responsibilities of pedagogical witnessing, is not straightforwardly hopeful. Although as witnesses to the testament of Vilna we must re-cite/re-site what we have read, heard, or seen, it is essential that this be done on terms that open the possibility of our own learning, of facing the past anew. Such a citational practice must resist the too easy assimilation of testamentary detail into either well-known historical emplotments or symbolic structures already invested with transferential attachments and collective identifications. Such a practice might begin with an indeterminate wandering of the semiotic ruins of Vilna; listening, reading, looking at what is before us, opening ourselves to the surprise, astonishment, and unsettlement that the juxtaposition of details can elicit.

Thus, it was in wandering Vilna's "ruins" that we found ourselves "addressed, challenged, and instructed" by the elective affinities we allowed ourselves to articulate (Gibbs, 2000). It was in such moments that images of the Vilna Ghetto became our concern, seizing us, disquieting our understanding, and loosening our emotional investments. They became dissonant images, which, in their memorial persistence, provided an insistence, a disruption of the ongoing time of the present, an interruption of "more of the same." In this disruption began the difficult learning of being instructed, not only about Vilna, but from within those moments in which we became assigned to its traces. In what follows, we present three such moments, three juxtapositions of citations that for us became recognized as significant instances of learning. These juxtapositions and their associated commentary are not offered as authoritative insights that attempt to secure historical meaning. Rather, they display a practice of witness-as-study—a practice of reopening the question of how to live in relation to the past. In each of these juxtapositions, there is a realization of a "concern" in which images of a distant time are "recognized by the present as being meant for it—not just in the sense of having meaning, but rather in the sense of being constitutive to/for its existence."[10] On such terms, this concern provoked our attempts to work through the unsettling effects of this memorial persistence, precisely binding remembrance and learning. Far from becoming a form of passive contemplation, this remembrance, this witness-as-study, promises a hopeful learning to the extent that it reopens the present, inaugurating the possibility of a new present (Wohlfarth, 1978, 158).

Juxtaposition One

To begin laying out what is at stake in the position outlined above, consider the first of the three juxtapositions enacted within this chapter. Two citations[11] are presented here. The first, from the video testimony of Samuel B., is a narration of a portion of Samuel's childhood experience during the forced relocation of Vilna's Jews to an enclosed ghetto. The second, from the video testimony of Mira B., is a narration of a particular technique she used for smuggling food into the ghetto. Both transcriptions are from the video testimony held in the Fortunoff Video Archives for Holocaust Testimony at Yale University.[12]

Video Testimony—Samuel B.

I remember very well on a very rainy day the police came . . . the German and Lithuanian police and they told us to take a suitcase something we could carry and to go down, . . . we had to leave the apartment I was alone with mother at home . . . there was also our Russian maid . . . and she was scared . . . my mother started in a very panicky way to take things and put them in a small suitcase and there was not enough place in that suitcase and she took another one . . . and then she took my hand and started to walk through door of the apartment and then suddenly she remembered something and ran back and took a pillow from the back so she took the suitcase, me and the pillow . . . in the courtyard of the apartment house there were many people standing, Jews—our neighbors . . . all quite amazed and not quite certain what was going to happen . . . it was raining and some were getting soaked and nobody really thought about opening an umbrella and when they had brought down all the Jewish occupants of that apartment house into the courtyard, we go out to the streets . . . there I saw sort of a caravan of people walking on the road . . . cause we were not permitted to walk on the sidewalk . . . and on the road near the sidewalk with the enormous rain . . . there was water . . . and everyone was walking in the water . . . and they were just walking . . . like a procession with everyone just carrying something, I had the pillow in my hand and it was becoming soaked and more and more heavy so that at a certain point I threw it away. . . . now with my mother . . . with this little suitcase . . . we arrived in a area that was once a very heavily populated poor part of the town . . . where mostly Jews lived . . . of the poor population . . . it was the old ghetto . . . from the middle ages actually . . . what happened there the day before, the police took out all the people living there and they brought them out to be exterminated . . . and all those apartments were empty . . .

Video Testimony—Mira B.

A month later I was fortunate enough that somebody lent me a pass *[authors' note: a pass to leave the ghetto for work during the day]* . . . she was sick and said take my pass for the day . . . maybe you can buy something . . . and this group went to a place . . . a Lithuanian garden school on outskirts of city . . . as we came in I began to speak Lithuanian and I went into the office and said well, I speak Lithuanian and I know German . . . and they said really you know both . . . how do you know both languages? . . . we need you . . . [I said] I don't have a pass . . . could you get for me a pass . . . Of course . . . they got a pass to work in their office . . . this saved our life for a while . . . because what we did, all those who went out of the ghetto learned quickly a certain trick . . . like a pillow case . . . we took a pillow case and took a machine and sewed straight lines . . . you got here channels [demonstrates this] . . . and farmers were there [at the school] they were glad to exchange a Russian pound . . . a unit . . . like 30/40 pounds . . . and we would put flour into those channels . . . and sowed flaps and made sure that we could put it on around our bodies . . . we all lost weight and our coats were big enough to accommodate our body plus the flour around it . . . we were carrying it two three kilometers and we were coming to the gates. . . . there were Jewish policemen who were supposed to ensure that nothing was smuggled in, they did not catch us to find if we had flour . . . only if there were German soldiers there, they would touch and try . . . and a friend of mine was taken, caught with some flour and was taken to Luskiski and was killed. Because she was caught with the flour . . . when I came in the evening with the flour, I went to the baker and I would give him the flour and would get in return a big loaf of bread which was slightly 2–3 lbs of bread.

In re-citing the testimony of Samuel B. and Mira B., staging them together in a juxtaposition, we are well aware that we are shifting the terms on which these texts are to be engaged. The juxtaposition of these two texts is not intended to supply an interpretation of their witness. Rather, it knots together these accounts in order to impart a moment of concatenation encountered as surprise and instruction, initiating thought that has no rest, that can neither be completed nor ended. We must speak then, if only briefly, of our own surprise, our own questions, our own instruction. The contiguity of detail here is what struck us as so surprising. Something as trivial as pillows are noticed, and they become not trivial at all. Rain soaked and too heavy to carry, young Samuel B. throws his away. Mira B. uses hers to save her family. And even though we perhaps force a similitude in knotting these testimonies together with pillows; no, they are not the same pillows. They never are, but that, in a way, is the point. We, the listeners, stand between the two stories. We join them together. They meet not in the synchrony of a single narrative, in one story, one history—but as stories of two lives, which, when remembered together, are not only made more vivid, but perhaps open us to something new. In what sense, then, is the staging of this juxtaposition, this remembrance-image, a moment of learning and perhaps hope?

There are, of course, differing levels of response to this question. On a basic demonstrative level, the juxtaposition of these two testimonies illustrates the indeterminacy and difficulty of planning for survival in the ghetto. How and what objects might have been useful for what purposes could not have been easily anticipated. At a narrative level, the juxtaposition functions as a device that helps individuate the histories of those subject to the genocidal intentions of the Nazis and their collaborators. The differences embodied by Mira and Samuel in relation to their pillows returns us to their very different bodies, forcing us to attend to the embodied character of their tellings. Sensing this embodiment, thinking this embodiment, reminds us again—as the collapse of singularity into the mass "the Jews of Vilna" cannot—that justice is never an abstraction but is to be condemned not because a law is broken, but because people have been hurt (Heschel, 1962, 195–220).

But neither of these observations addresses what is so astonishing to us about the appearance of pillows within these juxtaposed narratives, and what might be learned from this astonishment. Our astonishment begins in a "disjunctive continuity," bringing our attention to how similar objects become differently intertwined in lives lived within the same space/time. This astonishment elicits a rereading of the testimonial excerpts in which the details become more vivid in their singularity and historicity. This vividness heightens the specificity of that moment of address that summons us as witnesses to their accounts. The lives of the ghetto inhabitants are brought more in focus as lived within historical circumstances that are not simply "there," not simply "given," but the result of choices made by those committed to mass systemic violence and its attendant justifications. Furthermore, this astonishment returns us to an awareness of how the significance and use of the material of our lives are embedded in a forgetfulness, a taken-for-grantedness, regarding the created contingencies of our existence.

This learning was intensified when we came across yet another reference to pillows in the ghetto, albeit a strange and disturbing one. In Grade's memoirs, he tells the story that while wandering the ruins of the ghetto he met a woman who had survived by hiding in the sewers. He reports she told him that:

> Once she had gone out with a group to work outside the Ghetto and she had seen, among a group of Jews who were being taken to Ponary, an old man and an old woman. Each was carrying a pillow under one arm; they were holding hands like two children, and they were walking so quietly—never in her life had she seen such quietness. Her eyes had been dim with tears, but yet she had noticed that the pillowcases for the old couple's pillows were carefully ironed, fresh and white, as though they had just been put on. (374)

Grade asks "Why did the old people take along the pillows. . . . Didn't they know what Ponary was, or did they think they were being transferred to another ghetto?" The woman doesn't know, although she speculates that it is possible that they didn't realize where they were being taken, or perhaps they did—since she knows that, at such moments, very strange thoughts can enter one's mind. Grade offers that perhaps they had the notion that with the pillows they would lie more softly in their grave. What interests us most, however, is what Grade writes next:

> I start walking down Gitka-Toybe's Alley. . . . But ahead of me now walks the old couple, I do not see their faces—only their hunched shoulders and the pillows under their arms. They wander amidst the ruins, holding each other's hand. . . . (374) I sink back into my thoughts about the old couple: it may well be that they had children living somewhere overseas, who supported them in their old age. Fine children! And when they find out what happened here, they will say: "So many young lives were cut short, how can we complain? Our parents, after all, were already old." Something like this the children will say, and little by little they will forget the old man and old woman. But I, I shall not forget them—for the sake of their walking with their white pillows under their arms, I shall not forget them. (376)

It is the pillows under their arms that haunt Grade, that face him, that obligate him to remembrance. The details face, not names, not human figures. In a flash, the injustice of Ponar hits Grade, obsesses him. How to speak of it? What must be rescued from the past before it disappears irretrievably? Taught here is that what must be rescued are the details, but details now understood as the saying of one's life, the speaking, writing, and depicting of one's sensuous practice of living. The juxtaposition of the citations from Mira and Samuel enjoin us to this rescue, driving us back to hear their testimonies again. Thus, we are always learning how and why we must interminably ask: what more is there *to hear in* the testimonial excerpts re-cited/re-sited above and what more is there *to hear of* the tellings given but not yet "re-given."

Juxtaposition Two

As a second example of the memorial and pedagogical force of the juxtaposition of testimonial detail, consider the following six excerpts, two from ghetto diaries (Rolnikas, 1995; Kruk, 2002), three from video testimonies,[13] and a poem by Avraham Sutzkever written while he was in the ghetto (Sutzkever, 1991).[14]

Excerpt from Ghetto Diary of Macha Rolnikas

Toward evening, the clothes of the executed were brought back to the ghetto on carts.

The cart comes up the narrow pavement. The clothes move like human beings. A sleeve is dangling down. Yesterday morning, a man slipped his arm into it while dressing. Now this arm is already frozen. A small coat—how old was the child who wore it? A cap. It seems to be covering a cut off head. The cap slips . . . beneath a shoe appears. One feels like crying, screaming, biting, shouting: "It's yesterday only yesterday, that under these clothes hearts were beating warm bodies were breathing. Yesterday they still were human beings! Today they are no longer!! They were killed! Do you hear me: killed." The ghetto is plunged into a state of mourning.

Video Testimony: Paul K.

And You Never Saw Your Mother . . .?
Never saw my mother again since then. And our occupation was being in jail, when they took the people to Ponar, everyone has to disrobe before they shot them. And they used to bring all the clothing back to the jail. Now our job was to sort the clothing out. The good clothing like with jackets or shoes we used to put them on the side in different piles and soon they used to pack them and send them back to Germany. And the poor clothing, the old shoes and old things we used to bury right in the yard and we used to dig ditches and bury them.

What Was That like as a Job?
It wasn't a job, it was a heart, heart-broken. Plenty times when a father recognized the shoes of his little child or a father recognized this wife's dresses and it was heartbreaking story, but what could we do? We were under guard and that was our job. We stayed there for, like I said, for three, four weeks and then one morning they came with big trucks and they took us to another camp in Vilna, that was the last camp, it was called HKP.

A Wagon of Shoes

My every breath is a curse
Every moment I am more an orphan
I myself create my orphanhood
With fingers, I shudder to see them
Even in dark of night.
Once, through a cobblestone ghetto street
Clattered a wagon of shoes, still warm from recent feet,
A terrifying
Gift from the exterminators . . .
And among them, I recognized
My Mama's twisted shoe
With blood-stained lips on its gaping mouth.
—Mama, I run after them, Mama
Let me be a hostage to your love,
Let me fall on my knees and kiss
The dust on your holy throbbing shoe

And put it on, a *tfillin* on my head,
When I call out your name!
But then all shoes, woven in my tears, Looked the same as Mama's
My stretched-out arm dropped back
As when you want to catch a dream.
Ever since that hour, my mind is a twisted shoe.
And as once upon a time to God, I wail to it
My sick prayer and wait
For new torments.
This poem too is but a howl,
A fever ripped out of its alien body.
No one to listen.
I am alone.
Alone with my thirty years.
In their pit they rot—
Those who once were called
Papa.
Mama.
Child.
Vilna Ghetto, July 30, 1943—A. Sutzkever.

Excerpt From the Ghetto Diary of Herman Kruk

April 6, 1943

9 Wagons

The Labour Office in the ghetto soon received an order to send 9 wagons with 15 men to Ponar. Purpose: to bring Jewish objects from the cars?! . . .

This sounds strange. But the order is immediately carried out

. . .

Loot

. . . 9 wagons with the 15 workers were driven into the ghetto. 8 of the wagons were full of foodstuffs: potatoes, flour, bread, etc. 1 wagon was packed with clothing. Everything was turned over to the Winter Aid.

. . .

April 7 [1943]
"Loot"

All we have written so far about loot was the beginning of a big "gift" the Gestapo is preparing for us.

All day today, they brought masses of things and bundles, just as they were packed by their owners. They bring food, furniture, cutlery, and everything that was in the wagons. The inhabitants who watch all that are cursing that the ghetto takes it . . . Jews stand and shake their head, looking at the furniture:

"This is how they prepared for a life," says a Jew watching them take a washtub off a truck . . . "Meaning," he says, "That they will arrange a life here" . . . Some women cry and cannot watch. Others think it is disgusting to look at it, that all this is a profanation. Nevertheless, scoundrels who immediately try to share in the inheritance aren't lacking either. People snatch, take advantage of opportunities and steal—Sodom! . . .

. . .

April 8 [1943]

The Ghetto has lost its Bearings

All who still live and walk a round the streets of the Vilna Ghetto are truly lost and helpless, everyone is waiting for the end—for liquidation. Most workers don't go to work. Those who do, don't really work. Nothing is in your head—Anyway, it is all coming to an end! . . . This is the mood and this is how most Vilna Ghetto residents think. Naturally, this panic is the greatest reservoir of rumors and Jewish gossip.

Things, Things, Things

Meanwhile, the things of those killed are brought here. The ghetto warehouses are crammed with things. "Tatters" for many millions flow in here.

. . .

April 10 [1942]

About the Property of the Slain

Here, he [Kruk is reporting on Ghetto Chief Gen's speech about the recent slaughter] considers morale and reaches the conviction that the property must not be taken. Nevertheless, in the name of the ghetto, he argues that the ghetto inhabitants are naked and hungry, and here food and clothing are given. How to justify the refusal? Why provoke?

Then Mr. Gens comes to another conclusion: Rather than let strangers enjoy it, better it remains among Jews. . . . So, he decided to take the things.

What will happen next? He cannot guarantee that there will be no more *Aktsias* in the ghetto. There could be an *Akstia* of the non-productive element; qualitatively, the ghetto has deteriorated. The most important thing—to raise our productive capacity. Everyone who can work must work! Mr. Dresler and Mr. Broyde also spoke along these lines.

Altogether, the council didn't produce anything new. Everyone present was silent. What you think, you can't say. No one wants to justify the deal. We listened and went home depressed, because what has happened is still far from the end.

So we are once again in line.

Video Testimony: Zena G.

. . . before then I had a job . . . at Rossa. . . . Jewish people in Gestapo camp. . . . had a job for her I said ok I went there . . . I went to wash laundry. . . . I didn't know how . . . but you learn. . . . I was washing the laundry . . . came a whole bunch of clothes from Ponar . . . clothes were from children . . . deep with blood. . . . we were standing there washing and washing . . . like crazy . . . washing and crying. . . .

Video Testimony: Beba L.

After a while I was shifted to the Lithuanian unit, the Lithuanian unit was the execution unit, it was called the Ypatingi or Einsatzcommando. . . . the special unit . . . I was assigned to them . . . this were a group of about I don't know . . . 20 or 30 barbarians that the Germans commanded and they kept them drunk all the time . . . they had dormitories . . . in the dormitories you could see only big bottles of vodka and guns and bullets that's all . . . their faces were always flushed and always drunk . . . in the morning they were drunk and at night they worked, they killed Jews . . . [Interviewer: what did you do over there?] I cleaned . . . I . . . I don't know what I did . . . I cleaned their rooms and then there were rooms of the German officers. . . . and I was assigned 16 rooms I had to dust . . . and they would tell me to look at a paper . . . and they would ask me if I know German . . . I didn't know German . . . who knows German? I used to have to fire the furnaces . . . it was cold and I used to be responsible for putting wood in these furnaces . . . the most terrible thing is when they went killing Jews and they would bring back the clothing . . . and people who have to sort it. . . . I didn't have to sort it . . . but some of the people there would recognize the clothes of the people . . . it was a terrible thing . . .

These testimonial fragments obviously speak of returned clothes, piles of objects—remains that themselves testified to the murder of those to whom they once belonged. Reading these fragments, we were astonished by these citations in their disjunctive contiguity with the display of shoes, suitcases, eyeglasses, and hair presented in contemporary memorials and museums; object remains that have become central symbols of the human loss suffered in the Shoah. This association jolted us into an abrupt awareness of the space/time difference with regard to the return of objects as witnessed by the Jews of the Vilna Ghetto and the return of objects we have observed in museum display. In sharp contrast to ghetto witnesses, the objects for us are not fraught with, do not bear the burden of, an immediacy and urgency. We do not recognize them as those we saw yesterday. We are not required to sort them, nor to decide the appropriateness of their use in the service of our own survival. How, then, is remembering this difference implicated in how we listen and learn from Vilna testimony, as well as how we see and learn from museological/memorial presentations?

Visitors often report that standing in front of the "object survivors" in a museum display is an experience of profound absence. This response is assumed to result not only from the indexical relationship that these objects have with a historical "reality" but, as well, from our "negotiation" with these objects. As Alison Landsberg writes, "For at the same moment that we experience the shoes as their shoes—which could very well be our shoes—we feel our own shoes on our feet. . . . in the museum . . . we have an eerie lack of bodies and a pronounced sense of our own bodies" (1997, 81). Landsberg assumes that the memorial and pedagogical power of such objects results from a form of "de-realization" that produces a momentary split in the ego; those shoes are/are not our own. Such forms of de-realization vary, of course, with the differing forms of identificatory structures mobilized in the engagement with the experiences of others. But, in the face of the testament of Vilna, perhaps we might at least caution ourselves about indulgent transferences, about a complacent understanding, and, consequently, turn to a required vigilance with regard to what it might mean to bear witness.

The vigilance at stake here is the recognition of the hypothetical quality of our connection with the returned objects, in contrast with the responses of the various witnesses cited above. Imagining that such objects signify a murdered relative, or friend, or even ourselves, becomes foregrounded as self-serving, voyeuristic, and idle in our awareness that, for ghetto witnesses, these same thoughts are grounded in a horrible reality that we cannot possibly know. This renders the object-remains as incontestably artifactual. Rather than locating remembrance in an experience of a traumatic and mournful engagement with individual lives, we ask instead, what practice of witness would speak of what is being learned, but attendant to one's irremediable distance from the suffering of the past.

This is a practice that, in attempting to hear the details of testimony, returns me to the "details" of my life, implicating my experience in attending to the experience of the other. What implicates me in bearing witness to the testament of the Vilna Ghetto are not others' experiences, but rather, my inexperience in hearing the testimony that addresses me. Encountered is not a dramatic abundance of experience, or even the choking excess of a traumatic episode, but the very withdrawal of experience—the experience of my inexperience to hear and learn. In this moment, the enclosure that constitutes the presence of my present is pierced from the outside from a distance by those who, despite not being an interest of mine (i.e., who do not provide me with any useful information about my life, who do not serve my interests), remain my concern. In this light, the past is "relevant" despite its "irrelevance" to the present. By emphasizing the distance that separates me from these testaments—not the events themselves, but the very tellings—I find myself addressed and instructed. It is not what I share with the past that concerns me, but the very lack of commonality. It is always the very distance that implicates me, that concerns me in my "living on" after the event, after the telling. Thus, I must attempt to account for my learning as something that already incorporates my distance.

This means standing again in front of the object-remains in light of the juxtapositions staged above. What are these objects? Why are they here in front of me? What now is opened for me? How is my present different in the face of these contrasting practices of remembrance? Confronted again by these questions, I begin to answer differently. These objects are more than *memento-mori*, more than just surrogates for murdered bodies. They are the objects Jews had to literally deal with. They are traces of the acts of having to sort them, traces of decisions as to whether to use them or not. Thus, in making evident my own very different position vis-a-vis how I am obligated "to deal" with these objects, I am thrown back into my present on different terms, with regard not just to these objects (here in this museum in front of me now), but to the historically contingent character of my engagement with the details that make up the substance of my everyday life.

Juxtaposition Three

The third example enacted here comprises another set of six juxtaposed citations, including two from Rudashevski's diary, another ghetto poem by Sutzkever (1981)[15] a ghetto rhyme reported by Grade in his memoirs, an extract from the documentary *Partisans of Vilna* (Waletzky, 1986)[16] of interviews with Abba Kovner and Baruch Goldstein (both members of the armed resistance inside the ghetto), and a repositioning of Mira B.'s previously cited video testimony.

Video Testimony: Mira B.

All those who went out of the ghetto learned quickly a certain trick . . . like a pillow case . . . we took a pillow case and took a machine and sewed straight lines . . . you got here channels . . . And farmers were there . . . they were glad to exchange a Russian pound . . . a unit . . . like 30/40 pounds . . . and we would put flour into those channels . . . and sewed flaps and made sure that we could put it on around our bodies . . . we all lost weight and our coats were big enough to accommodate our body plus the flour around it . . . we were carrying it two three kilometres and we were coming to the gates . . . there were Jewish policemen who were supposed to ensure that nothing was smuggled in, they did not catch us to find the flour . . . only if there were German soldiers there, they would touch and try . . . and a friend of mine was caught with the flour . . . when I came in the evening with the flour, I went to the baker and I would give him the flour and would get in return a big loaf of bread which was slightly 2–3 lbs of bread. (Mira B.)

Written in the Vilna Ghetto

Flower

Because he wanted to smuggle a flower through the ghetto's gate

my neighbour paid the price of seven lashes. How precious it is to him now—this blue vernal flower and its golden pupil!

My neighbour bears the mementos with no regrets:

spring breathes through and colours his tortured flesh—that's how much he wanted it to flourish.

Vilna Ghetto—May 29, 1943

A. Sutzkever

Interwoven Excerpts from Interviews with Abba Kovner and Baruch Goldstein from the film "Partisans of Vilna"

K: Baruch Goldstein went out to work, as usual, and we remain inside. That evening we heard that there'd be a stricter search at the gate. And Baruch's work-group is about to be searched. We don't see Baruch. And now we see him, limping.

G: I was limping a little. This was a signal that I was carrying something.

K: Our people are approaching the gate. Suddenly the entire column stops. They say, `Hands up!' They search.

G: There were only two more ahead of me before they'd search me. They would undress you almost down to the skin. They only had to open my coat and there was the machine gun.

K: We tried to signal to him to go further back in the line.

G: Suddenly an officer comes over to me and tells me that I should go further back because I wouldn't be able to get through. I said, "How can I go back?" (He was one of the Jewish police). Then I saw the Jewish Police change positions. (We had our own people in the Jewish police.) They were already on guard at the gate to help me get through. But what could they do? I thought, What will be, will be.

K: We see Baruch is pale. He sees what's happening at the gate.

G: I knew I'd never survive the war. I was one hundred percent sure. But I had decided that I wasn't going to be taken to Ponar. They'd shoot me on the spot.

K: There's no retreating. He approaches.

G: Suddenly, Yashke Raff, my friend who didn't survive—on his own initiative—he comes dancing out of the Ghetto. The Germans saw him dance out of the Ghetto and got suspicious. They went for him. As soon as they went after him, I stepped into the Ghetto.

Excerpt from the Diary of Yitskhok Rudashevski

"Monday the 2nd of November (1942)

Today we had a very interesting group meeting with the poet A. Sutzkever. He talked to us about poetry, about art in general and about subdivisions in poetry. In our group two important and interesting things were decided. We create the following sections in our literary group: Yiddish poetry, and what is most important, a section that is to engage in collecting ghetto folklore. This section interested and attracted me very much. We have already discussed certain details. In the ghetto dozens of sayings, ghetto curses and ghetto blessings are created before our eyes; terms like 'vashenen,' 'smuggling into the ghetto,' even songs, jokes, and stories which already sound like legends. I feel that I shall participate zealously in this little circle, because the ghetto folklore which is scattered over the little streets, must be collected and cherished as a treasure for the future." (Rudashevski's Diary—pp. 90–91)

Spiderwebs—Excerpt from the Memoirs of Chaim Grade

The stall-keeper falls silent, and her eyes rest once again on the sewer-grating: she marvels endlessly at the miracle of her survival down there. Then she turns to me and begins to tremble, like the net of spiderwebs over my mother's doorway.

"In the ghetto," she says, "people used to sing this rhyme: 'The homes are empty and bare/But in the pits—all are there.' " And she walks slowly away down Jewish Street, until she disappears behind the piles of rubble. (Grade, 1984, 373–374)

Excerpt from the Diary of Yitskhok Rudashevski

"Wednesday the 10th of December (1942)

It dawned on me today is my birthday. Today I became 15 years old. You hardly realize how time flies. It, the time, runs ahead unnoticed and presently we realize, as I did today, for example, and discover that days and months go by, that the ghetto is not a painful, squirming moment of a dream which constantly disappears, but is a large swamp in which we lose our days and weeks. Today I became deeply absorbed in the thought. I decided not to trifle my time away in the ghetto on nothing and I feel somehow happy that I can study, read, develop myself, and see that time does not stand still as long as I progress normally with it. . . . I do not feel the slightest despair. Today I became 15 years of age and I live confident in the future. I am not conflicted about it, and see before me sun and sun and sun . . ." (Rudashevski's Diary—pp. 103–104)

Some of the details cited above were striking and unexpected given our various levels of familiarity with the history of the ghetto. Thus, there was the experience of surprise in reading that the ghetto was porous enough for arms to be smuggled in or that smuggling a flower would be something worth the risk of being caught. But to pose this montage of citations, this remembrance-image, as a site wherein a hopeful learning takes place, we need to attend not just to individuated details but to their juxtaposition. While each detail seems to offer a glimpse into how residents experienced the ghetto, in their juxtaposition, they begin to unsettle any certainties regarding that impression.

In Mira B.'s account, we read (again) of the preoccupation with obtaining sufficient amounts of food and of how dependent that effort was on successfully smuggling supplies into the ghetto. We are faced with testimony that bespeaks the care, intricacy, and time devoted to basic instrumental activities. Then, in Sutzkever's poem, we hear of a concern for a flower. Resisting the temptation to assimilate both accounts to the trans-historical theme of the necessity of "bread and roses," we found ourselves asking a troubling, perhaps obscene question. There, in the ghetto, where people were dying of starvation, what could impel the displacement of efforts to obtain food for efforts to obtain a flower? And in the very moment of asking, feeling the shame of a question that might revictimize those already subjected to more than is speakable, we learn that we must attend not only to possible answers to our questions but, more importantly, to the impetus for and crafting of their wording. Why write this query as a question of "displacement?" What judgments lie behind the unreflective use of this term?

We also learn from Kovner and Goldstein about those who smuggled hidden arms into the ghetto in anticipation of a time to come when Jews might have a different measure of control over their fate. But while we can read this conversation as a testament expressive of the audacity and bravery of ghetto partisans, in juxtaposition with other citations above, we also cannot easily let go of a reading in which we hear a self-conscious priority placed on the symbolic character of any possible armed struggle, a priority that for some superceded the immediate concerns of daily survival of one's family and community. Is this another judgment on our part? Another accusation of "displacement?" These are not necessary readings nor honorable ones. Thus, as we learn about how ghetto residents spent their time, from our time in the present, we find it necessary to wonder and worry about our own impulses to pass judgment, recognizing that doing so is neither our task nor our place. The issue here is not one of guilty readings. Rather, it is learning how to read within our unbridgeable distance from the past. And so, as we go about collecting and re-citing fragments of Vilna's testament, we notice too that Rudashevski writes of his fascination with collecting. In citing this detail, asserting and re-inaugurating its memorial importance, we also wonder about the source of our fascination with Rudashevski's familiar curiosity. From our hindsight, with some measure of extent of the Shoah and of the obligation to face up to its horror, we find ourselves immersed in a frame that too easily leaves us unsettled by what Grade refers to as the so-called "normal times in the Ghetto"—times that in moments of self-absorption we might term as escapist or perhaps even delusional. Thus, in the above citations, we not only learn about how ghetto residents convey their manifold experiences, we are also able to learn from our practice of juxtaposition of how the pastness of the past accuses us, challenging the authoritative position on which we read history (Clamen, forthcoming, 2005). But there is much more at stake here.

There is a disconcerting tension structured into Rudashevski's diary entry of December 10, 1942, re-cited above in two separate excerpts. At one moment, he writes:

Time runs ahead unnoticed and presently we realize, as I did today, for example, and discover that the days and months go by, that the ghetto is not a painful, squirming moment of a dream which constantly disappears, but is a large swamp in which we lose our days and weeks.

However, he immediately adds:

Today . . . I decided not to trifle my time away in the ghetto on nothing and I feel somehow happy that I can study, read, develop myself, and see that time does not stand still as long as I progress normally with it . . . I do not feel the slightest despair.

Astonishingly, Rudashevski hints at a problem with enormous implications for how we attend to the testimony of the ghetto. He seems to suggest that if ghetto residents maintain a form of productive human activity (whether in study, collecting ghetto folklore, smuggling arms, food, or flowers), time will not stand still. On the other hand, if one is mired in the passivity of despair, the conditions of existence become a swamp in which we lose our days and weeks.

But then what do we know of how and with what determinations ghetto residents experienced time? Without pursuing this question, we perhaps too easily take testamentary expressions of resistance at face value, valuing them for what they confirm of what we—perhaps unconsciously— need to understand. Despite his confident entry of December 10, we learn from the editor of his diary that Rudashevski himself will soon fall prey to despair, not because he forsakes productive activity, but plausibly because events surrounding the future of the Jews of Vilna will grow increasingly bleak in the coming months. Similarly, the previously cited diary of

Herman Kruk oscillates along these lines, foreclosing any reduction of his testament to expressions of pure optimism. So, we learn here that we must attend to each saying of testimony as rooted in ghetto time, a chronos wildly out of control, and veering from one moment to the next in different directions.

However, there is more at stake in this particular remembrance-image, for if the ghetto resident's witness is always given with respect to a position in time, how then does our own position "in time" implicate our listening to ghetto testimony? We know that there is a constant danger that the remembrance of the Shoah can become "a swamp in which we lose our days and weeks." This, perhaps, is one reason why so many people are cautious of any intense engagement with the details of what happened during the Holocaust, denying or choosing to ignore particularly painful and threatening experiences that beckon identification.

So, what is it that is determining our own sense of time—a time that is always already implicated in how it is we hear and learn from testimony? And how does our own commitment to the obligations and possibilities of witnessing testimony affect this sense of time? How does the time of writing this chapter, an act incorporating a practice of pedagogical witness, affect what we have read, seen, and heard of Vilna's testament? Does one listen differently if obliged to more than just personal reception, if obliged to find a way to teach, to teach how and what we learn not only about Vilna but from attending to its testimony? The implications of these questions run deep, opening the issue of a dialectical relationship between knowing and the social activity of sustaining a historical consciousness, an activity that neither closes nor promises closure. Indeed, perhaps these questions are unaddressable except in the form of a conversation that upholds the ongoing renewal of historical consciousness, a conversation sustained by relations of learning and teaching, by witness as a form of collective study.

Study and Witness

Witness-as-study as a form of collective learning might be best be grasped through, what is here, a necessarily brief consideration of the Jewish tradition of *midrash*. On traditional terms, midrash is a set of commentaries constituted within a particular practice of biblical interpretation developed by the Rabbis in Palestine during the first centuries of the common era. While much has been made of the affinities between midrash and contemporary literary theory, our particular interest is in midrash as a form of study.[17] David Stern maintains that the object of midrash is not so much to find the meaning of scripture as it is literally to engage its text and, in so doing, prolong a conversation—a conversation that in itself is an enactment of the covenantal relationship between God and Israel (1996, 31). In other words, midrash does not simply enact a private reading practice; most importantly, it stages a discourse, a particular form of collective study. On such terms, as Judah Goldin asserts, "Midrash is not just a device. It is a pedagogy" (1988, 280). In the interminable rereading of scripture, this pedagogy not only refuses to "close the book," but attempts to offer the hope inherent in a vigilant, wakeful, incalculable attending not just from my time but into my time.

The key point here is that midrashic study is able to make this offer because it recognizes its concern as *holy*. For Levinas, the "holy" is quite emphatically not that which is sacred. In a remarkable Talmudic reading, Levinas links the sacred with sorcery, finding perversion in a "world in which appearance falsifies that which appears [*l'apparence altère l'apparaître*]" (1990b, 153). In other words, the sacred enacts a displacement of one's relation to that which appears, by taking its appearance as its essence, limiting this relation to the world of images. Holiness (*sainteté*) in opposition to the sacred (*sacré*), puts forward the possibility of a desacralization of the world. This desacralization, for Levinas, is "a hope of holiness in the face of a sacred that cannot be purified . . . an irreducible modality of being present to the world" (153). This modality connects Levinas's thought to notions of midrash and pedagogical witness by gesturing toward a particular form of attentiveness that binds not only the human with the divine but also human beings with each other in an indeterminate relationship. This relationship elicits an obligation in which the appearance of the other is illimitable, irreducible to presence alone.

Within any consideration of the remembrance of the Shoah, the risks of deploying such explicitly theological language are considerable. The Shoah should not be made into a second Sinai. The testament of Vilna must not be approached and read as sacred text. Yet, in order for remembrance, learning, and hope to be bound, new desacralized forms of study are needed. As we offer each other our efforts to meet the interminable obligations the present owes the past, it is no small matter to support a collective study of testimony that attempts to grasp the many facets of its "face," not by attempting to secure its essence, but by guarding the face of the other in a practice of non-reductive remembrance. This is the heart of the matter, the moment when witness begins to enact a historical consciousness with radical possibilities. This would be a consciousness that, in the words of Levinas, "is the urgency of a destination leading to the other and not an eternal return to self. . . . [It is] an innocence without naivete, an uprightness without stupidity, an absolute uprightness which is also an absolute self-criticism, read in the eyes of the one who is the goal of my uprightness and whose look calls me into question" (1994, 48). Such a consciousness is built with practices of remembrance that unsettle enough to enable a reworking of one's relationship to the world and others, seeing the possibilities inherent in an incomplete present, and deepening one's commitments to justice now and in the world to come. This may indeed be a productive path toward new forms of Holocaust remembrance. Within this path, the lessons of the Shoah will not reside exclusively in the historical and sociological understanding of what was done by others, nor in the moral messages that encourage us to the civic courage needed to stand against injustice. These lessons will also reside in a practice of creative historical study that becomes a way of thinking the present, our present; a creative study that opens to a learning that cannot—without trivialization—be specified in advance.

CHAPTER SEVEN

Remembrance as Praxis and the Ethics of the Interhuman

WITH MARIO DI PAOLANTONIO AND
MARK CLAMEN

Atlas was permitted the opinion that he was at liberty, if he wished, to drop the Earth and creep away; but this opinion was all that he was permitted.

Franz Kafka, "The Fourth Notebook," 1991:41.

To be an I means then not to be able to escape responsibility, as though the whole edifice of creation rested on my shoulders.

Emmanuel Levinas, "Meaning and Sense," 1996:55.

For several months, we have been meeting biweekly. Eight men and women of varied ages and with diverse ethnocultural histories who share an interest in the position of testimony in the formation of historical memory. Each has read substantially regarding the history of the German occupation of Vilna (1941–3) during which most of the Jewish population of the city was incarcerated in a ghetto and systematically murdered. Independently, we have studied a myriad of documents that pertain to these events including diaries, poems, songs, video testimony, drawings, and photographs. For each meeting, one of us develops an array of testimonial material, documents, which through their very juxtaposition with one another, raise important questions integral to our attempts to think through and enact both an ethical remembrance and a practice of critical learning. This juxtaposition, along with a written commentary, is then electronically sent to all others and becomes the basis for further written responses that are distributed, read, and considered when we meet.

Irena has sent a juxtaposition composed of multiple images and text that document the decision by the Nazi command to have a brigade of Jewish slave labor dig up and cremate the bodies of over 60,000 Jews murdered since the German invasion and buried in the killing fields of Ponar, a wooded area on the outskirts of Vilna. This juxtaposition includes photographs of brigade workers digging up bodies, drawings of the scene of cremation by F. Segal (a survivor of the brigade), and the Nuremberg testimony of Solomon Gol (also a survivor) who provides a narrative describing the experience of being a member of the brigade.

Irena writes in her commentary on this juxtaposition: "I suppose that what I'm trying to think through in my engagement with the testimonies of Vilna—and the question of how photographic images might be used to inform this engagement—is how can I find ways of activating testimonial images such that they become more than either merely information, or disengaged voyeurism." This is a decisive, symptomatic question, carrying much of what is at issue in the proposal for an ethical practice and pedagogy of remembrance that is presented in this chapter. With regard to her juxtaposition, Irena wants to keep the photographic and graphic images cited from constituting either a site of spectacle or flattening into an evidentiary extension of Solomon Gol's narrative account. But, more generally, implied in her question is the challenge of considering on what terms a consciousness of history might become a responsible historical consciousness. Irena is asking not just what we might learn about the past, but also what can be learned from our attempts to face the traces of lives lived in times and places other than our own. Ultimately, at stake in such a practice is the question of one's attentiveness to the stories and images addressed to us that arrive from another space/time—stories and images that insist that remembrance be accountable to the demand for non-indifference.

One consequence of the recent "turn to ethics" in social and political thought has been a return to the question of what it could mean to live historically, to live within an upright attentiveness to traces of those who have inhabited times and places other than one's own. Substantively, this is manifest in the problem of how one attends to the experiences of others: how one reads, how one views, and how one listens. These are not simply pre-given capacities but are historically specific normalized practices, which, in any given epoch, are ingrained in what it means to live in consort with others, to live as though the lives of other people mattered.

As neoliberal logic increasingly fosters a narrow conception of what constitutes responsibility, a central question for cultural study in our times has become the ethical, pedagogical, and political implications of various practices of historical remembrance. While narrated memories are a sign of civic life, the motivated, authorized character of that *civitas* is very much an issue of how such memories might construct the substance and terms of one's connection to those who have gone before us. Public memory is not just that which contributes to knowledge of the past and/or underwrites a claim to group or communal membership. Quite divergently, public practices of memory can have a testamentary, transitive function; that is, they may be conceived as actions that "pass over" and take effect on another person or persons. On such terms, practices of remembrance are always caught up in the obligations expected by the transitive character of the testamentary act—the act of writing, speaking, imaging so as to bear an educative legacy to those who "come after."

It is how one conceives of this educative legacy and on what terms one is prepared to engage it that is the crux of the relationship between remembrance and civic life. The texts and images we are studying are commonly incorporated into two basic forms of remembrance, both of which, in quite different ways, attempt to address the problem of social adhesion. In the first of these forms, remembrance practices constitute collective rituals that attempt to build a social consensus by invoking iconic memories that mobilize affective structures of identification. In the second form, remembrance practices are more overtly hermeneutic in that they attempt to organize discursive structures within which basic moral collective commitments might be articulated, cultivating mutual understanding and social solidarity. Our attention to these texts and images, however, has been on quite different terms.[1]

Particularly concerned with their testamentary function, we argue that the demands initiated by this function open a cultural space within which a moment of "public time" might come into existence. While we shall elaborate on the notion of public time further on, we note here that in such a moment, relations are constituted wherein which "the ethical" becomes a question of how to read, view, and listen, "response-abilities" through which historical and cultural worlds become conceivable and concrete. In other words, the transitivity of testimony inaugurates a question of relationality—a question with the potential to re-situate human existence. Here, then, is a politics of hope[2]: an opening anew to the actuality of enacting or deciding the range of possibilities within which we live as purposeful human beings. What is at stake in the pregnancy of public time is a practical response to the question of how one might relate to the past, or, more precisely, how one might actualize a historical mode of being as a fundamental condition through which we inhabit the world as humans (Ziarek, 2000, 68–69). Remembrance, then, is a question of and for history as a force of inhabitation, as stories we live with, that intertwines with our sense of limits and possibilities, hopes and fears, identities and distinctions.

It is in this context that we are interested in new spaces of memoration, temporal and ontological boundary spaces that advance, encourage, and enable practices of ethical response and critical learning through which one might explore the fundamental terms of relation with an absent presence that—through testament—arrives asking, demanding something of us. This arrival initiates a potentially transformative supplement to conventional questions of power (questions of who gets to decide for whom, what privileges, opportunities, and resources will be made available and withheld within any given community). That is, the testamentary address, in posing the problem of inheritance, circumscribes a space/time for working through the politics and possibilities of the interhuman. As Krzysztof Ziarek puts it: "The shape into which the world is formed historically depends precisely on the modality, or modalities, of relating, *since these modalities never simply operate within the world but take part in the 'activity' of unfolding this world in the first place.* Differently put these modalities of relating are 'responsible' for how the world occurs" (2000, 77, emphasis ours).

How one responds in the face of the demand to read, view, and listen counts for something—indeed, counts for a great deal. Thus, our overriding question: what practices of response to the testamentary demand for non-indifference might enable an opening into learning? Learning, here, is understood not solely in terms of the acquisition of previously unheard of, unknown facts and stories, but also in terms of an opening of the present in which identities and identifications, the frames of certitude that ground our understandings of existence, and one's responsibilities to history are displaced and rethought. In other words, how might remembrance be understood as a praxis creating the possibilities of new histories and altered subjectivities (Frazier, 1999)? The consequence of such learning extends to reworking notions of community, identity, embodiment, and relationship. This is a move toward a hopeful yet risk-laden learning that seeks to accomplish a shift of one's ego boundaries, that displaces engagements with the past and contemporary relationships with others out of the inescapably violent and violative confines of the "I," to a receptivity to others, to (in Jacques Derrida's terms) a "welcome" of the other's difficult, onerous approach. On such terms remembrance enacts possibilities for an ethical learning that impels us into a confrontation and reckoning not only with stories of the past but also with ourselves as we *are* (historically, existentially, socially) in the present.

As Derrida suggests in the concluding paragraph of *Specters of Marx*, "[i]f he loves justice . . . , the 'scholar' of the future" should not just enlist the ghost to provide lessons about justice but should also learn from attempts to engage the ghost, not how to "make conversation with the ghost but how to talk with him, with her, how to let them speak or how to give them back speech, even if it is in oneself, in the other, in the other in oneself" (1994, 176). What practice constitutes talking with ghosts? What demands would such an ambition make on our modes of engaging aspects of testament? In its address, the testamentary act enacts a claim that, while providing accounts of the past, it may wound or haunt, interrupting one's self-sufficiency and demanding an attentiveness to an otherness that resists being reduced to a version of our own stories. This is a claim on our practices of reading and listening that enables the reassessment and revision of stories that are most familiar. For this reason, we have become interested in the pedagogical and political implications of the question of attentiveness; that is, what form of attentiveness, what mode of sensibility might support the possibility that memories of others be engaged as something other than documentary evidence or a spectacle of suffering, which (while it might move me emotionally and provoke what I hope might be helpful action) fails to fundamentally challenge the narratives with which I orient my commitments and social relations? And crucially, what educative relationships and institutional forms, what elements of new memorial practices, might be necessary to sustain such an attentiveness, such a sensibility?

In a recent issue of the journal *Race and Class*, John Berger contemplates the prophetic qualities of Hieronymus Bosch's *Millennium Triptych*. Focusing in particular on the right-hand panel that depicts Hell, Berger discusses how the form of the painting prefigures contemporary culture under the threat of globalization. He notes that in Bosch's vision of Hell, there is no horizon:

> The world is burning. Every figure is trying to survive by concentrating on his own immediate need and survival. Claustrophobia, at its most extreme, is not caused by overcrowding, but by the lack of any continuity existing between one action and the next which is close enough to be touching it. It is this which is hell. The culture in which we live is perhaps the most claustrophobic that has ever existed. (1998, 3)

Berger goes on to emphasize the lack of an elsewhere or otherwise in this vision of Hell, a condition that reduces "the given" to an imprisoning actuality justifying self-serving projects and unrelenting greed, however, it is his diagnosis of a contemporary cultural claustrophobia that we find most evocative; for what Berger is suggesting is a cultural dysfunction actualized by a specific readiness-to-hand of sound, image, and text that convey the narratives, sentiment, and sensibilities of other people's lives. Brought close through mediation of book publishing, broadcasting, film and video-tape distribution, and Internet webpages, the testament of people subjected to oppressive circumstances, who have struggled (not always successfully) to survive on historical terms not of their own making, is increasingly evident, present, nearby. Yet, this testament remains fragmented, neither touching nor touching us.

What would it mean for one to be "touched" by the testament of another? To be touched by the memories of others is, at first blush, a phrase that brackets a matter of affect. It is commonly used as a synonym for those occasions when one is "moved," when one begins to feel a range of possible psychic states in response to another's story: sorrow, shock, elation, rage. There is obviously some form of human connection referenced here. Most commonly characterized as an empathic response to stories and images of other's plight, this is clearly one trajectory through which an archive of narrative and images might be redeemed from its hellish construction as a set of disconnected fragments. But, there are other, less affect-laden possibilities. If "being touched" amounts to a negation of the fragmentation and isolation of experiences, then also redemptive is the contiguity and causality supplied by the historiographic impulse that seeks human continuity within historical narratives. Likewise, connectedness of experience is possible in the context of allegorical or emblematic readings wherein one set of experiences is understood through the representation of another. But all these interpretations of the event of being touched limit the force of Berger's observation. Edith Wyschogrod has suggested, "touch is not a sense at all; it is in fact a metaphor for the impingement of the world as a whole upon subjectivity . . . to touch is to comport oneself not in opposition to the given but in proximity with it" (cited in Jay, 1994, 557). The proximity she refers to here is not a spatial concept denoting an interval between two points or sectors of space. Not a state, nor repose, but rather it is, as Emmanuel Levinas would have it, a restlessness—a movement toward the other in which one draws closer (Levinas, 1998, 61–97). It is a welcome in which one becomes not just emotionally vulnerable (open to feeling), but where one exposes one's self to a possible de-phasing of the ego wherein the cognitive terms on which one makes connection with others are shaken, put up for revision. Thus, more than being moved or being able to integrate the stories of others into the communally established framework ordering one's grasp of the world (past and present), being touched commands taking the stories of others seriously, accepting such stories as matters of "counsel."

In his essay "The Storyteller," Walter Benjamin referred to counsel as, "less an answer to a question than a proposal concerning the continuation of a story which is just unfolding" (1968, 86). For Benjamin, in order to seek and receive counsel, one would first have to be able to tell this unfolding story. On such terms, for the lives of others to truly matter—beyond what they demand in the way of an immediate, necessary practical solidarity— they must be encountered as counsel. These would be stories that might actually initiate a de-phasing, a potential shifting of our own unfolding stories, particularly in ways that might be unanticipated and not easily accepted. Benjamin was attempting in this essay to reflect on the erosion of the very possibility of the exchange of experience. For him, this was actu- ally being prevented by the proliferation of news reports and the mass dissemination of stories and images that accompanied the media mediated transmission of experiences. Benjamin thought that the link between memory and experience was being threatened within what he termed a "phantasmagoric" flow of information that resulted in an age well informed about itself but, at the same time, knowing very little. Missing was the "wisdom" of experience, its non-indifference, its transitivity; that is, the possibility that the telling of a story would actually make a difference in the way one's own stories were told, either by opening one's existing narratives to assessment and revision or by influencing one's actions. This inability to "experience" the transitivity of the stories of others (something other than simply being able to read/hear and recount them) is a historical condition. And it is to the conceptualization of this condition that we now wish to turn.

Restaging Politics in the Space of the Spectacle

In order to communicate the intricacies of the transitive nature of testament—of stories and images of distant suffering and death that arrive in my time and demand something of me—our project implicates the giving and receiving of testament with the possibility of what Derrida terms "a spectral moment": a moment that no longer belongs to the present economy of coherent and integrated successions of "nows," of the "linking of modalized presents" (1994, xx). To think of the transmission of testament as a "spectral moment" incites a mode of historical apprehension that is distinct from the inclination to plot the past back in place—an inclination that in the process of uncovering the patterns and themes that impute historical meaning ends up, according to de Certeau, subsuming the dead into "the objective figure of an exchange among the living" (1988: 46). In this exchange relation between the past and present, we, thus, witness a closed-circuit reception that renders the past into an abstraction (of historiography), a phantasmatic foreclosure that resurrects the past as a finished object that can be buried within the terms/grounds of the present.

Yet, the spectral moment that invites us to make contact, to gain "counsel," from a haunting noncontemporaneity, with a haunting that overturns our ontological grounds, would trouble any mode of historical reception that (unwittingly) attempts to remain immanent to itself. To think of testament as a spectral instance, as a call that comes before and beyond the present, urges us to reckon with details that exceed the continuity of "our" present terms. It allows us to acknowledge that within the details of the testament, there always remain *remains* not yet accounted for or defined by the present terms of our discursive exchange.[3] Heeding that there are remains, that there exists the too troubling or, perhaps, the too shameful (the too much for now!), allows us to encounter the irreducible nature of testament. This is an instance that reminds us that it is the complexity of a living-life that often disappears in the typicality of historical abstraction. In the spectral moment, remembrance is challenged to rework the singularity of life from its absorption in some undifferentiated mass-theme of history. In this sense, being attentive to the living complexity of testaments implies, citing Avery Gordon, "making a contact [with ghosts/with what is beyond here] that changes you and refashions the social relations in which you are located. It is about putting life back in where only a vague memory or a bare trace was visible" (1997, 22). In other words, a transitive engagement with testament implicates a welcome to that which comes from beyond my time, to *instances* that expose us to what we are not, that engender a mode of being—a sociality of learning to live finally here, now—with ghosts that disjoin the exchange-order of presents.

But, to contemplate the possibility of a sociality of living with ghosts requires grappling with our present position of reception; for how and what constitutes the spectral instance or an appropriate welcome to testaments is not—at least at this point—apparent. Much depends on the structure of our mode of attention, on how we audience the stories and images that come before us. For the onlooker does not simply encounter testaments that speak for themselves. The stories and images of distant suffering come to us inherently through a form of mediated attention, through a process of meaning making within discursive limits that have particular implications. Drawing on what Benjamin terms the phantasmagoric, we seek to make a distinction between a mode of reception that makes room for the coming-and-going of the ghost and a phantasmagoric invocation that incarnates and transfixes the ghost into a parade of identical phantoms whose claim to presence undermines the possibility of developing a covenant with a non-present instance. Our assumption is that, before we can entertain the possibilities of an adequate reception of the ghost, we must grapple with the pervasiveness of the phantasmagoric form of encounter with the present operative means of structuring our attention to the stories and images of distant suffering.

The phantasmagoria of today can be glimpsed by how it circulates and structures our attention to the images and stories of the suffering and death of others primarily as news and information, granting them the lifespan of the moment. Its mode of presentation or preservation, thus, outstrips its content, its temporality foreclosed within the primacy of the present. "The value of information," Benjamin wrote in 1936, "does not survive the moment in which it was new. It lives only at that moment; it has to surrender completely and explain itself without losing any time" (1968, 90). Every moment a new item of information arrives before our eyes and (more often than not) passes away without much effect or with a fleeting momentary fascination—its urgent and frightful address instantly replaced by another item, leaving the basic assumptions of *our* place as the onlooker intact. Although we can feel deeply and endorse that we "do something," my response is short-lived—and, more gravely, it is contained: *I am not in question.*

By invoking the phantasmagoria in this way, do we not risk a straightforward dichotomization: with an earlier, pure and untainted form of experience, a nostalgic lament for "a once upon a time" when these stories could have been attended to and experienced *properly*? To be clear, we want to make no claims for a kind of "pure responsiveness" that precedes some supposedly "technological Fall of Man" (cf. Virilio, 2000). It is not a question of technological obstacles or filters—for this mode of circulation is not "in the way," but remains, in fact, the only way for these images and stories to arrive, to get to us at all. In this sense, what is of concern to us is less the mystification involved in the means of producing phantasmagoric apparitions, but rather the peculiar presentation of phantoms that structures a mode of reception that forecloses the transitive nature of testaments. In order to unfold what is at stake here, let us explore, in more detail, the operative principles of the phantasmagoria.

The term phantasmagoria first appeared in connection with a particular type of magic lantern show that became popular in early-nineteenth-century France, England, and the United States. It is generally acknowledged by historians of visual technology that the most accomplished showman to present phantasmagorias was Etienne-Gaspard Robertson. These multimedia manifestations, literally, conjured a parade of ghosts. As projections of painted slides, these ghostly images were created by what Robertson called a *phantoscope*—a movable magic lantern on wheels. Often the projector was behind a translucent screen, out of view of the audience.

Although the technology of the phantasmagoria is important in order to understand how it elicited a particular form of attentiveness, let us dwell for a moment on its content. While the apparitions that Robertson's phantasmagoria summoned drew on a variety of gothic narratives, literary specters, and mythic images, it is those that drew on French cultural memory and the traumatic history of the French Revolution that are perhaps most noteworthy in this context. Keep in mind that at the turn of the nineteenth century, Parisians were living in the traumatic aftermath of the Revolution and the Terror of 1793–4. Indeed, one might argue that Robertson's presentations exploited the memory of these events in order to evoke both fascination and dread. But also, we might speculate that Robertson's phantasmagoria contributed to the production of a particular form of cultural memory as much as it drew on one, and thus was very much implicated in the enactment of a particular form of historical consciousness.

Appearing along with the assassinated revolutionary Marat, one evening, were the apparitions of the founder of the Swiss republic William Tell, Virgil, Voltaire, and the images of victims executed as a result of the revolutionary court's denunciations and decrees. While Robertson turned "the bloody events of class warfare into [the] fantastic nightmares of an evening's entertainment," into aesthetic apparitions "divested of their material reality" as shadows who had lost their bodies, "these historical figures were more than just entertaining" (Cohen, 1993, 234). Robertson helped them enter into a structure of signification through which they could be integrated into a pantheon of cultural memory where they would play the role of either evil demons or proud heroes. Robertson's phantoms literally constituted a procession of images out of history that were in-scripted into an imaginative melodramatic recontextualization, presented within the enchantment of the supernatural.

Robertson never hid the fact that his performances were illusions. He gave interviews that stressed this fact. Nevertheless, he did create a technology of representation that assembled a public to witness one way of living with ghosts, of bringing back the dead. Whether people believed the phantoms to be "real" is not the issue, far more important is to consider the economy of exchange within the phantasmagoria: for the representational practice and the subjective processes is what made it intelligible and tolerable even if, at times, frightening. Thus, it is the terms on which the phantasmagoria structured a certain reception and relation to the past that is so crucial to understand if this discussion is to illuminate the problems of how contemporary practices of historical memory mediate our relationship with those whose stories reach us from times and places other than our own. Although the phantasmagoria appears to unnerve and frighten, profiting from its effect through its relation with what is radically other (the dead), in claiming to bring back the dead it ultimately betrays and subsumes any relation to what is incommensurable to and with the present. That is, nothing can ever be sufficiently "other" enough. As Benjamin might say, not "even the dead are safe from it" (1968, 255), everything can be brought back—resurrected and reanimated. This phantasmagoric process, which denies the loss of loss, which denies that there is anything that is radically beyond the recuperative power of the present, ends up accumulating and circulating all things through the principle of identity. There is an obvious resemblance here between the phantasmagoric form and the commodity form, for both are committed to an economy where all things—eventually—can be evaluated, interchanged or b(r)ought back through one universal equivalent.

In this sense, that which would otherwise remain incommensurate can be reduced—predicted in advance—to standardized objects or thematic events that facilitate a reciprocal undifferentiated exchange process. The principle of general equivalence, thus, cannibalizes the particular into an abstraction (identity), which then becomes suitable for (undifferentiated) exchange. This is precisely what happens within the mix of ghoulish, spectral history and phantasy that Robertson specialized in. Within his non-linear, melodramatic structure, which of necessity included figures of shining ideals juxtaposed with representations of terrifying images of evil, Robertson provided universal transcendent themes (good/evil; light/darkness; order/chaos) within which to place the specters on offer to his public.

In order for the universal-equivalence of exchange to operate between the past and present, for the past to enter (phantasmagorically) and incarnate the terms of the present, there must be present in representations of the past an identity and continuity that conforms to a recognizable and coherent structure of meaning. A universal shared signified is thus presumed in the phantasmagoric invocation and reception of the past, structuring our relationship to the past through a type of symmetrical one-to-one correspondence. In this abstracted sense, particular historical instances—which have the possibility of breaking up my time—are emptied of their specificity, and risk becoming fetishized and paraded as an "event" that is reducible to its comparable or readily understood thematic characteristics. There is *no transitivity* in this form of living with ghosts. For no particular obligation—that supercedes my time—is encumbered by the phantasmagoric mediation of images and stories from other times and spaces. Rather, the phantasmagoric activity of making the past present through a successive series of identifiable connections structures a particular attentiveness that thwarts the recognition that a learning from the past requires the present and the past to meet on a different time, through an active remaking of one's present historical consciousness.

If the phantasmagoria defines the terms of exchange between the past and the present, it then brings forth, precisely, questions of what might constitute *learning about* and *learning from* the stories of others. How is the suffering body presented to us, in our time? Consider in this context the great treatise on human social suffering, Terrence Des Pres's book *The Survivor: An Anatomy of Life in the Death Camps*. In this riveting study of memoirs of the Nazi concentration camps and the Soviet Gulag, Des Pres's subject is survival, "the capacity of men and women to live beneath the pressure of protracted crisis, to sustain terrible damage in mind and body and yet be there, sane, alive, still human" (1977, v). Although Des Pres recognized the limits of his project (see 1977, vi), it is the way he works with testimony that needs to be given a second thought.

Des Pres, first of all, decontextualizes individual narratives and reabsorbs them into various categories of "survivor experience." Perhaps, most vivid is his chapter on "Excremental Assault" where he writes: "How much self-esteem can one maintain, how readily can one respond to the needs of another, if both stink, if both are caked with mud and feces?" (1977, 66). Arguably, Des Pres's *Survivor* presents a phantasmagoria of pain and suffering. He does not deal with the *production* of those moments of pain; rather, through representation of individual descriptions of suffering, Des Pres returns to us the reality of the violence endemic to totalitarian regimes, presenting a viscerally moving presence of elemental degradation as it was experienced in the Camps and the Gulag. These accounts are narratively encoded as elements of the psycho-dynamics of *survival*, in effect the *phenomenality* of survival. In establishing the category of "survivor" as the meaningful frame in which we can receive and hold the shocking stories he re-presents for us, Des Pres produces an ontology, the *being* of the survivor. As we read on, we are certainly moved deeply—shocked and disgusted—*yet*, with an epistemological frame effectively in place: one that emplots our reception in a narrative that delivers the thematic terms for claiming that here indeed is the terrible damage that has been inflicted and against which the human capacity to survive triumphs. What might be made of such testamentary legacy engaged on these terms?

Raphael Rosen (2000), one of the winners of an annual essay contest for high school students designed to encourage and promote the study of the Holocaust, wrote the following:

> [T]he emotional connection we make to the descriptions [of survivor testimony] is fundamental to one's ability to feel suffering when we read horrifying images and descriptions of individual human suffering during this time. In describing dysentery in concentration camps, Terrence Des Pres says, "Those with dysentery melted down like candles, relieving themselves in their clothes, and swiftly turned into stinking repulsive skeletons who died in their own excrement" (1977, 59).

Rosen responds to this passage as follows:

> "Repulsive skeletons" dying "in their own excrement," is a powerful image by itself, but when we can imagine it occurring to individual human beings, and when we can connect on an emotional level to this image, it becomes extremely [powerful]. The forceful images [provided by] Des Press . . . take the connection to . . . the level of the visceral. . . . With Des Pres we can actually *feel* the suffering that so many went through. Survivor testimony and description will forever play the crucial role in the future of Holocaust remembrance.

As Rosen suggests, Des Pres's phantasmagoric representation solicits our attention on an emotional level providing a visceral connection to the degradation he has returned to us. Within this connection, Rosen imagines that he can "actually *feel* the suffering that so many went through." In this collapse of self and other, non-indifference is not an option. Rosen may indeed find ways of acting on this non-indifference, turning it concretely into positive (or perhaps relentlessly melancholic, destructive) forms of cultural memory. What is not likely, however, is that he receive the testament presented by Des Pres as counsel, as subject to the difficult work of opening up his own structure of attendance, his own unfolding story, to the demand that he explore and take into account the implications of being addressed by one "stinking . . . caked with mud and feces."

In this example of reception, phantasmagoria might be understood as a mode of regulation of the interhuman, one whose terms are defined by a particular mode of attentiveness, one that we have come to call *spectacle*. The particular mode of circulation and exchange between the past and the present that the phantasmagoria structures, circumscribes the task of inheriting testament and handing it onward within an economy that grants currency to the spectacle of presence. In order to theoretically extend the implications of the phantasmagoric reception, we, thus, draw out how its reliance on spectacle mediates our attention to what arrives from beyond the masterable grounds of the ego. Whereas the phantasmagoria allows us to forefront a particular relationship between the past and the present, our venture into the workings of the spectacle seeks to highlight the structure of attendance implicit within the phantasmagoria.

How then is the relationship we hold of the body in ruins (the suffering body) one of *spectacle*? In providing a few points in this regard, we are self-consciously reappropriating Debord's—imminently problematic—concept (1983), reworking its terms and the force of its insight.

(1) First of all, spectacle is not a thing, it is not an event or even a particular representation of an event. Nor is it something that is exclusively visual, that necessarily incorporates looking at images. Rather, spectacle is a particular mode of attentiveness organized within phantasmagoric relations. It is a way of entering the significations of social relations and, in this sense, may be understood as enacted through certain forms of thought (conscious and unconscious) as well as expressions of feeling.

(2) Spectacle accepts the incarnation of the ghost as the terms of its attention. Whether in novels, memoirs, diaries, recorded testimonies, films, or theme parks, its ambition is to recognize the past as present-at-hand, to accept the terms of the reduction of the past so that the ghost can be of our time—all its radicalness, its otherness gone. The ghost is thus manifested/staged as a phantom by means of a familiar and exchangeable set of present characteristics; that is, the terms of its welcome are within spectacle: within a spectatorial address that invites the sensationalized sense that "you are there," engrossed in a symmetrical relation with an "entified" other. This type of engrossment, according to Kaja Silverman, "encourages

us to apprehend other beings as present-at-hand entities because it implies seeing them from one uniform standpoint . . . through those perceptual coordinates which are most emphatically and frequently reiterated in our culture, and which therefore interpose themselves almost automatically between us and the world—through what might be called the "given-to-be-seen." Although we are at such inauthentic moments still in the world, we are not really "there" (Silverman, 2000, 32–33).

(3) Spectacle is the development of a technology of separation. "Spectacle is not primarily concerned with a *looking at* images but rather with the construction of conditions of attention that individuate, immobilize, and separate subjects, even within a world in which mobility and circulation are ubiquitous" (Crary, 1999, 74). Spectacle, thus, requires the individuation of attention. As a mode of attentiveness, it opens the object of my gaze to my individual involvement with it. Not at all pure passivity, the very basis of spectacle lies in eliciting an individual response. But—as a strictly individuated response—it pretends that there is no need to have the substance of my attendance reinscribed in a relational, publicly accountable manner. Rather, my encounter is naturalized into a collection that befits the private interior of "my experiences." That is, spectacle opens on to the melodramatic structure of phantasmagoria, thus, inviting identification and the reading of the particulars of images and narratives on the terms of the moral certainties we hold dear. Indeed, it is the very acceptance of this invitation that allows us to disavow any requirement that the terms on which we are moved by phantasmagoric displays might throw ourselves into question, into destabilization. The projections and identifications made within spectacle, and the consequent defences it elicits, both require and enact leaving ourselves intact, at a distance, protected from being called into question and altered through our engagement with the stories of others.

(4) Spectacle offers an attentiveness to suffering, which encourages or reproduces an illusory or fantastic mode of attention that endows *that* horror with a capacity to turn the praxis and process of human history into *its* thing. Our attentiveness while not "inactive," is compliant; it does not engage in the praxis of making and remaking our historical consciousness. Before the phantasmagoric scene we fall in awe—feeling deeply, but with nothing to say. Yet, though the light is not on us, within relations of spectacle we are assigned responsibilities; there are expectations. Assembled on terms of spectacle, we must behave as good audience members—leaving unthought the question of how this regulates our obligation to a testamentary legacy that demands a reckoning in the present.[4]

As a clear example of the contemporary logic of spectacle within the phantasmagoria, we refer to an article entitled "Seeking Answers Down in the Trenches" in the *New York Times* (November 19, 2000) by William Boyd, novelist and film director. In this article, Boyd is sketching his intention and mode of framing his film *The Trenches*—a feature presentation that depicts forty eight hours in the British trenches before the beginning of the four-month Battle of the Somme, which resulted in 420,000 British casualties, 195,000 French, and 600,000 German. Explaining his efforts, Boyd notes:

> We forget that the First World War took place in glorious Technicolor, so familiar are we with its monochrome version. We forget also that it wasn't mute. The silence of the silent film and the sepia of the images distance the event from us, visually, and it seemed to me one of the great advantages of making a film at the end of the 20th century about the trench experience of the First World War would be that, at the very least, we would see and hear it approximately as it must have been.

Boyd also refers to receiving, just as the filming began, information about his great uncle Sandy who had fought in World War I and had been wounded at the Battle of the Somme. He writes:

> My uncle had also sent a photograph of Sandy in uniform; I had never seen a picture of him before. So—as the world of the film began to cohere and come alive—if there was ever any ghostly presence haunting our replica trenches (and they were spookily evocative at times), I imagined it as being that of Sgt. Alexander Boyd, D.C.M.
>
> We say, casually, that life in the tre nches of the Western Front must have been "unimaginable." But it seems to me that the challenge to the artist, the challenge of art, is precisely to try to imagine the unimaginable—to set the imagination free and attempt to bring that bizarre, boring, filthy, terrifying world to life. . . . In filming
>
> "The Trench," I wanted to make the First World War personal again, to recreate a world that could have contained my grandfather and my great uncle, whose photographs sit today upon the mantelpiece in my study. I wanted more than anything else to represent the ordinariness and humanity of these boys and these young men, and in that way I felt we would understand all the better what they endured.

Yet, Boyd knows full well what the economy is within which his staging could circulate. In his film, the camera never rises above ground level, but rather "roves around the trench system with the actors, almost as a ghostly witness," as the clock ticks down the hours before the men go over the top and into battle. When they leave the trench to walk across the Somme valley, Boyd's aspiration is:

> that we have come to know them—and [that] the messy, desperate fates awaiting these particular young men would stand as symbols for the grotesque and enormous massacre that actually took place. My aim, my hope, was to make it authentic, to make it true, to make it real.

Here, again, are all the tropes of a spectatorial address. To make it authentic, to make it true, to make it real when it cannot be. To move us within the very move in which "particular young men would stand as symbols for the grotesque and enormous massacre." In this promise of the immediacy of presence, of our absorption in this presence, effaced is any notion of a "trace" as that which points to what is now gone, which ironically renders that which is not there, *there*. For the trace is not the terms of spectacle. The grounds of spectacle are far more empirical, eliciting excitement more than the anxiety of the sign, an anxiety mobilized not only by the slippage between the signifier and that which is signified, but also by the unbridgeable gap between what Levinas termed "the saying" and "the said." In the phantasmagoric return of the dead, what is lost, is loss itself with the result that—although we might weep, fear, and be shocked—the spectacle of presence becomes a mode of consolation.

The society of the spectacle has not only mobilized and supported an effusion of contemporary re-presentations but has also produced a narrowing of what counts as one's own experience with the result that the elemental structures of sociality are increasingly narrowed. But the promise of counsel, the potential for the experience of others to "touch" us is too important to the prospect of hope—to the possibilities of human futurity— to simply abandon within the hegemonic prerequisites of a neoliberal logic that would hermetically seal the possibility of the past and future within the actuality of the present. If there is to be an acknowledgment of a future to come—and not the resignation of thought to more of the same—central to our present concerns must be an openness to what Homi Bhabha (1994b, 223–229) calls "translating" cultures and histories in ways that make it possible to reassess and revise the means of receiving stories with which one is most familiar.

We cannot, however, step out of the phantasmagoria to some neutral, objective place. As Benjamin knew full well, "the unclouded innocent eye has become a lie" (cited in Cohen, 1993, 251). Emphasizing the force of Benjamin's words, Margaret Cohen writes: "Rational de-mystification can hence no longer be the critic's task. Rather, [one] must seek some form of activity using his/her immersion in the very objects of study to productive end" (1993, 251). With this in mind, we begin a reconsideration of questions of public memory. To work toward ethical and transformative pedagogical forms of remembrance, one must recognize that spectacle will be the initial mode through which testamentary remnants give themselves to us. As we read, listen, and view accounts of human-initiated suffering and death, we are brought into the orbit of a spectacular relationship with the body in pain that is humiliated, that perishes. A risk encountered in this relation is the abstraction of testament into a narrative of "man's inhumanity to man." Testament on phantasmagoric terms configures particular moments of anguish/suffering into a thematic formula in which the testamentary inheritance loses its specificity and historical grounding and, even more crucially, *loses its transitivity*. Within our twenty-first-century phantasmagoria, the ghost is called forth, but is yet reabsorbed into a history that is more troubled than troubling, delivered more as news than counsel. But the question remains, living within this phantasmagoria, can we work within it to find moments in which it can be undone, where there is something other than the terms of a spectacular attentiveness, one in which a specific relation between stories/images and their reception might begin to define the substance of the interhuman?

Remembrance, Pedagogy, and the Ethical Praxis of the Interhuman

The challenge of remembrance in our time is to create a sphere of human engagement and learning, to develop a social space and a practice where it becomes possible to engage with the stories of others on un-phantasmagoric terms. We now turn to our attempt to meet this challenge through ongoing work with a group of people attempting to enact a form of remembrance-*as*-learning, through what we have called a "historiographic poetics." Our efforts to work toward a nonspectacular mode of attending have found that it is only among others, only in working together, that this attending can become a genuine *practice*. The study group is thus not merely an assembly of individuals with common interests or commitments: more than just a "meeting," it is simultaneously a time, a site, and an opening up. Watchful of the many ways in which this mode of attending continues to be subject to forces of spectacularization (forces from which no *solitary* act of reading can ever entirely disengage), the group supports a space and a time within which one learns, one teaches how one learns, and one learns again. It is this space that inaugurates what we have earlier referred to as a moment of public time—a relationality that, in the very unpredictability intrinsic to open conversation between individuals, perennially keeps itself open. It is a community of rememberers and learners, an open community[5] of witnesses, both present and absent, living and dead.

Envisioned is a transitive sphere (or spheres) within which various and varied stories can be circulated, and where participation in such a sphere of public memory requires vigilance and attention to the instances conveyed of other people's lives. In the context of this vision, a particular diary—for example, Herman Kruk's diary of the Vilna Ghetto—can be approached as an instance of "testament." More generally, testament in this sense refers to images, text, and/or sound written and assembled to constitute (in the very movement of production) an address that attempts to initiate a *public* memory. But the "public" character of this memory is not something given in advance. Rather, the idea of a public is what is at stake in the *transitive* address: an address that seeks, but may not arrive at, its destination (Keenan, 1998). That is, the public character of the memorial demand of testament is inherent in the very dynamic called for by a testament as such: a waiting, a hearing, a response, a welcome of the arrival of that which—in its difference—opens the question of the interhuman. Thus, public here is neither a prescription nor prescribed. It is neither those with a "citizen" status, nor pre-given as a "we" that is amassed into something called "the public." Rather, the sense of a public we are mobilizing here is the we who "recognize the possibility of an open response" (Keenan, 1998) to a testamentary address, acknowledging membership in the generation (which could be any generation) for which this message was intended.

This transitive testamentary act (at every reading, at every listening) is an *occurrence*, an event that has a singular illocutionary force that subjects its addressee to a demand, to an obligation that can either be refused or differentially enacted. But, what is the pedagogical project inherent in this force? The temporal condition of the event of testament brings the past with it, charging this event with a future, a possibility; that is, the address of testimony opens the possibility of a site of difference and transformation whose contours are not preset, but brought into view and situated, situated anew at each testamentary instance of public time. This initiates a force that has the potential to instantiate the present as "already extended beyond itself into the future and carrying with it the past" (Ziarek, 2000, 84), implicating testament in the re-formation and renewal of historical consciousness. The transitivity of testament initiates a nonlinear temporality—a momentary complex of the has-been—the making-present and the coming-toward (Ziarek, 2000, 84). Thus, the pedagogical hope of this form of remembrance is that new things may happen if this moment includes the radical openness to the proximity of the other, one beyond a spectacular sensibility.

We have been exploring a practice of remembrance that attempts to provoke and support such an openness to testament and have termed this practice a historiographic poetics. This refers to a specific form of public work, a particular creative, reflective working with testimony that attempts to serve both ethical remembrance and critical learning. It describes the activities of a group working *together* to enact a new form of relationship to historical material. The sense of the poetic in this relation is not being invoked for any aesthetic eloquence, but for the active process of decomposing our expectations and recomposing our obligations to the testamentary traces. As our idea of historiographic poetics reveals, this is as much a creative act as a responsive one: it is an act of creation that *is* essentially responsive. And the *work* is thereby inherently and inexorably unfinished—called forth by and intended for the group itself, it *becomes what it is* only in being offered to others, in becoming other than whatever one had intended. In this regard, we offer a methodological triad of juxtaposition, commentary, and response as the primary terms on which a trans-activity is enacted in the process of reading and responding to the archive of testamentary materials.

We know, as Benjamin taught, that "every image of the past that is not recognized by the present as one of its own concerns threatens to disappear irretrievably" (1968, 255). However, this recognition of the past as one of one's own concerns is no simple task. Indeed, it is fraught with problems and risk. Within the space of our study group, as we read and listen to the testimony of Vilna, we are faced—we will perpetually be faced—with the problem of recognition[6]: how might the images of the Vilna Ghetto be recognized as one of our own concerns? The task cannot be reduced to the apprehension of *relevance*: the grasping of (from our time-of-the-present) themes or issues that seem to persist through time and into our own. Finkielkraut has rightly cautioned that "[m]emory does not consist in subordinating the past to the needs of the present . . . for he who looks to gather the materials of memory places himself at the service of the dead, and not the other way around" (1994, 54). So, one must proceed on grounds different from the typical investments one often finds at the root of the "use of history," the active adaptation of history to the social, emotional, and political needs of the present.

This means attending to the implications of Benjamin's astute paradox that "in order for a part of the past to be touched by the present, there must be no continuity between them" (1999, 470). This demands new, and perhaps less directive, forms of answering to the responsibilities of memory: for the work of a historiographic poetics will not be "about something," but rather that it will *be* something, a form of remembrance that attempts to clear the way for the arrival of the new, and emergent. This requires a focused conversation within which one is enabled to work with and through the dialogical and transferential relations evoked by the transitive demands of testimony. As Kelly Oliver suggests, "working-through is the process of articulating and diagnosing the ways in which we totalize or deny otherness; its aim is transforming our relations with others and otherness" (2000, 45).

This "method" is our exploratory response to the question: how does one read and listen differently to testamentary material if obliged to more than just personal reception, if obliged to find a way to teach, to teach how and what we learn not only about Vilna but from attending to its testimony? The implications of this question run deep, opening the issue of a dialectical relationship between knowing and the social activity of sustaining a historical consciousness. Indeed, perhaps these questions are unaddressable except in the form of a conversation that upholds the ongoing renewal of historical consciousness, a conversation sustained by relations of learning and teaching, by witness as a form of collective study.

As we described earlier, the basic operation that initiates—but does not complete—the work of historiographic poetics is the act of collage: the citation and arraignment of a finite set of testamentary texts and images in juxtaposition.[7] In historiographic poetics, the placing of each citation in relation to one another is intended to expose one's exposure to the address of testament, to my attempt to be responsible to that address. This citation of details in the form of a collage is a practice that attempts to give expression to what astonishes, what exceeds my horizon of expectations, what is contradictory and heterogeneous. As a gesture towards a nonreductive textual event, a juxtaposition will, in its most developed form, be a polylinguistic, polyvocal, and polytemporal[8] remembrance, which can include a juxtaposition of music, poetry and art with ghetto diaries, memoirs, and survivor testimony. It is a way of reintroducing incommensurability into linguistic and social structures—a constant remembering and reassertion of difference, whose purpose is to open the present to something new.

These juxtapositions will require proceeding from a rigorous listening and a certain attentive obsession with details. This means awakening to a humbleness that is also a form of vigilance: a being open to surprise, to an unsettlement, and then to an interrogation of why we are surprised, unsettled. Of the structure of this vigilance, Oliver writes, "vigilance is necessary to recognize the unrecognizable in the process of witnessing itself. To demand vigilance is to demand infinite analysis through ongoing performance, elaboration, and interpretation" (2000, 46). By staging aggregations of the testimonial details, we ask those addressed by our witness to engage with us in speaking (not *about* but) *to* these images as we attempt to recognize them as one of our own concerns. And this is why, included within this method, the juxtaposition must be accompanied by a "commentary." As an attempt to signify one's difficulties in working through the study of historical documents, this commentary is to be understood as a practice that attempts to discover what can be said about one's process of writing one's juxtaposition. In other words, a juxtaposition's commentary is an effort to deepen what is at stake for the one who remembers through the enactment of a collective, dialogical practice with those committed to the task of attending to the address of the past. To complete at least one cycle of the work of this poetics, the members of this community must, in turn, *write back*: responding to both the juxtaposition and its commentary within the contexts of their own attempts to engage an archive of testament, to respond to its demands.

Our interest is in the maintenance of a space of study that allows for, and provokes, an endless process of questioning and re-questioning, demanding greater and greater attention not only to the remnants themselves, but to our obligations and to our attempts to respond to those obligations. This open engagement with testament will always turn us back to our responsibility, to the work (and it *is* work) of foregoing the idealization or ossification of the approach, a rendering of this approach into a simple compensatory or consolatory formula. The obligation is to a constant rewriting of the face that approaches us—testifying to and out of my exposure to its demands, opening up in turn my own witness to the questioning of others.[9]

As we find in Levinas, "To study well, to read well, to listen well, is already to speak: whether by asking questions and, in so doing, teaching the master who teaches you, or by teaching a third party" (1994b, 78–79). To listen well is already to speak, and to speak is to open and sustain a space within which the (absent) voices of witnesses past might resound anew in and into our own time. It is to make possible the resonance, or echo, of what has not yet been spoken, of something that is not already contained *within* the document sitting in my hands. It is to make possible a space and a time within which something new can *happen*–inaugurating a hope for a future that might be more than merely "more of the same." As Benjamin writes in "The Task of the Translator," what is *essential* in an "original" work; what demands the attention and labors of the translator, "is not statement nor the imparting of information" (1968, 69). Rather, this essential quality is precisely what escapes the written-ness of the text—what demands translating is effectively what has not been said or recorded at all: its transitivity. For a story to survive as testament, it must continue to address. What the reader/rememberer is here called to do with a testament is keep it from disappearing *as* testament—and this means responding to its call, performing this response by exposing to others my exposure to its demands.

To receive a story as counsel is thus more than merely the question of garnering a piece of wisdom from the telling, nor is it to pass it on as if the social space across which voices are heard is a neutral and indifferent site of transmission and reception. To pass on a story is not only to pass on the content or information contained within it, but also the difficult experience of your attending of it. A living story does not pass from the mouth-of-the-teller to the ear-of-the-listener, but rather it moves—it *lives*—from mouth-to-mouth, from telling-to-telling (Benjamin, 1968, 87). Thus to properly "hear" a story *is* to tell it again—the wisdom of counsel is the wisdom of experience. It is, as Benjamin (citing Hofmannsthal) has written, "to read what was never written" (1999, 416).

Thus, it is important to emphasize that this citation of testimonial detail is not a simple privileging of the authority of the "eye-witness." It does not operate on the presumption that such testimony can bring one closer to the truth. Rather, we emphasize that citation is an act in which what is given, is given again and is given to another. Memoration through quotation is not simply repetition, but an iterative reworking with others in the site of the present (Benjamin, 1997, 50), a reworking that in its very work may unsettle the invested frameworks that help one grasp and negotiate present realities. The unsettlement that citation may provoke lies in the substance and method by which our citation provides details.

This feature of our historiographic poetics is what we describe as the "impoverished and impoverishing" potential of a juxtaposition. One may find the juxtaposition "impoverished" insofar as it presents an array of details that, in their very density, begin to diminish the surety that the signs emplot an adequate index of the events they reference. This opens to the possible registration that however detailed each passage might be on its own, the effect of reading them together on the page can "empty out" the contents of its substantiality. The result is the impoverishment of the reader/rememberer: one is left *poorer*, both in terms of what each account, in themselves, seemed to have communicated, and in terms of the knowledge, information, or structures of understanding that one may have taken for granted prior to this encounter. It is this structure of impoverishment that can perhaps open to the witnessing of that which necessarily escapes any particular telling or testimony: the singularity of the *telling* itself, beyond the content and information that any testament might bear.

The discussion that followed one specific juxtaposition is of particular interest on this point. It consisted primarily of references to the well-known Vilna singer, Lyuba Levitska, and her subsequent execution for the crime of smuggling food through the ghetto gate. The juxtaposition with its repetitions and contradictions between accounts of Levitska's "crime," arrest, imprisonment, and death, threw its readers into "a historiographic crisis." What to admit, what to refuse as reliable evidence, reliable information, reliable witness? But this is not merely a crisis of evidence, but one of interpretation. In the amassing of details about the circumstances of Levitska's death, readers encountered questions of how to be responsible to a life that has been lived, traced amidst and between testamentary referents.

One member of the group admitted that the profusion of details in this juxtaposition produces a text that "breaks the heart." He explained that, within the confusion of multiple accounts, the *presence* (perhaps we might talk here of the Levinasian "face"—the face without features) of Levitska comes through, something that is not available in the bare surface details of descriptive accounts often given in diaries, memoirs, and oral testimonies. In part, this can describe the escape of a *life* from the confines of a narrative— a narrative that is always a candidate for being the authoritative story. In this escape, what comes forth is the un-representable particularity of Lyuba Levitska, her face becoming visible precisely for having escaped the fixity of the citable details of the narration of her death.[10] The multiplicity of texts keeps unsettling the "story"—keeping the story open—and it is in that very unsettlement that the ghost, the facing that escapes all possible representations, enters.

It is in this spectral moment that one can begin to regard one's own facility for attending to testimony, for learning what it has to teach, and for helping formulate a responsible response not only to what is said but to its persistent moment of saying. For us, the importance of citation lies in the confluence of its indexical and delineative dimensions as this confluence is subjected to the discipline of a historiographic poetics.

But why call this method a "poetics"—a term historically loaded, pregnant with multiple associations? In order to address this question directly, we must clear away two possible misdirections that the use of the term poetics may initiate. First of all, within the humanities, there is a long tradition following Aristotle in referring to poetics as the study of the rules, codes, and procedures that operate in any given set of texts: that is, the study of the laws of effective composition. On such terms, to undertake a discussion of poetics is, most commonly, to describe and analyze (and, for some, historicize) the discursive conventions that inform the reading of, and response to, a particular set of texts. In poetics as a field of study, one "attends to all the moves, schemes, and conventions that govern writing, including the order of material, the choice of voice and point of view, and

stylistic matters such as diction and sentence patterns" in order to understand its effects (Carrard, 1992, xiv–xv). Yet, as is already evident, our interest
is far from the analysis of writing (testamentary, historical, or otherwise).

Second, the use of the term poetics might signal to some a gesture
toward a concern with philosophical aesthetics, particularly as the agenda
of this area of inquiry is taken up with the problem of expressive limits and
the notion of the sublime. However, in our work, we clearly depart from
approaching the Shoah as an event—a subject of contemplation. In our
wrestling with the responsibility of memory, we are not gesturing toward
issues of the sublimity of the Holocaust memory. Our concern is not with
the response of wonder, enormity, or astonishment that meditation on the
Shoah as an event elicits, making it alien to thought, leaving memory in
ruins, and reducing us to a stammer. We, indeed, disavow any notion of a
rhetoric of remembrance that constitutes a poetics of Auschwitz as an
"aestheticizing adornment" (Leslie, 2001). Indeed, quite differently, our
concern is with the risk inherent in "acts of predication" (Braiterman,
2000) that attempt to enact our obligation to respond to the demands of
testament—which needs always to be understood in its transitivity. For us,
the first instance of this response requires acts of communication addressed to
a community of others gathered to struggle with the question of the
responsibility of memory. Such communication must include speech and
writing that "give countenance" to those who have provided testament.
Silence is not permitted. Quite on the contrary, what is required are the
"naive" practices (Braiterman, 2000) of citation and detailed historiographic reference through which the responsibilities of remembrance can
be explored. As witnesses who stand in a transitive relation with the traces
of those who continue to speak through the material existence of testamentary documents, at minimum, we must in some medium—whether
print, electronic, or performance—cite (and hence point to) specific texts
or documents. In citing testamentary texts (be they diaries, memoirs, video
interviews, poems, art, or song), we stage a necessary indexicality.
Testamentary documents are signs that, first and foremost, are determined
by the events that produced them (Brinkley and Youra, 1996, 121–122).
Thus, in citation, attention is called not only to the presence of testamentary material but also to the testament's gesture beyond itself to past events.
In this sense, the citation of testamentary documents does—importantly—
"bring news," returning to attention that which has been missed, or
misplaced.

Thus, our interest in poetics seizes the term so that, for us, it stresses a
particular form of historiographic *poiesis*: an actual making or doing of
remembrance, the ongoing production of a radical historical consciousness
through a citational working with texts of testament in relation to the same
activity undertaken by others. This work, this poiesis, is the foundation of
remembrance as both a personal and social practice. As we know, remembrance resides not in monuments, images, and texts but in our *engagements*
with them. In this sense, the remembrance practice we are concerned with

is not simply a repetitive recycling of texts—a posting of signs as emblems. To write is to produce meaning and not reproduce a preexisting meaning— to write is always first to rewrite. As a poiesis, a doing, historiographic poetics carries the potential of something new, emergent, something not already predicated by a preexisting written form. *Historiographic poetics is never about something, it is something.* Historiographic poetics is not just a writing, but also performance, elaboration, interpretation that enacts the gift of testimony by, within the space of a community of memory, giving it again. This act of regiving is not as a simple textual re-transcription, but emerges essentially in the recognition that the gift of testimony lies precisely in its pedagogical force, its transitive demands.

To receive the gift of testament *is* effectively to be given a task; what is demanded is the interruption of this spectacle of full presence, which, in effect, demands nothing at all. Within the spectacle of the phantasmagoria, words, stories, and images require no metabolization, and thus make no demands upon their recipient. Offered as pre-interpreted, substantial, and with a life of their own, they short-circuit the very possibility of just such a demanding address. But, to attend to the transitivity of testament as *gift* means that something needs to be *enacted*: that lacking substance and any meaningfulness in itself, it demands our effort—even requires it. The language of the gift serves here to emphasize this transitive aspect of testament—like testament, all gifts make at least one bare originary demand (i.e, "receive me"); if this goes unheeded, it ceases to be (or rather, never was) a gift. Thus, it can perhaps be said that the inheritance of testament is the recep- tion of "the gift of the ghost." The ambiguous meaning of this phrase opens itself to the inherently paradoxical arrival of this "gift"—for testament is simultaneously the gift that is given and the face (or rather the fac-*ing*) of the giver. The ghost arrives to give itself to me, demanding (from the start) my attention and my response in order to arrive at all.

So, even when, or perhaps especially when, we are given explicit instruc- tions ("This is what I would like you to do with my words"), it is funda- mentally up to me to announce this obligation—I cannot simply submit to their authority, wishes, or hopes. This apparent disrespect is what marks the absolute character of the encounter. As Geoffrey Bennington (2000, 140) writes: "The structure of inheritance commits us to a view of the here and now as a moment when the past always still remains before us as an endless task." It is entirely up to me—in speaking for those who have passed, and those who have summoned me to speech "in the first place," I cannot ever defer to "the plain meaning" of an other's speech.

To offer a juxtaposition is thus not to inform others of historical facts, or confess autobiographical details about one's readings, but *is* the very open- ing up of that reading to an other, for an other. Attentive to those moments of interruption and address that mark every encounter with testament, the study group is called upon to emphasize the trans-actional significance of speech. Text near song, diaries next to poems, photographs alongside paint- ings or drawings—this mixing of media is designed to be neither additive nor thematic, but an attempt to negotiate and recount a moment of astonishment. To offer a juxtaposition is thus not intended to supply an interpretation of one's witness; rather, it is a knotting together of these various and distant accounts in order to impart a moment of concatenation encountered as surprise and instruction, initiating thought that has no rest, that can neither be completed nor ended. It by itself announces the obligation to speak then of our own surprise, our own questions, our own instruction. The experience of a juxtaposition and commentary is both a construction and an offering. It is a mode of speaking that cannot escape the intricate complications of *address*: for it is, at the same time, a speaking to and a speaking for.

Historiographic poetics is a response to the question of what one might do in order to listen and talk to ghosts. It is founded on the premise that when listening to ghosts and then giving them back speech, one must proceed in full acknowledgment that the gift of testimony is nonreciprocal. The only way to return the gift is by giving it to someone else. One gives back speech to a ghost by speaking *of* the ghost *to* others, speaking specifically of its teaching; speaking specifically so as to teach others what it is that the ghost has taught. Thus, to enact and live within public time, one must commit to a vigilant attention not only to the text in one's hands, but also to the world into which she or he will carry and teach its teachings. Levinas is prescient in reopening the question of the interhuman when he states:

> speech, in its original essence, is a commitment to a third party on behalf of our neighbour: the act *par excellence*, the institution of society. The original function of speech consists not in designating an object in order to communicate with the other in a game with no consequences but in assuming toward someone a responsibility on behalf of someone else. (1990a, 21)

CHAPTER EIGHT

The Audiovisual Supplement of Holocaust Survivor Video Testimony

The question of the archive is not . . . a question of the past, the question of a concept dealing with the past which already might be at our disposal or not at our disposal, an archivable concept of the archive, but rather a question of the future, the very question of the future, the question of a response, of a promise and of a responsibility for tomorrow . . . A spectral messiancity is at work in the concept of the archive and like religion, like history, like science itself, this ties it to a very singular experience of the promise.   (Derrida, 1996)

It is a rare event to confront a problem or question that seizes one in thought and launches the curious philosophical adventure of articulating and clarifying concepts adequate to one's query.[1] The following is intended as a preliminary report on such an adventure; its concern is the question of the substance of the audiovisual supplement with regard to the testamentary record of what is known in the English-speaking world as "the Holocaust"[2]—the Nazi genocide of European Jewry. Since the early 1980s, there has been a series of projects initiated by universities, museums, and private foundations to produce and archive video recordings of in-depth interviews with Jews and others[3] who had been subjected to the genocidal policies of the Nazi regime. This has resulted in archives of recordings in Canada, the United States, Israel, England, France, Belgium, and Italy. For more than two decades, the task of those responsible for these archives has been to complete the recording of testimony as fast as possible given the advancing age of survivors. As this task nears completion, attention is now being turned to the question of significance of this video documentation. In part, this means enquiring into the ways these audiovisual recordings might be productively studied and drawn upon for the contemporary public engagement with history. Given the extensive recognition the Holocaust has received in North America over the last three decades and, correspondingly, the increasing availability of historical studies, memoirs, photographs, museum exhibitions, films and video that pertain to this event, it is important to consider what it is that audiovisual testimonies might additionally contribute to the substance of our historical consciousness?

It is in the context of this question that I have evoked the problem of supplementation as an actuality[4] that we need to better understand in order to assess the full measure of the potential educational value of these recordings. It should be clear that in invoking the concept of supplementation, I am in no way rendering audiovisual testimony of residual significance to historical memory. Clearly, the importance of such testimonies is becoming increasingly evident in the deployment of testamentary excerpts in films and videos, museums, classroom curricula, and websites. However, in posing the problem of supplementation, I am explicitly acknowledging that through the last half of the twentieth century, the historical memory of the Holocaust has been instantiated primarily through written texts, documentary photography, and epic film and television narratives. There is, then, a specific chronological sense in which audiovisual recordings of survivors do come after an established degree of historical consciousness mediated through these media, and, therefore, are themselves viewed from within and potentially act upon such consciousness. Additionally, I am concerned with the reality that there is now available a richly multimodal testamentary record through which to engage questions regarding the significance of the Holocaust. As resource, this record opens new challenges regarding the relationships among visual images, texts, and sound, which may help us rethink practices of historical memory and the substance of the legacy of the relationships among these various testamentary forms.

Quite different from that which is residual, we might conceive of a supplement as pointing to something lacking and that which adds something new that carries an implicit sense of correction. On such terms, audiovisual testimony of Holocaust survivors is often welcomed as a corrective to a "lack" of a humanized picture of history perceived as missing from textual accounts. What is felt as missing is an encounter with the palpable character of historical experience, something that is perceived as made present, brought closer within the audiovisual register where the objectified subjects of history, in Irene Kohn's words, "appear more accessible by virtue of their corporeality" (Kohn, 2002), by virtue of their televisual enactment of the process of remembering. Such a view is exemplified by educator Jan Darsa who has written that "It is through . . . testimonies that one can be led closer to the center of that experience. A combination of the video testimonies together with history and literature blend well to create a synthesis that can take those of us who were never there nearer to those who were . . . History needs a human dimension, and there is the advantage now of having these testimonies on tape to bring out that dimension and the dilemmas that are encompassed in it in order to raise questions around this complex history."[5]

The sense conveyed here is that video testimonies fill a void making for a more complete historical record. This is not just a movement toward completion sustained by "living histories" that provide new information ("new pieces of the puzzle"), that add to, and possibly complicate, the store of historical knowledge of what happened to those victimized within Nazi Europe. Also, it is assumed that our historical consciousness of the Holocaust (as the partial grounds for constructing self and community) is amplified and complicated through the video presence of "survivors" conveying to us the details of their lives and evoking the memory of individuals, families, and communities that have been lost.

Yet, this "human dimension" is amply present in the multitude of diaries, memoirs, novels, poetry, photographs, songs, and visual art pertaining to the Holocaust—materials that may be read, heard, and/or viewed both for the historical information they provide, and the vivid, indelible, constructed *mise en scene* of experience rendered through descriptive detail, compelling figuration and narration, and the traumatic resonances that inform such practices of inscription. These inscriptions articulate a "visual" (and at times "tactile") sensibility enabling one to imaginatively experience the presence of the human lives and social suffering. So, given that the human dimension of history is certainly available in textual, image, and aural form, what is it then that video testimony specifically provides that such forms do not? To address this question, it is necessary to move the consideration of the audiovisual supplement to terms other than the logic of epistemological fulfillment. In saying this, I recognize that there are many historians who are fond of invoking Peter Geyl's (1955, 70) statement that "history is an argument without end." Nevertheless, I am taking the position that assumes historiographic work participates in a promissory project of an accumulated plentitude of knowledge, which presumes (although never reaches) a point of fulfillment. Concretely, this is manifest through both the accrual of various forms of documentation and the writing of narratives that make for a more complete and penetrating account of historical phenomena. On what other terms might we consider the concept of supplementation?

If there is something specific to the televisual mode of documentation, perhaps it is to be found in a notion of a supplement that, when added, shifts (perhaps disrupts) existing ways of reading historical documentation and writing narratives, opening the possibility of the transformation of contemporary frameworks of historical understanding. On such terms, the supplement would be an intervention that while still compensatory, rather than simply filling a void, potentially "hollows out" (Derrida, 1978, 212), ruptures, and transforms the authority and substance of the textual figures in place, thus, destabilizing the certainty of oneself as the one who knows, as one whose knowledge has depended on the authority of dominant discourses for framing an engagement with everyday life: past, present, and future.

On these terms, the supplement is not to be assessed on historiographic terms alone. Indelibly pedagogical in its force, it is not so much a question of "what" the audiovisual supplement is, but "when" the supplement is. That is, the supplement must be understood as a predicate form, as not having a determinate ontological substance, but rather a concept that references a particular communicative transitivity—a force that enables something to happen between people and across time and space. This makes the question of the supplement a question of pedagogy and pedagogy's politically transformative possibilities; that is, on these terms, we now ask when, and under what conditions, may the viewing of audiovisual testimony provoke a pedagogy of supplementation evoking new questions and conceptual reconsiderations with significant consequences for the social relations of everyday life. This means considering how supplementation might become implicated in the disorganization and reorganization of knowledge, opening up the dimension of time by making evident the spacio-temporal framing of the figurative representation of people and events as well as the conscious and unconscious affective and social investments in such framings.

In this regard, as part of my ongoing work on the pedagogical dimensions of practices of remembrance, I have been drawn to ask how video testimony might intervene in the way that one holds the historical memory of a particular time and place; that is, how video testimony might initiate a displacement—or at least a fundamental questioning—not only of what we think constitutes an adequate picture of another time and place, but also what we assume are the most appropriate forms for instantiating memory within particular practices of remembrance. What is at stake in such an intervention is a possible shift in one's way of reading, listening to, and viewing testamentary material, and as a consequence, the alterations in historical consciousness associated with such shifts. This would be the ground of opening new questions and perspectives, not only with regard to the adequacy of any given understanding of the past, but also as to how it is that we have been drawn to remember in particular ways, and in what ways the testamentary, transitive "face" of the past might "touch" us, breaking into our contemporary consciousness, opening it to new historical understandings, new forms of memorial significance, and new possibilities for thinking and acting in the present.

Toward the Audiovisual Supplement

In what follows, I will work through a detailed instance of what it might mean for video testimony to initiate a pedagogy of supplementation. As I have discussed here and in chapter six and seven, my colleagues and I at the University of Toronto have been developing new forms of study of, testamentary material, exploring ways of reading, listening to, and viewing the testamentary legacy of the ghettos of Vilna and Lodz (including memoirs, diaries, poems, photographs, art work, songs, official documents, audiovisual testimonies). In this context, I had begun to consider the frisson created by juxtaposing a constellation of written documents and photographic images referencing experiences in the Lodz ghetto with moments of video testimony drawn from interviewees who were interned in the ghetto at some point during the time between the winter of 1940 and the liberation of Lodz by Soviet troops in January 1945.

This constellation, the citation and arraignment of a finite set of testamentary texts and images, was intended to reveal my exposure to the address of testament and my attempt to be responsible to that address. In this collage of testamentary fragments, I endeavored to give expression to that which exceeded my horizon of expectations and, at times, struck me as either contradictory or, at least, significantly heterogeneous. Neither additive nor historically thematic, my juxtaposition was a performative knotting together of diverse moments of expression regarding life in the ghetto in order to impart something of a moment of study that left me unsettled, necessitating an examination of what frameworks might be limiting my encounter with traces of the past and the legacy they offered. In this sense, the juxtaposition announces and enacts my obligation to speak of my own astonishments, questions, and subsequent instruction; being open to unsettling surprise and further, the consideration of the basis of such a response.

Writing juxtapositions of this kind have become central to the form of study that I have termed "historiographic poetics." A reflective working with testamentary records that aspires to a practice of ethical remembrance and critical learning, historiographic poetics is to be understood as a situated social activity—a mode of working together to enact a new form of relation to historical material. Hence, the juxtaposition I created was initially intended for a study group of which I was a member. It was one moment in my ongoing attempt to engage the considerable material indexical to life in the Lodz ghetto and wrestle with its difficulties with regard to coming to know something of the lives of those who experienced it. It is this engagement, this education of our sensibilities, that Sam Wineburg (2001) calls "historical thinking." Wineburg suggests that "what allows us to come to know others is our distrust of our capacity to know them, a skepticism toward the extraordinary sense-making abilities that allow us to construct the world around us" (23–24). He argues that "the awareness that the contradictions we see in others may tell us more about ourselves is the seed of intellectual clarity . . . [a clarity needed to] go beyond our own image and the fleeting moment in human history into which we have been born" (24).[6]

Historiographic poetics is then, perhaps, one means of attending to the implications of Benjamin's insight that "in order for a part of the past to be touched by the present instance (*Aktualität*), there must be no continuity between them" (1999, 470). This seemingly paradoxical requirement demands a new, and perhaps less directive, form of answering to the responsibilities of memory. At stake is the possibility of working with and through the dialogical and transferential relations evoked by the transitive demands of testament. As Kelly Oliver observes in relation to historical thinking, "working-through is the process of articulating and diagnosing the ways in which we totalize or deny otherness; its aim is transforming our relations with others and otherness" (2000, 45).

It is on the above terms that I may have made some insight with regard to the supplementation possible within an engagement with video testimony. Thus, in setting forward the following juxtaposition and its associated commentary, I make no claim that it provides new historiographic insight or illustrates the determinate effects of all forms of audiovisual testimony. Rather, my interest is to simply note how the thought initiated by this juxtaposition has helped me to begin to think through the pedagogical force of the audiovisual. Each component of this juxtaposition I am about to discuss bears on the fact that in the streets the Lodz ghetto children sold sweets. These citations came together as I was exploring my curiosity and puzzlement regarding this aspect of life in the ghetto.[7] The juxtaposition, however, represents only one instance of unsettlement in my study of these sources, one in which I have registered the what and when of the audiovisual character of a video testimony that not only gave me pause with regard to my understanding of the images and written texts, but also opened the question of the cultural expectations through which the historical memories of the ghetto might be held.

The juxtaposition is composed of two photographs—one brief text excerpt from a memoir, and a short "clip" from a video testimony. When presented to study group members, I first provided written copies of the memoir excerpt, then the photographic images, and finally the video clip. In previous oral presentations of versions of this chapter, where there were severe time constraints, I simultaneously presented the photographic images and a recording of a colleague reading the memoir before presenting the video clip. This turned out to be unsatisfactory as it reduced the photographs to an illustration of the memoir. Each element of this juxtaposition is nonidentical, and meant to resonate in relation to each other. At the end of the chapter, I provide the memoir excerpt, the audio transcription of the video clip with accompanying "stills" that sample the video images that make up this excerpt, and one of the two photographs. The photographs are from the extraordinary collection of images illicitly taken in the Lodz ghetto by Mendel Grossman (1970), the text is from *Through the Window of My Home*—a memoir by Sara Selver-Urbach (1986)—and the excerpt of video testimony is taken from a two-and-a-half hour interview with Rita Hilton, which is archived at the United States Holocaust Memorial Museum.[8] This selection from Hilton's interview in no way represents the significance and character of her entire testimony. I did not choose it to be representative of her testimony, nor do I intend it to be a metonymic narrative of what life was like in the ghetto.[9] The transcription of Hilton's testimony, grasped as the life account it provides, is a document added to the historical record that, under the conventions of disciplinary rigor, must be subjected to a critical reading of its "writing," its moment of inscription in the oral text of testimony, and subsequent transcription into written form. But this not a matter of the audiovisual and its supplemental force. I am on the trail of something different here—something quite divergent from conventional historiographic considerations.

Desire and Proximity—The Disruptive
Dimensions of the Televisual

This extended commentary on my juxtaposition is to be understood as a practice that attempts not only to pursue what might be the force of an audiovisual supplement, but how this supplementation can open the touch of the past, transforming the possibilities of living within history. In the juxtaposition, there is, at first glance, a simple thematic alignment among the textual excerpt, photographic images, and the video clip. In other words, the extraction of these citations and my grouping them together is thematic, at least in the sense of their referent: all refer to children selling sweets in the ghetto. In this sense, I have engaged in the process of compiling of "pieces of the (historical) puzzle," the gathering together of documentation that might be thematically understood, and on these terms, either confirm or modify historical accounts of ghetto life. Yet, when this particular audiovisual segment of Hilton's interview becomes part of the collection, it does more than simply add to a store of previous documentation and understandings.

Selver-Urbach's writes in her memoir: "After the numerous 'Aktions', they [the children street vendors] vanished from the Ghetto streets. And though their mere presence had testified to unspeakable misery, dereliction and suffering, their disappearance turned our streets still gloomier." A presence of unspeakable misery disappears and is missed. It is clear that to Selver-Urbach the presence of children—even children of misery—offered something of a hopeful significance amid an indescribable existence. Grossman's images testify similarly. This, too, seems to be a sentiment conveyed in Hilton's testimony. Does Hilton offer in her video interview anything of significance with regard to our historical memory of the Lodz ghetto that is not available in the images and written text I have placed with this video excerpt? And, if it does, how can this be accounted for?

To address these questions, I will begin with a few comments on my initial response to this brief moment in Hilton's interview. While watching the entire interview, when it came to this segment, I was initially very much surprised and perplexed. It was not so much what Hilton says that was surprising, but how she said it.[10] I am referring here to the audiovisually conveyed performative recounting of her experience of children in the ghetto, offering viewers both an animated version of the sales-song of the sweet sellers and a humorous story of mispronunciation by a young boy who worked in one of the ghetto factories. At least at first viewing, I experienced this moment of the interview as evoking a "delightful," or better a "bittersweet" memory. Yet, as I had studied the written texts portraying the plight of street sellers of the Lodz ghetto, describing orphaned, starving children struggling to survive, there was nothing conveyed that might be considered delightful—nothing particularly bittersweet.

This frisson instantiated by the facial expressions and prosodic register of Hilton's testamentary address presented a problem that I attempted to explore, creating this juxtaposition as an initial mode through which I might begin to communicate (to those willing to join in study) my difficulty in stabilizing a clear understanding of what it was that I had heard in this testimony. Again, the point of this juxtaposition was to illuminate what I experienced as a moment of contradiction rather than negate or sublate the tension among instances of various modes of conveying something of ghetto life. Thus, the juxtaposition was meant as a starting point with which to consider the nonidentity of various testamentary records, attending to what might be learned in the spaces between these texts and images.

On the one hand, by placing the specific text, images, and video in a thematic relationship to each other, I placed a controlling frame on this portion of Hilton's testimony. In effect, I was reducing Hilton's excerpt to a relatively simple thematic in which incarcerated children simultaneously mark grotesque violence against the innocent and the remarkable hope that youth's innocence and resilience signifies. This reductive thematic has the potential for deflecting the difficulties in this excerpt and foreclosing thought, not only on the limits of my capacity for experiencing a portrayal of the everyday life in the ghetto, but also as a consideration of what makes this portion of her testimony so difficult hear, so difficult to bear witness to. Yet, on the other hand, this juxtaposition—taken as a moment in the process of study, a "reader response" that requires its own problematization—allowed me to open just such considerations.[11] Thus, I am, here, considering what it is in the audiovisual supplement in Hilton's video-based recounting of aspects of the lives of the children of the ghetto that makes apparent the limitations of my a priori interpretations and investments regarding such material, and, indeed, encourages me, requires me to consider modifying them?

Quite different from the titillating shock initiated by subjecting the senses to an immediacy that either is abject or makes no sense (which may be received as both horrifying and pleasurable), the experience of surprise always refers back to the substance and structure of anticipation and desire that evokes it. It is this anticipation and associated desire that Hilton's testimony helps bring forth; that is, her testimony was a violation of what I desired to see and hear, a violation of my own tacit anticipations of how the story of life in the Lodz ghetto would be told by one of those incarcerated. To the extent that these anticipations and desires are not just idiosyncratic, but anchored in a socially shared, contemporary form of historical consciousness, the excerpt of the testimony I presented in my juxtaposition may be considered "improper" or at least "unsuitable" for Holocaust memory, destabilizing the authority of its author and threatening to diminish not only the magnitude of Nazi violence against Jewish existence, but the tremendous loss conveyed in testimony, consequently risking public anxiety and confusion.[12]

Thus, what is at stake in this audiovisual supplement is not simply the reflexive consideration of how my engagement with Holocaust video testimony might be influenced by my assimilation of cultural expectations regarding how such accounts might look and sound. If we pursue the pedagogical force of the supplement, it is necessary to work through the basis of such anticipations. One might suggest that my anticipation of testimony was invested with a desire for an account consistent with a particular dominant representational trope, specifically what David Slocum has termed the pervasive melodramatic structure of North American Holocaust memory—one shaped by heightened emotion and moral polarization. Melodrama, of course, is not dependent on visual representation but as Slocum (2003) reminds us is "a mode of organizing experience and telling stories that emerged in the early nineteenth century novel and popular theatre and has remained central to popular cultural narratives in the twentieth". In his work on the incorporation of survivor video testimony into popular documentaries, Slocum offers that in video testimony, the viewer is addressed by the images on the screen so as to heighten her or his experience of pathos. Underscoring the audiovisual gestures that convey heightened emotionalism, he suggests that these televisual moments do not necessarily elicit pity, but crucially lend an aura of "authenticity" and unmediated access to the survivor experience. Such moments in testimony constitute a series of culturally constituted anticipated performatives that may be taken as symptoms of survivors coping with or working through trauma while reconstituting self and memory during the process of providing testimony. What might be at stake for viewers in such a structure of anticipation?

Building on Slocum's insights, I am suggesting that viewers often anticipate and desire that the audiovisual performative character of testimony be fulfilled in certain ways, once one grasps that what one is watching is a "survivor interview." In this sense, we might be said to not only have a cognitive structure of perceptual expectations but a specific form of eidetic desire, that is, a desire for a particular figural form of temporal image within video testimony that is recognizable within the frames used to make sense of our world. In this respect, the melodramatic structure of much of contemporary historical memory of the Holocaust provokes an eidetic desire, which, with regard to audiovisual testimony, defines "preferred" or at least satisfactory temporal images recognizable within the frameworks within which we constitute our historical memories and negotiate our identities. If we are to understand the very substance and structure of one's historical consciousness as itself a historical phenomena subject to the social processes that normalize specific discourses and the contingencies of the psychosocial consequences of the circulation of such discourses, we then must pursue a consideration of the constitution of this consciousness as the grounds of our memorial expectations and desires.

Marianne Hirsch (2001) argues that the dominant frames of the remembrance of the Holocaust have already been cast by a relatively small number of well-known photographs depicting violence and violation—either those photographs taken by the Nazis or the troops that liberated the concentration camps. Rather than becoming desensitized to these images or dismissing them as "clichés, empty signifiers, that protect us from the event," she argues that they are fundamental to existing frameworks of Holocaust memory. Her argument is that these photographs, in making present an inconceivable violence, initiate a rupture that has considerable significance for historical consciousness. While Hirsch may downplay the importance of literature and film in the establishment of contemporary memory of the Holocaust (for me, more than photographs, it was reading Andre Schwartz-Bart (2000) and Ka-Tzetnik (1977) that was pivotal), her point is applicable to a range of documents depicting genocide and mass violence, documents that while rendering a picture of an event are unable to prevent its meaning from unraveling. Because they are present to us but inconceivable, such representations resist assimilation to the terms of meaningful experience and consequently compulsively return as a psychic break. As Kaja Silverman suggests, on such terms, "to remember other people's memories is to be wounded by their wounds . . . to let the traces of other people's struggles, passions, pasts, resonate within one's own past and present, and destabilize them" (1996, 185). The implication here is that for us—the generations who have come after the event—the fundamental structure of historical consciousness of the Holocaust is not just melodramatic, but also traumatic. As a consequence, Hirsch suggests, it is as trauma that such memories enact a particular articulation of history and identification. And furthermore, to maintain this articulation, which realizes a particular form of connectedness with past events, one requires the circulation of a delimited range of historical representations—images and narratives that return the rupture, the incomprehensibility of genocide and mass violence. This spells problems for the viewing of Rita Hilton's testimony, particularly in those moments in which her telling cannot be contained in these well-established structures of historical consciousness. Even more so, the juxtaposition of the excerpt from Hilton with the photographs and text puts forward a contradictory structure of testamentary traces incommensurable with an investment in a melodramatic and traumatic historical consciousness. The memoir and the photographs depicting children selling sweets obtain significance in an already structured historical consciousness, one that has little place for a video testimony which, in the flow its narrative, at times, evokes the possibility of pleasure in the ghetto.

The very possibility that there is an eidetic desire mobilized at the moment of viewing Holocaust video testimony, indeed, requires some caution with regard to the place of such testimony in the development of historical consciousness. At minimum, it is necessary to guard against ceding historical authority to accounts in which those identified as "the victims of history" meet the socially constituted expectations of how they should speak or act on videotape. But we should also be cautious of privileging exemplary excerpts of testimony with the result of flattening of memory, either for fear that its moral pedagogic force may be compromised by the circulation of certain images and accounts that do not fit the melodramatic structure of Holocaust memory, or in aid of the identifications made within repetition of the traumatization instantiated by the compulsive return to stories of unambiguous victimization.

Dwelling within the Televisual

Part of what I'm arguing is that the pedagogical force of the audiovisual supplement puts forward a consideration of eidetic desire and its consequences. But, you might argue, the possibility of an eidetic desire is not limited to video, and certainly may exist in relation to the specific media of photographs and even literary texts. Accepting this point means we still need to further pursue the singularity of the medium of video testimony, both to clarify the force of its supplementation and how it might come to complicate eidetic desires specific to this medium. To do this, it seems to me, requires a theorization of the televisual, what I understand to be the production of a particular audiovisual experience of an unmediated "being there." In the context of video testimony, this takes the form of the virtual making present, bringing into presence a figure whose corporeality and narrative performance might elicit a series of ethical and pedagogical considerations. These considerations include an exploration of the possibilities and limits of viewer response structured within elicited identifications and transferential relations, as well as the study of those conditions that foster the problematic spectacularization of the video image within a logic, which suggests the equivalence of various instances of testimony as these stand for and illustrate a specific theme. Such spectacularization is the logic that underwrites much of the use of video testimony in documentary films such as Steven Spielberg's *Last Days* and Joshua Greene's *Witness: Voices from the Holocaust*. However, quite differently, the televisual being there may also initiate a consideration of those conditions that foster the opening up of difficult questions of viewer responsibility in the face of that which is not fully assimilated within existing frameworks of cultural memory.

To the degree that the televisual image is associated with the live broadcast, it retains an aura of immediacy and directness of an address. Indeed, this was the production premise of one of the very first television programs to address the question of historical experience. Aired during the 1950s, the program titled *You Are There* provided mock "on the spot interviews" with actors playing historical figures in the midst of undergoing events that had lasting historical significance. The conceit of this program was that it brought us closer to the center of the experience of these events.[13] In the frame of the experienced immediacy of the televisual image, a videotape recording is commonly received as an archived record of the video image that was coincident with the live event it conveyed. In addition to its association with the experience of "live" events, another key aspect of the televisual is the experience of duration initiated by watching a video. To consider this specifically, in the context of video testimony, what such video initiates is a viewing of a conversation that unfolds over time. In this viewing, those watching the tape are positioned literally as a witness, a third within the triangle of interviewee, interviewer, and the viewing audience. Even though the interviewer is off-camera, the gaze of the interviewee most often implies the presence of another who has initiated and sustained the occasion of speaking. As the viewer takes the position of the camera, the *mise en scene* of video testimony always includes three actors.

The video image produces a synchronous movement of sound and image such that a dynamic figural presence becomes manifest over the course of interviews that may last as long as two or three hours. As this presence changes over time—shifts position, grows weary, expresses different emotional states, and so on—as viewers we experience ourselves not just as being there, but "being with" the interviewee as he or she makes their way through the difficulties of speaking of experiences undergone during the Shoah. This is a moment in which the televisual annihilates itself as a medium, where the audiovisual testimony is no longer a sign but a thing-in-itself.[14] This sets the condition for the fantasy that the televisual image is direct and direct for me (Esch, 1993), producing a spatial sense of virtuality within which a viewer relates to a screen image as an individuated presence signifying to her or him through the enactment of the narrative of a story of subjection and survival. This virtuality of being with the person on screen—of participating in a form of televisual inhabitation—provides viewers with a sense of the palpable usually far in excess of the photograph and text. This palpability is a form of surplus or excess that occurs as a result of viewing the televisual interview, a viewing in which a nonspatialized, existential distance is both established and overcome. In this sense, the viewing of the interview on screen is a temporal opening in which something can be near and far; I recognize the image on the screen as exemplifying and confirming my existing experience and suppositions regarding the Holocaust and those who survived it, while still offering an unarticulated excess uncontainable within my available frames for understanding. But rather than being a traumatic rupture that serves as a point of identification, this excess offers a different set of possibilities.

While it may be said that the experience of *being with* may indeed draw one closer, it is not to the center of the historical experience of the Shoah, but to the interviewee in the immediacy of the interview. Yet, this relation of proximity is double-sided. While one may feel closer to image on the screen, this televisual experience also creates a condition within which the experience of alterity and distance may come forth. On these terms of response and responsibility, terms that Levinas (1998) insists are necessary for a relation of proximity, the narration of experience undoes itself. This, indeed, is what I experienced in relation to my viewing of Hilton's video testimony. What interested me about that moment in which she speaks of the children in the ghetto is that what was spoken (to me, as I experienced *being with* her) was far in excess of what she said. This is not just a matter of the non-textual pragmatics of communication, but what Levinas terms the excess of the saying of the said within a televisual relation of being with developed over the time of the unfolding interview. Her words in the video testimony (aligned thematically with other testamentary documents within the logic of historiographic rationality) bore a surplus that, as Michael Levine suggests,[15] exceeded the very opposition of life and death, requiring for its translation a nonexistent language beyond the bounds of my resources for easily repeating here the addressed message sent in Hilton's testimony. In other words, melodramatic forms of memory, despite their implication in psychic demands of traumatic repetition, cannot contain what is potentially available in the supplement of video testimony. This is a doubled, deeper understanding of my experience of surprise (when I first viewed the segment of Hilton's testimony under discussion here). While the first significance of my surprise may be traced to how the testimony failed to meet my expectations, there is a second significance, rooted in the plentitude of the interview, the experience that Hilton's testimony contains more than one can hold. It is this surplus and its concomitant requirements that destabilized my understanding of her testimony and its relation to the testamentary texts I had been reading. It is why the video clip is not reducible to the text and photographs I have placed alongside it.

Furthermore, as I have tried to show through the commentary on my juxtapositonal response to this video in relation to other instances of testamentary documentation, it is this destablization of understanding that can provide the viewer of video testimony with both the occasion and challenge of beginning to speak/write to others about the project of remaking one's relation to the past. This endeavor is an opening beyond the acknowledgment of the realities and difficulties of reading image/texts, which trace the actualities of the lives of others. It is a demand and responsibility for thought instigated by finding oneself, not just receiving the text as information, but positioned so that in order to preserve the memory of those lives,[16] one must enter into conversation with still others regarding the grounds of one's epistemological limits. In a similar vein, Levine suggests that in order to take responsibility for the very excesses of witnesses' stories, bearing testimony must be viewed as an incomplete act requiring a "witness to the witness," one who might "hold open the very space of translation" altering this space into another scene of witnessing. The very possibility of such a translation, such speaking/writing, is no mere retranscription of information. This witness to the witness is the enactment of thinking without the solidifying over-determination of meaning and the refusal of contradiction (Simon, 2000). It rests on the opening of a register through which to think the limits of testament and the limits of thought, and hence the limits of language and the limits of self. One is required to speak/write on behalf of the Other to others, and in addition is also required to consider and work within the stakes, issues, and challenges implicated in the practice of making a relation with the testament of another.

The audiovisual supplement, then, occurs in that moment when one is enacting a performative, praxiological conception of historical consciousness, very much dependent on opportunities to speak/write to others. In this sense, the supplement "happens" with a pragmatic conception of knowing. This places the very possibility of supplementation in the orbit of Franz Rosenzweig's framework of "new thinking" where in the "method of speech appears in place of the method of thought," a difference that does not "lie in loud or quiet, [but] rather in the need for another, and what is the same, in taking time" (cited in Gibbs 2000, 231).[17] Knowing that is not a timeless attunement to timeless truths but rather a temporal process needing others not only takes time but is risky as well (Gibbs, 2000, 229, 232). One must risk time, effort, exposure, and the unwillingness or incapacity of others to verify the significance of speech/text. As Gibbs notes, "Rosenzweig made theory risky in order to preserve the futurity of meaning . . . this leads to the problem of how to use signs to indicate what is properly pragmatic: the qualities of signifying and not the sign" (248). Key here is the notion that one is to respond to the call of the witness, but in the context of others to whom one is also responsible. Such a form of knowing is the basis of a community of memory in which relationships with others (concretely expressed in the dynamics of action–thought) are integral to what it means to found a public world on one's responsibilities to others.

If it is possible to speak of hope at all,[18] perhaps, then this is the most hopeful component of the audiovisual supplement of video testimony, that which requires one to implicate oneself in this relation to the video witness, respecting one's necessary distance from, while moving toward, the alterity of the Other. Rather than simply recycling a traumatic fixation, which serves to shield against thought in the service of identification, video testimony also offers the possibility of a fall into thought. While this might begin with a critical engagement with existing forms of historical consciousness that serve as the basis for and limit of one's own comprehension and investment in the understanding of past events, this thought must move beyond remembrance as a resource for the psychosocial demands of identification in order to confront the complex, contradictory multiplicity of human experience within histories of genocide and mass state violence. It is not that we can do away with the acutalities of trauma and identification in our engagement with a violent past, but rather we must learn new ways to integrate that violence into the structure of historical consciousness, ways that might teach us something "new"—something we do not yet know about being human. In this respect, the supplementary promise of video testimony lies in our continual exploration of its pedagogical potential. Thus, in my view, what one might experience as the incommensurable relation between video testimony, photographic images, and written text is best taken as an incitement to study and speech, to enjoin with others in taking on the problem of receiving that legacy bequeathed to us within multimodal archives that bring together various forms of expression of the actualities of social existence. Indeed, perhaps such an incitement is a condition of possibility for what Derrida's terms the "spectral messiancity" of the archive—a condition that might open participation to the "very singular experience of the (archival) promise."

Appendix: *Juxtaposition (Children Selling Sweets in the Ghetto)*

An Excerpt from Sara Selver-Urbach (1986) Through the
Window of My Home: Recollections from the Lodz Ghetto.

Many children had been cast out . . . in the Ghetto streets and were
forced to fend for themselves. Some . . . tried to get along with
singing, others tried their hands at "commerce," filling the streets with
their shrill cries while offering their miserable wares: "Saccharine,
genuine saccharine" their thin, reedy voices merged together as in a
children's choir. The children who sold a funny kind of sweet—God
knows what it was made of—emphasized its "dimensions," since size and
quantity were of the utmost importance: "One for only five pfening!"
They would shout, "Just look at the big chucks, the huge lumps!" Who
can forget those pitiful waifs who loitered usually around Brzezinska
street, the site of their "commercial ventures?" After the numerous
"Aktions," they vanished from the Ghetto streets. And though their
mere presence had testified to unspeakable misery, dereliction and
suffering, their disappearance turned our streets still gloomier.

Of all these street waifs, I remember particularly the "Glücks,"
perhaps because they appeared frequently on our corner, and perhaps
because their sorrowful singing touched my heart. I've forgotten most
of their song, but the words that I still recall blend perfectly with my
memory of those two little boys.

> There is boundless luck in this world
> Though not for me or for you . . .
> Or is my end that near?
>
>> I've never known luck in my life
>> Nor a moment of friendship
>> No hope was promised me—
>> Oh, where are you, my luck?
>
> Fortune, you have cheated me so badly
> I've been waiting for you so longingly,
> Or is my end that near?
>
>> Will the sun still shine for me?
>> Will something good still happen to me?
>> Or will my luck go on mourning over me
>> Sadly and heart brokenly?

The song seemed to stick to the boys as though they had become one
with the words that expressed so perfectly their wretched and hopeless
existence. For though they would sing other songs as well, all of us
thought of them and remembered them for this one song: "Glück."

Transcript: Rita Hilton (USHMM RG 50.030*002)
(Tape 2 02:36)—Cited with Permission of the United States
Holocaust Memorial Museum

Q: When you would take walks, what would you see?

A: People very often, you saw people lying on the ground. They found
    bodies on the street. The children, they used to sell saccharine [smiling]
    and there were children, there was a little chant, the little children
    would sell saccharine, saccharine, *fifn* for a mark, or *drie* for a mark, and
    that's three for, for one mark. This was almost like a, like a ghetto song,
    those little children selling. Children were working. My mother was
    working in a factory where children were working. I don't know what
    jobs they had, sorting something, putting something together . . . little
    children. And I remember once she told a story about a little boy and
    he said he saw a goose, but he said it in Jewish, and he says I saw a *gants*,
    and he said not something whole, a gants!, he meant a goose and he

Figure 8.1 Video image sampling of interview with Rita Hilton—reproduced with the permission
Courtesy of the United States Holocaust Memorial Museum, Washington, DC, USA

Figure 8.2   Mendel Grossman Photograph—Children selling sweets in the Lodz ghetto (I)—reproduced with the permission of Ghetto Fighters' House Museum, Israel

started flapping with his wing and trying to say what the goose was. And he saw a *gants*, and my mother said the eyes were big because it was an animal. And even the little children, I mean the ones who were finally eventually, maybe were evacuated, but at one time they had little factories for them. Even they had to work to get a little soup. Life was in . . . there were wives who fought with husbands about food. The husbands would threaten wives or steal. People would steal the food from each other. People would sell the bread for cigarettes and then they were *starving*. I mean, it was *so* difficult to live. (Tape 2 04:16)

Figure 8.1 shows the video image sampling of the interview with Rita Hilton. Figure 8.2 is a photograph by Mendel Grossman of children selling sweets in the Lodz ghetto.

NOTES

Introduction   Remembering Otherwise: Civic Life and the Pedagogical Promise of Historical Memory

1. Weisel's remarks were made during the speech "God and Man On Trial," sponsored by the Canadian Friends of Hebrew University, Toronto, Ontario, May 20, 1993.

Chapter One   The Pedagogy of Remembrance and the Counter-Commemoration of the Columbus Quincentenary

1. Speaking of the cultural activity spawned by the counter-commemorative movement, artist James Luna made this point abundantly clear stating that in 1992, "curators want a certain kind of Indian and a certain kind of Indian art. They want you to be angry, they want you to be talking it up. It's the same rush to say let's have a multiculturalism show. Now everyone is saying let's have an Indian show or let's have a colonialism show. So when people call me [to participate] I have to ask why didn't you call me before? You're calling me now but are you going to call me in '93?" (Durland, 1991, 34–39).

2. The issue here is not that there is evidence of previous landfalls by other mariners prior to the arrival of Columbus but rather how Columbus's landfall is to be understood. The voyage of Columbus was indeed significantly different from any prior contact with the peoples of "the Americas" in that it initiated a set of events that were a significant turning point in the lives of millions of people. Whether or not Columbus made first contact is a deflection of what is centrally up for revision: the nature of the foundational event for the contemporary "civilization" in which we live.

3. Translation of this passage by Michael Hoechsman—personal communication.

4. Of course, the question is not just whether we are going to listen, but how. What horror is to be grasped as we "read with hands over eyes peering through the gaps made by our fingers" (Reynolds, 1991). This question of how one listens to, reads, and views testamentary expressions of systemic mass violence will be a pervasive theme throughout this book.

5. This does not, however, explain why in the 1800s certain groups, most notably Irish Catholics and Italian immigrants in the United States, sought to enshrine Columbus as the discoverer of the New World. See Trouillot (1990).

6. This is not simply a matter of representing Columbus in his historical context. To take seriously questions that pose queries about the motives, justifications, and assumptions of historical actors have been one of the dictums of historical research. Thus, the well-known importance of the search for an "imaginative understanding" of the historical actor. This seems like a positive step although, by focusing on individual actors, such work may produce a distancing: a "them/not me" character to the study of history. It quite often becomes a way of avoiding any serious educative dialectic between the past and the present.

7. Understanding the rights claimed by the crown of Castile does not mean accepting these rights, but, rather, is essential to tracing the specific supremacist logics of the European conquest and colonialization.

8. For commentary on the problems of rendering of de Vitoria as a progressive legal humanist, see Todorov (1984, 149–150, 181–182). For broader assessments of de Vitoria as one of the founding fathers of international law, see Scott (1934), Grisel (1976), and Padgen (1982).

Chapter Two   Pedagogy and the Call to Witnessing Marc Chagall's *White Crucifixion*

1. The *White Crucifixion* first appeared publically in a photograph published in a 1939 issue of the Paris based *Cahier d'Art* and was exhibited at La Galerie MAI during January and February of 1940, four months prior to the fall of Paris to Hilter's army.
2. As Michael Bodemann has pointed out to me, while referencing events that were happening to Jews in Germany, all Chagall's images concern the world of the *Ostjuden* (Eastern European Jewry). Bodemann sees this as a dual displacement: the suffering/helpless Christ associated with Jewish suffering and the Eastern Jewish suffering associated with German Jewish persecution.
3. As is well known, Chagall was anything but a realist painter. A difference in the photograph of the *White Crucifixion* published in 1939 and that taken at its first exhibition in early 1940 shows that the sign hung on the man in the lower left corner of the painting originally included the words "*Ich bien Jude*" (I am a Jew). There are several speculations as to why Chagall erased these words for the 1940 exhibition, one of which is that he felt that the scenes of persecution were too literal.
4. The translation here is drawn from two sources: from Awad Ibrahim (personal communication) and from the one provided by Amishai-Maisels.
5. For brief discussions of efforts to include remembrance of the Nazi oppression of Romani, as well as gays and lesbians in the United States Holocaust Memorial Museum, see Linenthal, 1995.
6. I refer here to the important work of scholars such as Gregory Baum, James Crossen, Roy and Alice Eckhart, Darrell Fasching, Paul Knitter, Franklin Littell, John Pawlikowski, Karl Plank, Johan-Baptist Metz, James Moore, Rosemary Reuther, and Paul van Buren. For a useful discussion of a number of these and other authors, as well as pivotal reading of aspects of the gospel of Matthew, see James F. Moore (1989).
7. What is well recognized in this work is that a causative factor is *not* a cause. Fully acknowledged are the complex, intersecting determinations that historian's have suggested as explanations for the Shoah. However, as theologians addressing the Christian community, their emphasis has been to clarify and confront the implications of the complicity of Church doctrine in the formulation of the *Endlösung*.

Chapter Three   Remembering Obligation: Witnessing Testimonies of Historical Trauma

1. The elaboration of different modes of apprehending testimony would require distinguishing practices of mimicry, voyeurism, and spectatorship from witnessing. The former practices depend upon divorcing the testimonial referents and forms of emplotment from the transactional enunciation of lived engagements with the past. As a result of this splitting, testimony is heard or read as a phenomena to be rendered meaningful within classification and analysis, or it becomes a source of compulsive fascination. Rarely do such modes of apprehension call into question the epistemological and ethical frames through which one apprehends history.
2. An example of such commentary on this incident can be found in Langer "Preliminary Reflections on Using Videotaped Interviews in Holocaust Education" in *Elements of Time*, pp. 291–297.
3. Open for speculation here is whether or to what extent the woman's credibility as a witness may have been influenced by gender dynamics, which may have structured the historian's apprehension of her testimony. In raising this issue, we are underscoring the problematic practice of universalizing discussions of testimony and witnessing. How one gives testimony and how such testimony is heard or seen, as transactional practices, will always be infused with consequences of the social markings rendered by power relations that structure difference on terms such as gender, class, and race.
4. The Hebrew term *kavannah* has no simple English equivalent. In traditional use, one may speak about the extent and nature of one's *kavannah* during the act of prayer or when doing *mitzvot* (performing commandments).

5. For a similar list, see Johnson and Stern Strom, *Elements of Time* (1989).

6. This implies a relation to a text that is a "caress." "The caress consists in seizing upon nothing, in soliciting what ceaselessly escapes its form toward a future never future enough, in soliciting what slips away as though it were not yet. It searches, it forages. It is not an intentionality of disclosure but a search: a movement unto the invisible" (Levinas, 1969, 257–258). See also Ouaknin (1995, 220).

7. Remembrance is one communal practice addressed to the overcoming of temporality; another is communal law, particularly the enshrinement in legal codes of social forms, responsibilities, and injunctions. When the State or religious hierarchies attempt to mobilize and define practices of remembrance through such enshrinement, remembrance risks slipping into closed thematic frameworks that provide little room for the double attentiveness necessary to witnessing. Indeed, taken to the extreme, commemoration on this basis becomes integral to the articulation of a fascist public sphere.

8. As Sharon Todd (1977) suggests, "difference and disparity go hand in hand as conceptual tools, for without maintaining a notion of disparity of the material conditions which structure differences *differently*, difference can—and often does—collapse into an individualized and psychologistic rendering of what is often labeled as "diversity."

9. The pedagogical mindfulness required when one is working with or within a community of memory also extends to the recognition that students carry their own particular sets of histories in their encounters with testimony. In this sense, historical memory is always a mix of public history and personal remembrances. Given this understanding, in certain circumstances, those who carry memories of personal violence and abuse may transfer these memories and their accompanying emotions onto their apprehension of testimonies of historical trauma. Such transference may, consequently, create forms of identification with victimization that specifically structure what might be heard in testimony but also collapse some of the necessary defenses people have built up to contain prior traumatic experiences. In a similar vein, when people's lives appear full of events beyond their control and they seem to have few constructive resources for effectively dealing with everyday problems, without considerable work, helping students (personally and collectively) to develop such resources, testimonies of mass violence, and destruction may simply amplify feelings of loss of agency and hope. The result may then be an increase in cynicism that underwrites a fixation on one's own immediate needs and interests and a refusal of the obligations that testimonies attempt to initiate. Situations such as these, if not successfully addressed, may signal the practical and pedagogical limits of such encounters with testimony.

Chapter Four Beyond the Logic of Emblemization: Remembering and Learning from the Montréal Massacre

Thanks go to Tara Goldstein who took risks with us with very little by way of assurance, and for the cooperation and enthusiasm of the B.Ed. students in 3161/3210, without whom this essay would have been impossible to write.

1. The letter, detailing antifeminist sentiments and a "hit list" of prominent Québec women, was released by authorities a few weeks prior to the first anniversary of the murders. It was first printed in *La Presse*, a French-language daily newspaper in Montréal, November 24, 1990. It is reprinted in English (translation) in Malette and Chalouh (1991).

2. The anniversary markings in 1995, e.g., additionally included a women-only act of civil protest in downtown Toronto against continuing cuts to services for assaulted women, and a call to action by an alliance of feminists on university campuses in British Columbia, calling for province-wide demonstrations against, and institutional accountability for, the violence against women that continue in universities.

3. Documentation of memory has taken many forms. These forms include art shows such as *Art against Violence against Women: A Personal Statement* (Halifax, Nova Scotia: Eye Level Gallery, 1990); *Don't Remain Silent* (Toronto, Ontario: The Woman's Common, 1990); *Threnody* (Vancouver, B.C.: The Lateral Gallery, 1990). Poetic responses include: Allison Campbell, "Not One Step Back," *Contemporary Verse 2*, *14*, No. 4 (Spring 1992), 26; Maggie Helwig, "Flashpoint," *Matriart: A Canadian*

Feminist Art Journal 1, No. 1 (Spring 1990), 12; Rita Kohli, "Musings of a South Asian Woman in the Wake of the Montréal Massacre," *Canadian Woman Studies* 11, No. 4 (1991), 13–14. Memorialization in video form includes Gerry Rogers, *After the Montréal Massacre* (Montreal: National Film Board, Studio D, 1991); Maureen Bradley, *Reframing the Montréal Massacre* (Toronto: Full Frame Film and Video Distribution, 1995); Ling Chiu, *Tee Hee Hee* (Vancouver: Moving Images Distribution, 1996).

4. Left open to question, however, is whether this historical framing also enhances the likelihood of marking and bringing to the fore other pervasive acts of such violence, since a risk of emblemization is that it absorbs into its structure the specificities of other occurrences, diminishing what it is that can be learned in remembrance. This is a risk to which we will return.

5. This response was largely mobilized by women, drawing on feminist analyses of violence against women. While we do not forget this in our writing, we are cautious about evoking the label "feminist response" as if it referenced a singular and cohesive position. This is not simply a matter of being generally attentive to language. Although the arguments of this paper are calling into question positions of remembrance of the Massacre that have been understood as feminist, they do so not from a disavowal of the horror of violence against women. Instead, we are interested in contemplating other terms for remembering the event of the Massacre in the hope of coming to terms with these horrors more fully.

6. "The Act of a Madman or a Tragedy? [Headline]," *The Globe and Mail* (December 6, 1990).

7. Barbara Frum in "The Journal," December 7, 1989 in Lakeman (1992, 98).

8. We might note that this is a practice that risks a terrible echo to Lepine's act itself: for he did not target fourteen specific and particular women, he killed the women as emblems themselves—emblems, on his terms, of feminism. Our thanks to Nicholas Burbules for drawing this point to our attention.

9. For examples of this position, see Marusia Bociurkiw (1990, 6–10) and Caffyn Kelley (1995, 6–11).

10. We wonder, however, if the issue of repetition is perhaps an indicator that the initial reading of the Massacre as an act of violence against women has been losing the force of its meaning as this emblematic structure becomes more and more commonplace. What is being lost, we sense, is the legacy being bequeathed in this memorial stance, and is the reason why we feel some urgency in writing now.

11. There were thirty eight students in the class—thirty one women and seven men. Most students were in their early-to-mid-twenties. The class appeared to be predominately White; however, its ethnocultural composition was not recorded.

12. This line comes directly from the Wyrd Sisters's song, "This Memory," which contains lyrics referencing the likely substitutability of other women for those murdered, ending with the lines: "don't let us lose this memory/because it could've been you or me" (on The Wyrd Sisters, *Leave a Little Light* [sound recording] (Manitoba: Oh Yah! Records, 1992). This theme of instantiating substitutability within the event structure of the Massacre is not limited to this particular song, but has been prevalent across feminist memorial response. We note, also, the installation series, "Murdered by Misogyny," by artist Lin Gibson, which paired the names of the women murdered in Montréal with the names of fourteen living women, anchoring the second list with the phrase, "guilty as charged" (Yeo, 1991, 8–11). Working slightly differently within the same remembrance pedagogy, Pati Beaudoin created a horizontal panel of photographs of the fourteen murdered women, completing the panel with a mirror (installed as part of the show, *Don't Remain Silent*). For a sustained discussion of each of these works, see Sharon Rosenberg (1997).

13. Obviously, normativity is not singular—what is expected/anticipated for women in different positions and locations may differ substantially.

14. In exploring what learning might be staged in and through traumatic awakening, we, of course, recognize that such awakenings may be too troubling to be consciously sustained. In other words, the "shock of the known," the return of the repressed, will inevitably be repressed again. In this essay, we set out the pedagogical significance of traumatic awakening; however, it is beyond the bounds of the essay to pursue the question of what social and institutional forms might sustain moments of pedagogical engagement with such awakenings.

15. What is at stake in these questions is quite different from those instances where school authorities have provided trauma counselling for students who have experienced, in their own schools, the aftershocks of mass violence (such as at the Columbine High School).

16. We are using the term "survivor" here not in the usual feminist sense of "the survivor"—an identity category that marks a state of being. Rather, what we want to underscore through our deployment

of this term is that an awakening into survivorship is an awakening into a relationship not only with the dead, but also with others who have experienced the Massacre as a trauma.

17. We note here the importance of recent scholarship that is calling attention to the ways in which certain feminist discourses regarding violence against women become inadvertently complicit with structures of intimidation and subordination. See in particular the work of Marcus (1992), Brown (1995), and Burton (1999).

18. Invoked here as relevant to questions of testament and witness is Levinas's distinction between the saying and the said (Levinas, 1998). This distinction is discussed more fully in Chapter Three.

Chapter Five   The Touch of the Past: The Pedagogical Significance of a Transactional Sphere of Public Memory

1. To speak of touch here is to emphasize the primacy of a response that reveals the vulnerability of the self to the approach of another. As Wyschogrod has suggested, "touch is not a sense at all; it is in fact a metaphor for the impingement of the world as a whole upon subjectivity . . . to touch is to comport oneself not in opposition to the given but in proximity with it" (cited in Jay, 1994, 557).

2. As Appadurai (1996) comments "sentiments whose greatest force is in their ability to ignite intimacy into a political sentiment and turn locality into a staging ground for identity, have become spread over vast and irregular spaces as groups move, yet stay linked to one another through sophisticated media capabilities." It is, perhaps, ironic to note that the practices of globalization have made many diasporic formations increasingly stable and the central loci of learning and identification.

3. This is not to say that an observer operating with a spectatorial sensibility is without obligations. One may be obligated within the norms of historiography, by principles of research ethics, or by a series of a priori affiliations and identifications, which requires attentiveness to what another is attempting to communicate. However, none of these obligations are founded in that instant of regard in which I face another who in that moment addresses me.

4. One viewer, upon seeing a videotape of Ila Bussidor providing testimony to the Royal Commission, exclaimed: what is new in this? What am I do with this story? Haven't we heard all this before? The Sayisi Dene relocation is just another version of what happened at Davis Inlet (referring to another incidence of forced removal initiated by the Canadian government).

5. For an extensive example of how the normative structure of judgments, mobilized when listening to testimony, limit what can be heard, see Chapter three "Remembering Obligation: Witnessing Testimonies of Historical Trauma."

Chapter Six   Witness as Study: The Difficult Inheritance of Testimony

1. Conformism, with regard to practices of remembrance, is most often linked to those social forms that seek to regulate the relation between identity and memory. That such regulation serves a practical political function there is no doubt. Also, groups attempting to secure new practices of remembrance in the face of centuries of suppression of silenced histories may, indeed, have good reason to suspect the call to a continual reopening of remembrance.

2. Both history and memorialization may be present in historical representations such as films or novels. That the pedagogies implicit in these very different forms of memory may actually work against each other is often ignored in discussing the use of such forms for learning about the past. For a discussion of different pedagogies associated with the use of audiovisual testimony in public memory, see Simon (1998).

3. For a brief introduction to this radical character of remembrance, see Paul Mendes-Flor's (1987) discussion of Gershom Scholem's project of moving beyond the impasse of historicism by "overcoming history through history."

4. Our pronominal variation throughout this chapter is quite deliberate. While the use of the term "we" references our collaborative voice, following Levinas, the singular form is used to emphasize the specific character of responsibility as that which only "I" can enact in my response to the other. See, e.g. Levinas (1991).

5. On the history of Jewish Vilna and the extensiveness and significance of that which was lost in the Shoah, see Roskies (1984) and Ran (1974).

6. During these months, under indescribably horrific conditions and constant threat of individual execution and mass elimination, the Jewish population reorganized itself into a complex and multifaceted community. The ghetto developed its own economic order, health policies, and services, and a vast and varied educational and cultural life. Also, various groups formed that vied for public support as to how best to meet the constant threat to daily existence enforced by Nazi policy and practice. These included those who were part of the ghetto administration and those operating "underground." This period of so-called "stability" lasted for approximately sixteen months. In June 1943, Himmler gave the order for the final deposition of Lithuanian Jewry. The Vilna Ghetto was liquidated on September 23, 1943. Most of its remaining inhabitants were transported to work camps and then subsequently to concentration camps. The city of Vilna was liberated by Soviet troops on July 13, 1944.

7. For a comprehensive history of the history of the Vilna Ghetto, see Arad (1980).

8. Without denigrating the importance of the active pursuit of retributive and/or compensatory justice, in our view, situating the memory of the events of the Shoah in judicial or economic terms does not exhaust their significance.

9. In saying this, our very first steps toward a remembrance of the Vilna Ghetto already begin to rub against the grain of much contemporary Holocaust commemoration. As this chapter argues, hope cannot be reduced to the affirmation of continuity as, e.g., in the collective contemporary singing of "*Zog Nit Keyn Mol*"—the anthem of the Partisans, whose ringing refrain "mir zayen do"—"we are here"—affirms the collective continuity of Jewish life. This position does not suggest that such forms of remembrance are unimportant nor that we would demur in our own participation in them. Hope, however, is of a different order.

10. Retranslation of excerpt of Benjamin's Thesis V by Franz Eppert, personal correspondence. The text in Benjamin's *Gesammelte Schriften 1–2*, V, p. 695 reads: "*Denn es ist ein unwiederbringliches Bild der Vergangenheit, das mit jeder Gegenwart zu verschwinden droht, die sich nicht als in ihm gemeint erkannte.*"

11. The text of these citations were transcribed by Roger Simon from videotape recordings housed at the Fortunoff Archives at Yale University. I gratefully acknowledge the Fortunoff Archives for granting permission to publish these transcriptions.

12. T-618, Samuel B. and T-257, Mira B. Fortunoff Video Archive for Holocaust Testimonies, Yale University, cited with permission.

13. T-1399, Zena G. Fortunoff Video Archive for Holocaust Testimonies, Yale University and T-426, Beba L. Fortunoff Video Archive for Holocaust Testimonies, Yale University, cited with permission. Paul K. (Tape 221, Canadian Jewish Congress Archives, Montréal), cited with permission.

14. Sutzkever's poem "A Wagon of Shoes" cited with permission of The University of California Press.

15. Sutzkever's poem "Flower" cited with permission of Mosaic Press.

16. Cited with permission of Aviva Kempner, Ciesla Foundation.

17. See, e.g., Hartman and Buddick (1986) and Boyarin (1990).

Chapter Seven   Remembrance as Praxis and the Ethics of the Interhuman

1. Our interest in not in adjudicating which among differing forms of remembrance is the superior, reducing remembrance to one correct form. Rather, we are concerned here with expanding the range of possibilities regarding the practices that constitute a mature form of public memory. On such terms, the "lessons" of history will not reside exclusively in the historical and sociological understanding of what was done by others, nor in the moral messages that encourage us to the civic courage needed to stand against injustice. These lessons will also reside in a practice of creative historical study that becomes a way of rethinking the present and the terms on which commitments and responsibilities are constituted.

2. For a discussion of the notion of hope as that which resides in the rethinking of the present, and hence the possibility of futurity, see Andrew Benjamin's "Hope at the Present" in Benjamin (1997, 1–25).

3. de Certeau lends insight to the problematic being glossed here. The writing of history promotes a selection between what can be *understood* and what must be *forgotten* in order to obtain the representation of a present intelligibility. But, whatever this new understanding of the past holds to be

irrelevant—shards created by the selection of materials, remainders left aside by an explication—comes back, despite everything on the edges of discourse or in its rifts and crannies: "resistance," "survivals," or delays discreetly perturb the pretty order of a line of "progress" or a system of interpretation. These are lapses in the syntax constructed by the law of place. Therein they symbolize a return of the repressed, that is, a return of what, at a given moment, has *become* unthinkable in order for a new identity to *become* thinkable (1988, 4).

4. In an attempt to emphasize that the transitivity of testament is not held fetishistically in the text itself, we highlight the active role of various modes of reception and its effects on meeting the ethicality implicit in the testamentary address. Our work, at this stage, does not directly discuss the constitutive role of different forms of mediation, i.e., the various apparatuses of dissemination and their associated technologies, in certain modes of reception/reading. However, we want to note the importance of considering the specificity of media in enabling us to ask more concrete questions regarding the production of attention, and how these media structure the limits and possibilities of our engagement. In another stage of our work, we plan to take up the specificity of mediated transmission, i.e., the way in which particular forms for circulating testaments are implicated in contextualizing our audiencing practices. An initial exemplar of this concern can be found in chapter eight "The Audiovisual Supplement of Holocaust Video Testimony."

5. An "open community"—i.e., one founded in openness—would not be an exclusive grouping, but rather a coming together: sociality is thus never private, never simply two. With respect to the study group, e.g., the group comes together to gather around testament and near testament, a "third" whose absence perennially keeps the doors of the meeting place/time open.

6. See the critique of recognition in Oliver's *Witnessing: Beyond Recognition* (2001).

7. Drawing on Benjamin's insight that the citation "summons the word by its name, breaks it destructively from its context, but precisely thereby calls it back to its origin" (qtd in Weigel, 1996, 38), this juxtaposition of disparate and sometimes contradictory elements is offered in order to open testament to its "origin" as *saying*—allowing it perhaps to *address* once more.

8. Polylinguistic: since the juxtapositions potentially offer a disparate mix of "languages": both natural language (testimonies translated from Yiddish, Hebrew, German, Lithuanian, Spanish, some originally in English) and different representational languages (poetry, prose, plays, photos, songs, the visual arts, etc.). Polyvocal: insofar as a juxtaposition will include passages and images from multiple sources and individuals, whether or not they describe the "same" event or time. Polytemporal: insofar as these "quotations" will each have their own temporal index—some inscribed temporally proximate to the events depicted, some months later, and some as much as fifty years from the events.

9. Of this conception of study, we might also say, along with Levinas, that "study is not the activity of a lone individual and that essentially truth must be communicated, that the 'I think' is sociality, and that that communication is not an addendum to truth but belongs to the reading itself and is part of the reader's concern" (1994c, 66).

10. In this movement of "emptying out," this "more" that addresses the contemporary witness to testament makes its invisibility visible. It is a disorientation that can open to a genuinely new orientation: beyond the movement within the page, outward, toward the singular voice of the "original" witness, and toward the others, in the room, reading with you.

Chapter Eight   The Audiovisual Supplement of Holocaust Survivor Video Testimony

1. I draw inspiration here from D.N. Rodowick's notion of what it means to "have an Idea." See Rodowick (2001, 1).

2. This instance of event-naming of a vast array of specific policies and practices with genocidal intent and consequence is, of course, a historically and geographically situated act of cultural memory. As in any such instance of event-naming, the use of "the Holocaust" as specific terminological convention is not without consequence. Of chief concern in the context of my query here is the use of the term Holocaust for defining the boundary terms of archival collections of testamentary memories of Jews subjected to Nazi genocidal policies and practices and their subsequent consequences. This is a term that organizes a specific referential identity among memories, which because of the vast substance of their referent are inherently diverse and divergent. Thus, it is important to proceed under the caution that the notion of a "Holocaust testimony" cannot be easily drawn into a figural unity. However, I am writing under the presumption that the noun, the Holocaust, has the

same terminological specificity as "the Shoah," that is, it refers to the consequences of policies and practices initiated against Jews by the Nazi regime and their allies. At the very least, this delimitation clears a linguistic space within which to acknowledge and grapple with the specificity of the *Porrajmos*, the experiences of the Romani people subjected to Nazi-initiated genocide. It also marks a point of departure for considering other instances of systemic mass violence initiated by the Nazi regime as well as other historical instances of state-initiated genocidal violence.

3. While videotaped interviews with Jewish survivors are by far the most numerous, it is important to note that many archives include interviews with a broad range of non-Jewish survivors and witnesses to Nazi policies and persecution. For example, the Fortunoff Archives at Yale University includes video interviews with political prisoners incarcerated at work and in concentration camps, Sinti and Roma survivors, people who survived subjection to Nazi eugenics policies, people persecution based on their homosexuality or suspected homosexuality, those persecuted because of their beliefs and expressed convictions as Jehovah's Witnesses, liberators and liberation witnesses, rescuers and aid providers, and war crimes trial participants.

4. I use the term "actuality" here in sense of Walter Benjamin's *Aktualität*, following his insight that memory and action find articulation from, and in, images. For an important discussion of this aspect of Benjamin's thought, see Weigel (1996, 3–15).

5. Darsa, "The challenge of memory—video testimonies and Holocaust education" in *The Memory of the Holocaust in the 21st Century*. http://www.yad-vashem.org.il/education/workshop/workshop_toc.html

6. "History educates ('leads outward' in the Latin) in the deepest sense. Of the subjects in the secular curriculum, it does the best in teaching us those virtues once reserved for theology—the virtue of humility in the face of limits to our knowledge and the virtue of awe in the face of the expanse of human history." Wineburg (2001, 23–24).

7. My questions included: why did it make sense to try to make a little money selling sweets in a place where people were starving? Why were the Jewish police in the ghetto harassing the children? What is the significance of the images of these children within Holocaust memory? Why is it that I am asking these questions?

8. Testimony of Rita Hilton (USHMM RG 50.030★002).

9. I assume that any responsible use of audio visual testimony implicates one in the need for context. In choosing to include in my juxtaposition only two minutes of a four-hour interview, I run the risk that those who engage its transcript and associated sampling of still images taken from the video may falsely assume that through this excerpt they might understand what Rita Hilton remembers and how she remembers her experiences in Lodz.

10. Some readers of previous versions of this essay have been surprised by my "surprise." Of course, there is a frame within which Hilton's bittersweet moment of recall can be understood and appreciated as part of the spark of humanity surviving in deeply oppressive circumstances. However, rather than totalize this moment so that it settles into a comfortable comprehension, I am here preserving the fleeting experience of surprise in order to see how it might be rubbing against the grain of accepted forms of understanding.

11. In working from my own response to the Hilton video, there is clearly a phenomenological frame to my method of analysis and argumentation in this chapter. What is certain is that the value of this method must be tested against its facility for opening questions of visible evidence that have considerable generality. On such terms, the forebearers of the approach taken here would have to include among others both Proust and Barthes. In this regard, Barthes's (1981) interest in thinking about photography is particularly appropriate: "I wanted to explore it not as a question (theme) but as a wound: I see, I feel, hence I notice, I observe, and I think" (21).

12. The issue of an "improper representation" in the context of Holocaust memory is no small problem. Certainly, it has arisen in the context of representations incorporating aspects of the comedic in which, as Kundera (2003) observes, "reality is abruptly revealed as ambiguous, things lose their apparent meaning." Indeed, it is ambiguity that is often here the source of anxiety. See, e.g., Weber (2001) in which he discusses the reluctance of Henryk Ross, a photographer and survivor of the Lodz ghetto, to make available during his lifetime, the majority of the pictures he took in the ghetto.

13. For a discussion of the televisual mediation of history, see Edgerton and Rollins (2002).

14. The virtual experience of "being with" requires sustained moments of technological transparency. Those moments when the interview is stopped to change tapes, or when the adjustment of tracking on the tape disrupts the virtual.

15. Michael Levine (personal communication). See Levine's *The Belated Witness*.

16. Understood on these terms, the practice of historiographic poetics is not secondary to testament but is needed for the very possibility of a testamentary legacy to have an existence. In this sense, historiographic poetics might be related to the Freudian concept of *Nachtraglichkeit*, relevant in this context as a belated retranscription of the impact of that event to which testament attempts to give expression. This is a retranscription that opens new pedagogical possibilities for grappling with the significance of historical actualities. Key to this practice is differentiating between acting out and working through as forms of response to a testamentary legacy.

17. See the recent translation of *The New Thinking* by Udoff and Galli (1999). The following is a translated excerpt of Rosenzweig's essay from their volume. "The method of speech takes the place of the method of thinking, as developed in all earlier philosophies. Thinking is timeless and wants to be timeless. With one stroke it wants to make a thousand connections; the last, the goal, is for it the first. Speech is bound to time, nourished by time, [and] it neither can nor wants to abandon this ground of nourishment; it does not know beforehand where it will emerge; it lets itself be given its cues from others; it actually lives by another's life, whether that other is the one who listens to a story, or is the respondent in a dialogue, or the participant in a chorus; thinking by contrast is always solitary . . . the difference between the old and the new . . . does not lie in sound and silence, but in the need of an other and, what is the same thing, taking time seriously" (86–87).

18. Invoking the possibility of hope with practice of remembrance of the Shoah is, of course, fraught with problems. In *Negative Dialectics*, Adorno (1973) proposed a new categorical imperative for our age: to arrange our thoughts and actions in such a way that Auschwitz (or anything like this event) would never happen again. Sara Kofman (1998) argued that this includes the memorialization of the Shoah without "result" or profit for speculative thought. By this she meant thought regarding the Shoah that masters the event, enclosing it "in the clarity and happiness of daylight" (10). As an method of witness and study, the historiographic poetics discussed here and in chapters six and seven presumes no such mastery, but rather an infinite conversation. For a philosophical approach to the prospect of hope consistent with the thoughts expressed here, see Benjamin (1997).

REFERENCES

Adorno, Theodor. *Negative Dialectics* [trans. E.B. Ashton]. New York: Continuum, 1973.

Adorno, Theodor. *Minima Moralia* [trans. E.F.N. Jephcott]. London: Verso, 1974.

Adorno, Theodor. "What does coming to terms with the past mean?" In *Bitburg in Moral and Political Perspective*. Edited by Geoffrey Hartman. Bloomington: Indiana University Press, pp. 114–129, 1986.

Amishai-Maisels, Ziva. "Christological symbolism of the Holocaust." In *Remembering for the Future Volume II*. Edited by Yehuda Bauer. Oxford: Pergamon Press, pp. 1657–1671, 1989.

Amishai-Maisels, Ziva. "Chagall's *White Crucifixion*." *The Art Institute of Chicago Museum Studies*, vol. 17, no. 2, pp. 138–153, 1991.

Appadurai, Arjun. *Modernity at Large: Cultural Dimensions of Globalization*. Minneapolis: University of Minnesota Press, 1996.

Arad, Yitzhak. *Ghetto in Flames: The Struggle and Destruction of the Jews in Vilna in the Holocaust*. Jerusalem: Yad Vashem Martyrs' and Heroes' Remembrance Authority, 1980.

Atkinson, Karen. "Tales of desire." *New Observations*, no. 88, March/April 4–9, 1992.

Avni, Ora. "Beyond psychoanalysis: Elie Wiesel's Night in historical perspective." In *Auschwitz and After: Race, Culture and "The Jewish Question" in France*. Edited by Lawrence D. Kritzman. New York: Routledge, pp. 203–218, 1995.

Barthes, Roland. *Camera Lucida*. New York: Hill and Wang, 1981.

Bauman, Zygmunt. *In Search of Politics*. Stanford: Stanford University Press, 1999.

Beiner, Ronald. "Hannah Arendt on judging." In Hannah Arendt, *Lectures on Kant's Political Philosophy*. Chicago: University of Chicago Press, pp. 89–156, 1992.

Benjamin, Andrew. "Hope at the present." In *Present Hope: Philosophy, Architecture, Judaism*. New York: Routledge, pp. 1–25, 1997.

Benjamin, Walter. "The storyteller." In *Illuminations* [trans. Harry Zohn]. New York: Schocken Books, pp. 83–109, 1968.

Benjamin, Walter. "Thesis on the philosophy of history." In *Illuminations*. New York: Schocken Books, pp. 253–264, 1969.

Benjamin, Walter. *The Arcades Project* [trans. H. Eiland and K. McLaughlin]. Cambridge: Belknap Press, 1999.

Bennington, Geoffrey. *Interrupting Derrida*. New York: Routledge, 2000.

Benois, Alexandre. "Chagall, Oeuvres Recentes." *Cahiers d'Art*, vol. 15, no. 1–2, 33–35, 1940.

Berger, John. *Keeping A Rendezvous*. New York: Vintage Books, 1991.

Berger, John. "Against the great defeat of the world." *Race and Class*, vol. 40, no. 2/3, October–March 1–4, 1998.

Bhabha, Homi K. "Of mimicry and man: the amivalence of colonial discourse." In *The Location of Culture*. New York: Routledge, pp. 85–92, 1994a.

Bhabha, Homi K. "How newness enters the world: postmodern space, postcolonial times and the trials of cultural translation." In *The Location of Culture*. London and New York: Routledge, pp. 212–235, 1994b.

Bigelow, Bill. "Discovering Columbus: re-reading the past." In *Rethinking Columbus*. Edited by, Bill Bigelow, Barbara Miner, and Bob Peterson. Milwaukee: Rethinking Schools Ltd, pp. 6–9, 1991.

Bociurkiw, Marusia. "Je me Souviens: a response to the Montréal killings." *Fuse* XIII, no. 4, Spring, 6–10, 1990.

Boyarin, Daniel. *Intertextuality and the Reading of Midrash*. Bloomington: University of Indiana Press, 1990.

Boyd, William. "Seeking answers down in the trenches." *New York Times*, pg AR13, 22, November 19, 2000.

Braiterman, Zachary. "Against Holocaust-sublime: naive reference and the generation of memory." *History and Memory*, vol. 12, no. 2 (Fall/Winter), 7–28, 2000.

Brickman, Julie. "Female lives, feminist deaths: the relationship of the Montréal massacre to dissociation, incest, and violence against women." *Canadian Psychology*, vol. 33, no. 2, April, 128–147, 1992.

Brinkley, Robert and Youra, Steven. "Tracing *Shoah*." *Publications of the Modern Language Association of America (PLMA)*, vol. 111, no. 1, 108–112, 1996.

Britzman, Deborah. *Lost Subjects, Contested Objects: Toward a Psychoanalytic Inquiry of Learning*. Albany: State University of New York Press, 1998.

Brown, Wendy. *States of Injury: Power and Freedom in Late Modernity*. New Jersey: Princeton University Press, 1995.

Burton, Nadia. *Tools Not Rules: Cultivating Practices of Resistance to and Prevention of Sexualized Violence*. Ph.D dissertation, University of Toronto, 1999.

Bussidor, Ila and Bilgen-Reinart, Üstün. *Night Spirits: The Story of the Relocation of the Sayisi Dene*. Winnipeg: University of Manitoba Press, 1997.

Butler, Judith. "Review essay [*Spirit in the Ashes*. Edith Wyschogrod (1985)]." *History and Theory*, vol. 27, no. 1, 60–70, 1998.

Carey-Webb, Allen. "Transformative voices." In *Teaching and Testimony: Rigoberta Menchu and the North American Classroom*. Edited by Allen Carey-Webb and Stephen Benz. New Brunswick, NJ: Rutgers University Press, pp. 3–18, 1996.

Carrard, Philippe. *Poetics of the New History: French Historical Discourse from Braudel to Chartier*. Baltimore: Johns Hopkins University Press, 1992.

Caruth, Cathy (ed.) *Trauma: Explorations in Memory*. Baltimore: Johns Hopkins University Press, 1995.

Caruth, Cathy. *Unclaimed Experience: Trauma, Narrative and History*. Baltimore and London: John Hopkins University Press, 1996.

Cassou, Jean. *Chagall*. New York: Praeger Publishers, 1965.

Castoriadis, Cornelius. "The Greek polis and the creation of democracy." In *The Castoriadis Reader*. Edited by David Ames Curtis. Oxford: Blackwell, pp. 267–289, 1977.

Clamen, Mark. "Who am I to speak for the dead? A Levinasian encounter with Holocaust testimony." In *Practicing Levinas*. Edited by L. Bove and L. Duhan-Kaplan. Amsterdam: Rodopi (forthcoming).

Cohen, Margaret. *Profane Illumination: Walter Benjamin and the Paris of Surrealist Revolution*. Berkeley: University of California Press, 1993.

Cohen, Richard A. *Elevations: The Height of the Good in Rosenzweig and Levinas*. Chicago: University of Chicago Press, 1994.

Conley, Tom. "De Bry's Las Casas." In *Amerindian Images and the Legacy of Columbus*. Edited by Rene Jara and Nicholas Spadaccini. Minneapolis: University of Minnesota Press, pp. 103–131, 1992.

Crary, Jonathan. *Suspensions of Perception: Attention, Spectacle, and Modern Culture*. Cambridge and London: MIT Press, 1999.

Critchley, Simon. *The Ethics of Deconstruction*. Cambridge, MA: Blackwell, 1992.

Darsa, Jan. "The challenge of memory—video testimony and Holocaust education." In *The Memory of the Holocaust in the 21st Century—The Challenge for Education*. Educational workshop, Yad Vashem, October 14, 1999, http://www.yad-vashem.org.il/download/education/cont/darsaday4.pdf

Debord, Guy. *Society of the Spectacle*. Detroit: Black & Red, 1983.

de Certeau, Michel. *Heterologies: Discourse on the Other*. Minneapolis: University of Minnesota Press, 1986.

de Certeau, Michel. *The Writing of History* [trans. T. Conley]. New York: Columbia University Press, 1998.

Derrida, Jacques. "Freud and the scene of writing." In *Writing and Difference* [trans. Alan Bass]. Chicago: University of Chicago Press, pp. 196–231, 1978.

Derrida, Jacques. *Specters of Marx: The State of the Debt, the Work of Mourning, and the New International* [trans. Peggy Kamuf]. New York: Routledge, 1994.

Derrida, Jacques. *Archive Fever: A Freudian Impression*. Chicago: University of Chicago Press, 1996.

Derrida, Jacques. *The Politics of Friendship* [trans. G. Collins]. London: Verso, 1997.

Derrida, Jacques. "Intellectual courage: an interview." *Culture Machine 2*, March 2000, http://culturemachine.tees.ac.uk/articles/art_derr.htm

Derrida, Jacques. "The future of the profession, or the university without condition (Thanks to the 'Humanities,' what could happen tomorrow)." In *Jacques Derrida and the Humanities: A Critical Reader*. Edited by T. Cohen. Cambridge: Cambridge University Press, pp. 24–57, 2002.

Des Pres, Terrence. *The Survivor: An Anatomy of Life in the Death Camps*. New York: Pocket Books, 1977.

Durland, Steven. "Call me in 93': an interview with James Luna." *High Performance*, no. 56, Winter, 34–39, 1991.

Dwork, Deborah and van Pelt, Robert Jan. "Reclaiming Auschwitz." In *Holocaust Remembrance: The Shapes of Memory*. Edited by Geoffrey H. Hartman. Oxford: Basil Blackwell, pp. 232–251, 1994.

Eckardt, A. Roy and Eckardt, Alice L. *Long Night's Journey into Day: Life and Faith after the Holocaust*. Detroit: Wayne State University Press, 1982.

Edgerton, Gary R. and Rollins, Peter. *Television Histories: Shaping Collective Memory in the Media Age*. Lexington: University of Kentucky Press, 2002.

Eppert, Claudia. *Learning Responsivity/Responsibility: Reading the Literature of Historical Witness*. Doctoral dissertation, University of Toronto, 1999.

Erasmus, George. *Address for the Launch of the Report of the Royal Commission on Aboriginal Peoples*. Department of Indian and Northern Affairs: Canada, 1996, http://www.ainc-inac.gc.ca/ch/rcap/spch_e.html

Esch, Deborah. "No time like the present." *Surfaces*, vol. 3, 1993, http://pum12.pum.umontreal.ca/revues/surfaces/vol3/esch.html

Ezrahi, Sidra DeKoven. "Representing Auschwitz." *History and Memory*, vol. 7, no. 2 (Fall/Winter), 121–154, 1996.

Felman, Shoshana and Laub, Dori. *Testimony: Crises of Witnessing in Literature, Psychoanalysis and History*. New York: Routledge, 1992.

Finkielkraut, Alain. *Remembering in Vain: The Klaus Barbie Trial and Crimes against Humanity (European Perspectives)* [trans. Roxanne Lapidus]. New York: Columbia University Press, 1992.

Finkielkraut, Alain. *The Imaginary Jew* [trans. K. O'Neill and D. Suchoff]. Lincoln, NB: University of Nebraska Press, 1994.

Frazier, Lessie Jo. "Subverted memories: countermourning as political action in Chile." In *Acts of Memory: Cultural Recall in the Present*. Edited by Mieke Bal, Jonathan Crewe, and Leo Spitzer. Hanover, Dartmouth: University of New England Press, pp. 105–119, 1999.

Friedlander, Saul. "Trauma, transference and 'working through' in writing the history of the Shoah." *History and Memory*, vol. 4, no. 1, 39–59, 1992.

Frisch, Michael. *A Shared Authority: Essays on the Craft and Meaning of Oral and Public History*. Albany: State University of New York Press, 1990.

Fuller, Mary C. "Ralegh's fugitive gold: reference and deferral in the discoverie of Guiana." *Representations*, vol. 33, 42–64, 1991.

Geyl, Pieter. *Use and Abuse of History*. New Haven: Yale University Press, 1955.

Gibbs, Robert. *Correlations in Rosenzweig and Levinas*. Princeton, NJ: Princeton University Press, 1992.

Gibbs, Robert. *Why Ethics? Signs of Responsibilities*. Princeton: Princeton University Press, 2000.

Gibson, Charles. *The Black Legend: Anti-Spanish Attitudes in the Old World and New*. New York: Knopf, 1971.

Giroux, Henry A. *Border Crossings: Cultural Workers and the Politics of Education*. New York: Routledge, 1992.

Giroux, Henry A. "Public time versus emergency time: politics, terrorism and the culture of fear." *The Abandoned Generation: Democracy Beyond the Culture of Fear*. New York: Palgrave Macmillan, pp. 1–15, 2003.

Goldin, Judah. *Studies in Midrash and Related Literature*. Philadelphia: Jewish Publication Society, 1988.

Gordon, Avery F. *Ghostly Matters: Haunting and the Sociological Imagination*. Minneapolis and London: University of Minnesota Press, 1997.

Grade, Chaim. *My Mother's Sabbath Days: A Memoir* [trans. Channa Klenerman Goldstein and Inna Hecker Grade]. New York: Alfred A. Knopf, 1986.

Greenblatt, Stephen. *Marvelous Possessions: The Wonder of the New World*. Chicago: University of Chicago Press, 1991.

Grisel, Etienne. "The beginnings of international law and general public law doctrine: Francisco de Vitoria's *De Indiis Prior*." In *First Images of America: The Impact of the Old World on the New* (2 vols). Edited by Fredi Chiappelli, Michael J.B. Allen, and Robert L. Benson. Berkeley: University of California Press, pp. 305–325, 1976.

Grossman, Mendel. *With a Camera in the Ghetto*. Israel: Ghetto Fighter's House, Hakibbutz Hameuchaud, 1970.

Guillaumin, Colette. "Madness and the social norm" [trans. Mary Jo Lakehead]. *Feminist Issues*, vol. 11, no. 2, Fall 1991.

Handelman, Susan A. *Fragments of Redemption: Jewish Thought and Literary Theory in Benjamin, Scholem, and Levinas*. Bloomington, ID: Indiana University Press, 1991.

Handelman, Susan A. "The 'Torah' of criticism and the criticism of Torah: recuperating the pedagogical moment." In *Interpreting Judaism in a Postmodern Age*. Edited by Steven Kepnes. New York: New York University Press, pp. 221–239, 1996.

Hartman, Geoffrey H. and Buddick, Sanford. *Midrash and Literature*. New Haven: Yale University Press, 1986.

Hartman, Geoffrey H. "History and judgment: the case of Paul de Man." *History and Memory*, vol. 1, no.1 (Spring/Summer), 5–84, 1989.

Hartman, Geoffrey H. *The Longest Shadow: In the Aftermath of the Holocaust*. Bloomington: University of Indiana Press, 1996.

Heschel, Abraham J. *The Prophets*. New York: Jewish Publication Society of America, 1962.

Hirsch, Marianne. "Surviving images: Holocaust photographs and the work of post memory." *The Yale Journal of Criticism*, vol. 14, no. 1, 5–37, 2001.

Huyssen, Andreas. "Monument and memory in a postmodern age." *The Yale Journal of Criticism*, vol. 6, no. 2, 249–262, 1993.

Huyssen, Andreas. *Twilight Memories: Marking Time in a Culture of Amnesia*. New York: Routledge, 1995.

Irwin-Zarecka, Iwona. *Frames of Remembrance: The Dynamics of Collective Memory*. New Brunswick, NJ: Transaction Publishers, 1994.

Jay, Martin. *Downcast Eyes: The Denigration of Vision in Twentieth-Century French Thought*. Berkeley: University of California Press, 1994.

Johnson, M. and Stern Strom, M. *Elements of Time: Holocaust Testimonies*. Brookline, MA: Facing History and Ourselves Foundation, 1989.

Ka-Tzetnik. 135633 *Phoenix Over Galilee*. Jove Publications, 1977.

Keenan, Thomas. "Publicity and indifference (Sarajevo on television)." Shorenstein Center, Harvard University, March 30, 1998, http://www.bard.edu/hrp/keenan/sarajevo.htm

Kelley, Caffyn. "Creating memory, contesting history." *Matriart*, vol. 5, no. 3, 6–11, 1995.

Kofman, Sara. *Smothered Words* [trans. Madeleine Dobie]. Evanston: Northwestern University Press, 1998.

Kohn, Irena. "Beyond self-evidence: engaging with photographic traces of the Shoah outside a logic of simulation." Presented at the symposium, *History in Words and Image*. Turku, Finland, 2002.

Kruk, Herman. *The Last Days of the Jerusalem of Lithuania: Chronicles from the Vilna Ghetto and the Camps, 1939–1944* [trans. Barbara Harshav]. Edited by Benjamin Harshav. New Haven: Yale University Press, 2002.

Kundera, Milan. "The Theatre of Memory." *The Guardian*, Saturday, May 17, 2003.

LaCapra, Dominick. *Representing the Holocaust: History, Theory, Trauma*. Ithaca, NY: Cornell University Press, 1994.

Lakeman, Lee. "Women, violence and the Montréal massacre." In *Twist and Shout: A Decade of Feminist Writing in This Magazine*. Edited by Susan Crean. Toronto: Second Story Press, pp. 92–102, 1992.

Landsberg, Alison. "America, the Holocaust, and the mass culture of memory: toward a radical politics of empathy." *New German Critique*, no. 71 (Spring–Summer), 63–86, 1997.

Langer, Lawrence L. *Holocaust Testimonies: The Ruins of Memory*. New Haven, CT: Yale University Press, 1991.

Las Casas, Bartolomé de. *A Short Account of the Destruction of the Indies* [trans. Nigel Griffen]. New York: Penguin, 1992.

LeFort, Claude. *Democracy and Political Theory* [trans. David Macey]. Minneapolis: University of Minnesota Press, 1988.

Leslie, E. Book Review in *Radical Philosophy*, vol. 105, January/February, 52–53, 2001.

Levinas, Emmanuel. *Totality and Infinity: An Essay on Exteriority* [trans. Alphonso Lingis]. Pittsburgh, PA: Duquesne University Press, 1969.

Levinas, Emmanuel. *Otherwise Than Being or Beyond Essence* [trans. Alphonso Lingis]. Boston: Kluwer, 1981.

Levinas, Emmanuel. "Diachrony and Representation." In *Time and the Other (and Other Additional Essays)* [trans. Richard Cohen]. Pittsburgh: Duquesne University Press, pp. 97–120, 1987.

Levinas, Emmanuel. "Toward the other." In *Nine Talmudic Readings*. [trans. Annette Aronowicz]. Bloomington: Indiana University Press, pp. 12–29, 1990a.

Levinas, Emmanuel. "The temptation of temptation." In *Nine Talmudic Readings* [trans. Annette Aronowicz]. Bloomington: Indiana University Press, pp. 30–50, 1990b.

Levinas, Emmanuel. "Desacralization and disenchantment." In *Nine Talmudic Readings* [trans. Annette Aronowicz]. Bloomington: Indiana University Press, pp. 136–160, 1990c.

Levinas, Emmanuel. *Otherwise Than Being or Beyond Essence* [trans. Alphonso Lingis]. Dordrecht, Boston, London: Kluwer Academic Publishers, 1991.

Levinas, Emmanuel. "The Pact." In *Beyond the Verse: Talmudic Readings and Lectures* [trans. Gary D. Mole]. Bloomington: Indiana University Press, pp. 68–85, 1994a.

Levinas, Emmanuel. "Contempt for the Torah as idolatry." In *In the Time of the Nations* [trans. M.B. Smith]. Bloomington: Indiana University Press, pp. 55–75, 1994b.

Levinas, Emmanuel. *Otherwise Than Being or Beyond Essence* [trans. Alphonso Lingis]. Pittsburgh: Duquesne University Press, 1998.

Levine, Michael. *The Belated Witness: Literature, Testimony and the Question of Holocaust Survival*. Stanford: Stanford University Press, 2005.

Linenthal, Edward T. *Preserving Memory: The Struggle to Create America's Holocaust Museum*. New York: Penguin Books, 1995.

Lyotard, Jean F. *The Differend: Phrases in Dispute*. Manchester: Manchester University Press, 1988.

Maclear, Kyo. *Beclouded Visions: Hiroshima-Nagasaki and the "Art of Witness."* M.A. thesis, Ontario Institute for Studies in Education, University of Toronto, 1995.

Malette, Louise and Chalouh, Mario (eds). *The Montréal Massacre* [trans. Marlene Wildeman]. Charlottetown: Gynergy Books, 1991.

Marcus, Sharon. "Fighting bodies, fighting words: a theory and politics of rape prevention." In *Feminists Theorize the Political*. Edited by Judith Butler and Joan Scott. New York and London: Routledge, pp. 385–403, 1992.

Martinez, Ruben. "On the north-south border patrol, in art and life." *New York Times*, Section H, 1, 35, Sunday, October 15, 1991.

Mays, John Bentley. "The end of innocence or a new beginning?" *The Globe and Mail* [Toronto], Section C Arts Weekend, 1, 15, October 19, 1991.

Mendes-Flor, Paul. "History." In *Contemporary Jewish Religious Thought: Original Essays on Critical Concepts, Movements and Beliefs*. Edited by Arthur A. Cohen and Paul Mendes-Flor. New York: The Free Press, pp. 371–387, 1987.

Meyer, Franz. *Marc Chagall*. London: Thames and Hudson, 1964.

Miller, Laura. "Columbus and the quest for truth." *SF (San Francisco) Weekly*, 21–22, April 1, 1992.

Minerbi, S.I. "Pope John Paul II and the Shoah." In *Remembering for the Future*. Volume III. Edited by Yehuda Bauer. Oxford: Pergammon Press, pp. 2973–2985, 1989.

Mitchell, William J.T. *Picture Theory*. Chicago: University of Chicago Press, 1994.

Moore, James, F. "The Holocaust and Christian theology: a spectrum of views on the crucifixion and the resurrection in light of the Holocaust." In *Remembering for the Future Volume I*. Edited by Yehuda Bauer. Oxford: Pergammon Press, pp. 836–843, 1989.

Morrison, Toni. *Beloved: A Novel*. New York: Knopf, 1987.

Nelson-McDermott, Catherine. "Murderous fallout: post-Lepine rhetoric." *Atlantis*, vol. 17, no. 1 (Fall/Winter), 124–128, 1991.

Oliver, Kelly. "Witnessing otherness in history." In *What Happens to History: The Renewal of Ethics in Contemporary Thought*. Edited by Howard Marchitello. New York: Routledge, pp. 41–66, 2000.

Oliver, Kelly. *Witnessing: Beyond Recognition*. Minneapolis: University of Minnesota Press, 2001.

Ouaknin, Marc A. *The Burnt Book: Reading the Talmud* [trans. by L. Brown]. Princeton, NJ: Princeton University Press, 1995.

Pagden, Anthony. *The Fall of Natural Man: The American Indian and the Origins of Comparative Ethnology.* Cambridge: Cambridge University Press, 1982.

Plank, Karl. "Broken continuities: *Night and White Crucifixion.*" *The Christian Century,* 963–966, November 4, 1987.

Ran, Leyzer. *Jerusalem of Lithuania: Illustrated and Documented.* New York, 1974.

Rathjen, Heidi and Monpetit, Charles. *December 6: From the Montréal Massacre to Gun Control: The Inside Story.* Toronto: McClelland and Stewart, 1999.

Retamar, Roberto Fernandez. "America, descubrimientos, dialogos." In *Nuestra America: Contra El V Centenario.* Edited by Dietrich S. Heinz. Navarra: Txalaparta Editorial, pp. 89–97, 1991.

Reynolds, Anna "Review of *Children of the Flames.*" *The Times Saturday Review,* London, October 5, 1991.

Rodowick, D.N. *Reading the Figural, or Philosophy after the New Media.* Durham and London: Duke University Press, 2001.

Rolnikas, Macha (Diary Excerpt) in Laurel holliday *Children in the Holocaust and World War II: Their Secret Diaries.* New York: Pocket Books, pp. 185–199, 1995.

Rosen, Raphael. "Untitled." Berkeley: Holocaust Remembrance Project. Holland & Knight Charitable Foundation, Inc., 2000. http://holocaust.hklaw.com/essays/2000/200016.htm

Rosenberg, Sharon. *Rupturing the "Skin of Memory": Bearing Witness to the 1989 Massacre of Women in Montréal.* Ph.D. dissertation, University of Toronto, 1997.

Rosenzweig, Franz. "The new thinking." In *Franz Rosenzweig's "The New Thinking"* [trans. Alan Udoff and Barbara E. Galli]. Syracuse: Syracuse University Press, pp. 67–102, 1999.

Roskies, David G. *Against the Apocalypse: Responses to Catastrophe in Modern Jewish Culture.* Cambridge: Harvard University Press, 1984.

Roth, Michael S. *The Ironist's Cage: Memory, Trauma, and the Construction of History.* New York: Columbia University Press, 1995.

Royal Commission on Aboriginal People. *Looking Forward, Looking Back (Royal Commission Report Volume I).* Ottawa: Canada Communications Group, 1996.

Rudashevski, Yitskhok. *The Diary of the Vilna Ghetto* [trans. Percy Matenko]. Israel: Beit Lohamei Haghetaot [Ghetto Fighters' House], 1973.

Scanlon, Jennifer. "Educating the living, remembering the dead: the Montréal massacre as metaphor." *Feminist Teacher,* vol. 8, no. 2 (Fall/Winter), 75–79, 1994.

Schmidt, Lisa. "Sorrow, anger after Montréal." *Kinesis* (Vancouver) February 1990, p. 7.

Schwartz-Bart, Andre. *The Last of the Just.* Overlook Press, 2000.

Scott, James Brown. *The Spanish Origin of International Law: Francisco de Vitoria and his Laws of Nations.* Oxford: Clarendon Press, 1934.

Selver-Urbach, Sara. *Through the Window of My Home: Recollections from the Lodz Ghetto.* Jerusalem: Yad Vashem, 1986.

Silverman, Kaja. *Threshold of the Visible World.* New York: Routledge, 1996.

Silverman, Kaja. *World Spectators.* Stanford: Stanford University Press, 2000.

Simon, Roger I. "The contribution of holocaust audio-visual testimony to remembrance, learning and hope." *International Journal on Audio-Visual Testimony of Victims of Nazi Crimes and Genocide,* no. 1, 141–152, 1998.

Simon, Roger I. "The paradoxical practice of *Zakhor*: memories of 'That Which Has Never Been My Fault of Deed.' " In *Between Hope and Despair: Pedagogy and the Remembrance of Historical Trauma.* Edited by Roger I. Simon, Sharon Rosenberg, and Claudia Eppert. Lanham: Rowman and Littlefield, pp. 9–25, 2000.

Simon, Roger I. and Armitage-Simon, Wendy. "Teaching risky stories: remembering mass destruction through children's literature." *English Quarterly,* vol. 28, no. 1, 27–31, 1995.

Simon, Roger I. and Eppert, Claudia. "Remembering obligation: pedagogy and the witnessing of testimony of historical trauma." *Canadian Journal of Education,* vol. 22, no. 2, Spring, 175–191, 1997.

Simon, Roger I., Rosenberg, Sharon, and Eppert, Claudia (eds). *Between Hope and Despair: Pedagogy and the Remembrance of Historical Trauma.* Lanham: Rowman and Littlefield, 2000.

Sklarew, Myra. *Lithuania: New & Selected Poems.* Falls Church, Virginia: Azul Editions, 1995.

Slocum, David. "Melodramatic imaginings of the holocaust: survivor testimony and popular documentaries." Unpublished manuscript, 2003.

Small, Deborah and Jaffe, Maggie. *1492: What is it Like to be Discovered?* New York: Monthly Review Books, 1991.

Steedman, Carolyn. *Dust: The Archive and Cultural History.* New Brunswick: Rutgers University Press, 2002.

Stern, David. *Midrash and Theory: Ancient Jewish Exegesis and Contemporary Literary Studies.* Evanston: Northwestern University Press, 1996.

Suchecky, Bernard. "The carmelite convent at Auschwitz: the nature and scope of a failure." In *Discourse of Jewish Identity in Twentieth-Century France.* Edited by Alan Astro. *Yale French Studies* vol. 85, 160–173, 1994.

Sutzkever, Abraham. *Burnt Pearls: Ghetto Poems of Abraham Sutzkever* [trans. Seymovr Mayne]. Mosaic Press, p. 37, 1981.

Sutzkever, Abraham. *Selected Poetry and Prose* [trans. Barbara and Benjamin Harshav]. Berkeley: University of California Press, 1991.

Szondi, Peter. "Hope in the past: on Walter Benjamin." *Critical Inquiry.* Spring, 491–506, 1978.

Todd, Sharon. "Looking at pedagogy in 3D: rethinking difference, disparity, and desire." In *Learning Desire: Perspectives In Pedagogy, Culture and the Unsaid.* Edited by Sharon Todd. New York: Routledge, pp. 237–260, 1977.

Todorov, Tzvetan. *The Conquest of America: The Question of the Other* [trans. Richard Howard]. New York: Harper and Row, 1984.

Trend, David. *Cultural Pedagogy: Art/Education/Politics.* New York: Bergin and Garvey, 1992.

Trouillot, Michel-Rolph. "Good-day Columbus: silences, power and public history (1492–1892)." *Public Culture,* vol. 3, no. 1, Fall, 1–24, 1990.

Virilio, Paul. *Polar Inertia* [trans. P. Camiller]. London and Thousand Oaks: Sage, 2000.

Vulliet, Armand. "Letters to Claude Lanzmann and to the *Grand Larousse*." In *Discourses of Jewish Identity in Twentieth-Century France.* Edited by Alan Astro. *Yale French Studies,* vol. 85, 152–159, 1994.

Waletzky, Josh [director and editor]. *Partisans of Vilna* [videorecording]. Produced by Aviva Kempner; Screenwriters, Josh Waletzky and Aviva Kempner. Washington, DC: The Cielsa Foundation, Inc., 1986.

Weber, Thomas. " 'There was no Beauty in the Ghetto': The Visual Self-Representation of Holocaust Survivors." Paper presented at the 12th Annual Graduate Student Conference "The Visual Turn," Yale University, 2001.

Weigel, Sigrid. *Body- and Image-Space: Re-reading Walter Benjamin* [trans. by Georgina Paul with Rachel McNicholl and Jeremy Gaines]. New York: Routledge, 1996.

Wineburg, Sam. *Historical Thinking and Other Unnatural Acts: Charting the Future of Teaching the Past.* Philadelphia: Temple University Press, 2001.

Wieviorka, Annette. "On Testimony." In *Holocaust Remembrance: The Shapes of memory.* Edited by Geoffery H. Hartman. Cambridge, MA: Blackwell, pp. 23–32, 1994.

Wohlfarth, Irving. "On the Messianic structure of Walter Benjamin's last reflections." *Glyph: Johns Hopkins Textual Studies,* No. 3, 148–212, 1978.

Wyschogrod, Edith. *An Ethics of Remembering: History, Heterology, and the Nameless Others.* Chicago: University of Chicago Press, 1998.

Yeo, Marian. "Murdered by misogyny: Lin Gibson's response to the Montréal massacre." *Canadian Woman Studies,* vol. 12, no. 1, Fall, pp. 8–11, 1991.

Yerushalmi, Yosef. *Zakhor: Jewish History and Jewish Memory.* New York: Schocken Books, 1989.

Young, James. *The Texture of Memory: Holocaust Memorials and Meaning.* New Haven: Yale University Press, 1993.

Ziarek, Kristof. "The ethos of History." In *What Happens to History: The Renewal of Ethics in Contemporary Thought.* Edited by Howard Marchitello. New York: Routledge, pp. 67–93, 2000.

INDEX

Page numbers in *italics* refer to figures and the number in parenthesis refer to figure number.